CW01521965

Re-imagining North Korea in International Politics

The global consensus in academic, specialist and public realms is that North Korea is a problem: its nuclear ambitions pose a threat to international security, its levels of poverty indicate a humanitarian crisis, and its political repression signals a failed state.

This book examines the cultural dimensions of the international problem of North Korea through contemporary South Korean and Western popular imagination's engagement with North Korea. Building on works by feminist-postcolonial thinkers, in particular Trinh Minh-ha, Rey Chow and Gayatri Spivak, it examines novels, films, photography and memoirs for how they engage with issues of security, human rights, humanitarianism and political agency from an intercultural perspective. By doing so, the author challenges the key assumptions that underpin the prevailing realist and liberal approaches to North Korea.

This research attends not only to alternative framings, narratives and images of North Korea, but also to alternative modes of knowing, loving and responding, and will be of interest to students of critical international relations, Korean studies, cultural studies and Asian studies.

Shine Choi is Korea Foundation Visiting Professor at University of Mississippi, USA.

Interventions

Edited by:
Jenny Edkins, Aberystwyth University and Nick Vaughan-Williams, University of Warwick

As Michel Foucault has famously stated, 'knowledge is not made for understanding; it is made for cutting'. In this spirit the Edkins–Vaughan-Williams Interventions series solicits cutting edge, critical works that challenge mainstream understandings in international relations. It is the best place to contribute post disciplinary works that think rather than merely recognize and affirm the world recycled in IR's traditional geopolitical imaginary.

Michael J. Shapiro, University of Hawai'i at Mãnoa, USA

The series aims to advance understanding of the key areas in which scholars working within broad critical post-structural and post-colonial traditions have chosen to make their interventions, and to present innovative analyses of important topics.

Titles in the series engage with critical thinkers in philosophy, sociology, politics and other disciplines, and provide situated historical, empirical and textual studies in international politics.

Critical Theorists and International Relations
Edited by Jenny Edkins and Nick Vaughan-Williams

Ethics as Foreign Policy
Britain, the EU and the other
Dan Bulley

Universality, Ethics and International Relations
A grammatical reading
Véronique Pin-Fat

The Time of the City
Politics, philosophy, and genre
Michael J. Shapiro

Governing Sustainable Development
Partnership, protest and power at the world summit
Carl Death

Insuring Security
Biopolitics, security and risk
Luis Lobo-Guerrero

Foucault and International Relations
New critical engagements
Edited by Nicholas J. Kiersey and Doug Stokes

International Relations and Non-Western Thought
Imperialism, colonialism and investigations of global modernity
Edited by Robbie Shilliam

Re-imagining North Korea in International Politics

Problems and alternatives

Shine Choi

Routledge
Taylor & Francis Group

LONDON AND NEW YORK

First published 2015
by Routledge
2 Park Square, Milton Park, Abingdon, Oxon OX14 4RN

and by Routledge
711 Third Avenue, New York, NY 10017

Routledge is an imprint of the Taylor & Francis Group, an informa business

British Library Cataloguing in Publication Data
A catalogue record for this book is available from the British Library

Library of Congress Cataloging in Publication Data
A catalog record for this book has been requested

ISBN: 978-1-138-79168-8 (hbk)
ISBN: 978-1-315-76154-1 (ebk)

Typeset in Times New Roman
by Taylor & Francis Books

Printed and bound by CPI Group (UK) Ltd, Croydon, CR0 4YY

Contents

Illustrations

Acknowledgements

I do not think I would have persisted without the small but over-zealous group of cheerleaders rallying me on. I am sure this role was especially difficult to fulfil for Debbie Lisle and Dan Bulley, not because of their predisposition to bad cheer but also because they had the hard task of supervising me as a PhD student. I would also like to thank all those who were involved in reviewing my PhD research from its proposal stage to defence at Queen's University Belfast: Roland Bleiker, Vince Geoghegan and Ephraim Nimni. I would especially like to thank Roland Bleiker, who has been amazingly generous as an intellectual and professional mentor. Roland also introduced me to Skype. I don't know how this technology passed me by all those years! Special mention must also be made of the Belfast crew, especially Maria Andrea Deiana, Laura Mills, Elena Bergia and Esmorie Miller, who participated in perfecting the art of potluck dinners, long lunches and 'wee' coffee breaks. In Seoul, many, many thanks first to Moon Hyuna, Kwon Hee-Kyung, Hanna Kim, Shinwoong Choi and Sue Myung for their friendship and support, and especially Professor Moon for her help with this book project even before we knew it as such in 2008. I am also indebted to the support and care of and conversations with Professor Lee Geun and Professor Chung Chinsung in Seoul National University, and Professor Koo Kap-woo, Professor Lee Woo-yeong and Professor Lee Soo-jung in the University of North Korean Studies. Students, especially those studying soft power in East Asia at Seoul National University Graduate School of International Studies, also taught me a lot: thank you. Last, but definitely not least, thanks to my long-time partner in crime, cat carer and roommate, Peter Straghan, and my old friend and new roommate, Ruth Kim, for putting up with me in the (seemingly unending) final months of birthing this book. This book is dedicated to Peter.

I acknowledge the generous funding from Queen's University Belfast (Non-EU International Studentship 2008–12) during my postgraduate research, when a significant portion of research for this book took place. I also acknowledge the summer fellowship support from Kyungnam University Institute for Far Eastern Studies in the completion of this manuscript.

Lastly, I must thank the following publishers and authors/photographers for allowing me to use their work:

Landscape of the Everyday North, by Seok, Im-aseng (pseudonym: Ri, Man-geun), 2005, originally published in Korean by Hyeunshil Munhwa Yeongu.
North Korea, by Philippe Chancel, 2006, originally published by Thames and Hudson.
Pyongyang Project, by Oh, Young-jin, 2006, originally published in Korean by Changbi Publishers, Inc.
Pyongyang: Journey in North Korea, 2005, and *Shenzhen: A Travelogue from China*, 2006, by Guy Delisle, originally published by Drawn and Quarterly.

Note on translation

Original texts in languages other than English, which is the official language of this publication, are presented in translation. This book does not follow the McCune-Reischauer romanticization system preferred in the Korean studies field. Instead, it uses widely used and somewhat inconsistent conventional romanticization formats found in everyday and popular use. Perhaps this reflects my uneasy relationship with the academic Korean studies field.

For exceptional cases, such as in the case of proper nouns, formats used by the originator are used. Following the name order in Korean, the names that are originally in Korean are given with the surname first, followed by a comma and the given name. This order is followed unless the author uses a different order, in which case I follow the author's preferred name order.

Introduction
What North Korea problem?

The international problem of North Korea is that North Korea is a work of fiction. Despite the widespread use of the name 'North Korea' in international media, foreign policy pronouncements and academic research, it is a controversial term and a creation that itself spurs fiction from those hailed by or compelled to respond to it. When we attend to how the name is disowned by the referent, the fiction of North Korea is telling of the divisions in international politics more than the place, people and phenomenon that become associated with the name. If 'North Korea' is common international parlance for the Democratic People's Republic of Korea (DPRK), the relationship between the two is not one of direct correspondence but instead a contest of whose story of the country should be believed and who the legitimate (main) characters are. When speaking or writing in the Korean language, there are at least two different informal ways of referring to DPRK which bring to the fore at least two different North Koreas: '*Bukhan*' and '*Buk-chosun*'. This split makes explicit what kind of North ('*buk*' means North in Korean) is in reference, or more accurately, is in creation. '*Bukhan*' mobilizes '*han*' of '*Dae*han *Minguk*', which translates into the Republic of Korea (South Korea). '*Buk-chosun*' uses the suffix '*chosun*' of '*Inmin* Chosun *Konghwa Gukdan*', which would be DPRK. In other words, North Korea is either '*Bukhan*', which privileges ideologies and spaces associated with South Korea, or '*Buk-chosun*', which privileges the northern network; it is never one and the same thing, as too easily implied when thinking only in English.

Unpacking the full implications of the fiction of North Korea is vast, and this is a book that examines the relational dimensions of the fiction. Thus, this book is not *about* North Korea or DPRK, but the *relations* that come to the fore when we understand North Korea, and for that matter DPRK, as fiction in the making. The global consensus in academic, specialist and other public realms is that North Korea is a problem: its nuclear ambitions pose a threat to international security, its levels of poverty indicate a humanitarian crisis and its political repression signals a failed state. While opinions on the causes of this problem differ, North Korea, like many foreign policy or international issues, is largely seen as a problem that requires solutions from diplomatic and expert communities. Tracing the fiction of North Korea involves seeing the country as a complex site of statehood, identity, space, history and culture that is so easily 'Othered' in the powerful discourses of international politics (e.g. security, development, human rights and humanitarianism) and everyday social life.[1] Importantly, the fiction of North Korea crucially extends beyond the 'official' channels of policymakers, politicians and experts. Various popular engagements with North Korea have always proliferated, which include not only organized activities such as public campaigns and street protests, but also personal engagements that are often relegated as 'leisure' and 'trivial', namely creative (re)imaginings in books, films and other cultural products. This book begins from the assumption that cultural forms of popular/personal engagements with North Korea constitute an important dimension of the fiction of North Korea and political responses to it. To be clear, it is not my argument that North Korea is a fiction spun by those outside it which is a baseless, hallucinatory figment of outsider imagination. Even hallucinations are responses to or of some things, and in the chapters that follow I draw attention to the role that North Korean mediation and interlocutors play in our (hallucinatory) responses. North Korea is a product of encounters between various 'us's' and various 'North Koreas', but this various, diverse, fragmented, ambiguous 'us' remains a particular 'us' on one side of politics along the line reified by the Cold War binaries of (neo)liberal US–Western Europe versus the communist-socialist Soviet bloc.

Through a thick engagement with culture, this book interrogates the theoretical foundations that undergird prevailing constructions of North Korea as a problem of security and a failed state. It does so in two ways: by attending to how this 'North Korea problem' is mediated in cultural sites, which means following various genres, recurring narratives and images as well as the affective needs and desires articulated in the cultural realm. It also attends to cultural processes and differences related to the politics of identity/difference that comes to the fore in international relations involving North Korea. Of interest here are contemporary[2] cultural formations in English and Korean to explore the transit between East and West and the importance of location and cultural differences in articulations about North Korea.[3] What gets foregrounded in a cultural exploration is how the distinctness of International Relations (IR) frameworks – security, development, human rights, humanitarianism – becomes less important than how these frameworks converge to produce narratives that sustain particular relations of power, difference and identity. As such, I follow themes that predominate in cultural sites, namely demystification, modes of detection, suffering, visuality, love, sentimentalism and survival. Problem-solving modes in encounters with North Korea pervade in cultural sites, which admittedly is expressed differently from problem-solving practices in policy or academic sites. From the most academic to the most creative, they share common dreams of resolution, redemption and a safe return to normalcy, order and prosperity.

Focusing on the mediated nature of what we call the 'North Korea problem', I begin by understanding cultural representations as an illustrative site of intercultural encounters. This is to contend that international relations are instances of intercultural relations that require interrogation of how a particular position (e.g. the culture, subjectivity, perspective of the 'self') gets privileged and how the figure of the 'Other' operates in these cases. In short, arguing that issues of desire, suffering, conflict and violence – which conventional IR understands in the language of human rights, security, governance and development – are problems of inter*cultural* relations is to highlight how the study of the international demands attention to issues of translation, cultural mediation and in-between-ness. I explore the exclusionary, consolidating, miniaturizing, constraining and containing forces that prevail with respect to the 'North Korean problem' in these encounters and processes.

At the same time, I am concerned with the productive, creative and fictive effects of cultural efforts to address the 'North Korea problem'. I explore how the realm of culture in particular prompts us to think more critically about the ways in which North Korea is always represented as a 'problem'. Thus alternative modes and terms of intercultural encounter, and the alternative spaces and scenarios that they open up, comprise significant parts of Chapters 2 to 5. I am mainly concerned here, to borrow Homi Bhabha's (1994: 212–35) phrasing, with how newness enters the world that has no outside to the already contaminated and to that which is already present in and is part of the circulation of power. I ask, what makes alternatives *alternative*, rather than simply another reproduction of the existing hierarchic terms of intercultural relations? As delineated in the next chapter, this question is an attempt to register a shift in the very terms of intercultural encounters that create the possibility of transforming the culture of self-centrism and self-referentiality. This is not a normative argument that sets out the criteria for a 'better' or a more ethical construction of North Korea. Moreover, this cultural exploration into alternatives aims to reflect on, interrogate and broaden out not only *what* we seek (i.e. resources for re-thinking existing approaches and responses), but also *how* we seek and inadvertently go about evaluating alternative responses as useful, political or meaningful.

Contextualizing theory

Under the subheadings problems and alternatives, I provide an overview of the main arguments developed in this book. To be clear, the turn to culture and issues of representation, narratives, affect and aesthetics in this book is not an uncritical faith that the cultural realm offers better solutions to 'a problem like North Korea' than social scientific research with its focus on policy and diplomacy. Rather, it is an effort to interrogate more seriously the hierarchic terms of intercultural relations and how they are maintained and reproduced in an effort to relate to cultural Others differently. As part of this effort, alternative narratives and images are sought which can register, amplify and pluralize the shifts and the terms of intercultural encounter, however inescapably ambiguous, fleeting, fraught, inadequate. The critical question in examining cultural expressions is not only about producing disruptions and challenges that keep the possibilities in intercultural encounters open through privileging heterogeneity, ambiguity, creativity, contingency and so on. An integral part of the critical question of this book is to examine to what extent such disruptions and challenges also decentre the very terms of how possibilities are kept open, political and creative. In other words, I ask how self-disruptive and self-decentralizing the various efforts are which seek to create conditions that recognize alterity. Such concerns must be raised if we are more seriously to attend to and prepare for transformation of intercultural relations that heterogeneity, ambiguity, contingency and creativity (i.e. politics) have brought about and are continually bringing forth.

Problems

To say that the dominant understanding of North Korea as a problem is fictive and constructed is unrelated to the truth or falsity of what we know about North Korea. This statement is not a truth claim arguing that the dominant claim is wrong because it is false. Rather, it refuses the terms upon which true and false claims are distinguished, and insists that the dominant understanding of North Korea as a 'problem' is unacceptable because of the mediation of power in how the claims are made and how this work of mediation is itself erased from view by entrenched power relations. I argue that addressing 'North Korea' within dominant rational and technocratic problem-solving language is not only delimiting, but is also at the heart of the problem. The next chapter, 'International relations, interrupted: issues of positionality and intercultural relations', constructs a theoretical discussion to enable an exploration of where this refusal of the terms of truth can lead us. It introduces theoretical, methodological and political dimensions of how the predominant terms constrain, and argues for turning to expressive sites of culture and politics in order to create alternative languages, strategies and modes of engaging with and responding to the complex signifier that is 'North Korea'. A central part of this argument is that the international problem of North Korea has an intercultural dimension that is often occluded by mainstream approaches. I explore the collective need for fuller engagement with the intercultural dimensions of relations, positions and transformation by examining critical spaces created by poststructuralist, postcolonial and feminist scholars. Trinh Minh-ha, Rey Chow and Gayatri Spivak are introduced in Chapter 1 as important scholars for any study of international relations concerned with issues of intercultural processes. In Chapter 1, I focus on the concepts of 'translation', 'in-between spaces' and 'speaking nearby' which foreground interculturality of mediation, mediators and culture. This discussion has a strong practical dimension and seeks to move beyond discussions of theoretical concepts and bring in the everyday contexts and dilemmas of what we are discussing.

As already mentioned, the main sites from which international relations is problematized in this book are culture and popular culture. As argued by many, culture is a rich site for building, performing and circulation international realities, encounters and relations (e.g. Weldes 2003; Lisle 2006; Shih and Lionnet 2005; Chow 1995). It is through culture as a process, and its artefacts as resources, that we construct and make sense of our 'reality'. Although science, politics, art, psychology and popular culture are often thought of as separate, we cannot deny the intertextuality between them. They utilise and produce common cultural resources. Thus, by examining the different myths, narratives, imageries and metaphors that are enacted and performed in the cultural realm, we gain a deeper understanding of the complex and intricate workings of the 'global' consensus on the 'North Korea problem'. Here I am not only referring to the identities enacted for 'official' political activities (e.g. national identities such as citizens, or international identities such as diplomats and statesmen), but all identities (e.g. a modern man, a good mother, a real lover), and of myths about peace, the good life, gender and agency, among others. In other words, there is a very delicate but nonetheless powerful relationship between official 'political-collective' and everyday 'apolitical-private' modes, myths and realities that prop up existing hierarchies along gendered, racial and civilizational lines.

I explore this delicate relationship in four themes located in four specific genres that are widely mobilized in international encounters with North Korea, namely: mystery/detective fiction that travels to North Korea; photography of suffering in North Korea; films about love in inter-Korean relations; and North Korea defector memoirs. Chapter 2, 'Displacing the detective eye/I: seeing translation and mediation', critically examines how a mysterious, unknowable and recalcitrant North Korea is produced through a particular mode of encounter that seeks to detect, ascertain, know and see North Korea as an object from a position above and at a distance. In intercultural contexts such as those involving North Korea, seeing, uncovering and exposing are inescapably forms of translation that require mediators. I introduce the concept of the 'detective eye/I' to illustrate how visuality is of particular importance to how mysterious North Korea is produced. Using James Church's Inspector O mystery series and Guy Delisle's graphic travelogue *Pyongyang*, I focus on moments of translation and the various narrative functions that North Korean mediators play in the construction of North Korea. Central to these texts is the idea that knowing North Korea better, and enabling North Koreans to communicate their message to the world, will solve the North Korean problems of poverty, human rights abuses and international ostracism. I examine hierarchies established by modes of detection shared across genres, and consider how the concept of translation complicates the key tenets of these knowledge-driven productions. In particular, this chapter focuses on fictional and non-fictional texts that intersect on a basis that they have 'been there'.

This critical engagement with the mode of detection through the concept of the 'detective eye/I', and the chapters that follow, build on and contribute to the postcolonial insight that colonialism and imperialism are not just outdated practices of the past that 'have been consigned to the dustbin', as a prominent IR scholar on East Asia, Samuel Kim (2002: 11), claims. This chapter and those that follow are illustrative of how colonial and imperial logics of the 'West' remain alive and well in radically more complex and discontinuous forms than their predecessors. In other words, we live in the age of post-coloniality, which is a contested term but nonetheless useful in considering the historical context of the current global order, i.e. the historicity of the particular form of today's 'globality' and its power relations (see Krishna 1999; Ahmed 2000; Orford 2003). Mainstream IR accounts use standards or criteria set by their own coordinates (the Western modern self), which in turn universalize their particular image and deal with difference by doing violence to it. Such an approach insists that Others must conform to 'our' standards rather than, for instance, creating a dialogical space in which both positions learn or gain from the contact. The postcolonial critique is that this demand for sameness is a way of denying the need for translation between different worlds when encounters in contact zones occur. Mary Louise Pratt's (1992) idea of the 'contact zone' is cited most widely in IR, which is understood as a shifting space wherein subjects previously separated by geographic and historical disjuncture experience otherness. Historically, it has been a space of colonial encounters infused with inequalities of power.[4] Important to register here is how postcoloniality is '*a failed historicity*: a historicity that admits of its own failure in grasping that which has been, as the impossibility of grasping the present' (Ahmed 2000: 9, emphasis in original). Failed historicity means working fully with complexity of relations between the past and present, and tracing the continuities as well as the disjuncture between the colonial past and the contemporary international politics.

Chapter 3, 'What "seeing" suffering demands of us: photographic engagements with North Korea(ns)', turns to the case of international responsibility and action in response to the problem of North Korea's poor human rights record and economic poverty. Human rights and humanitarian discourses are the most prominent sites for postcolonial politics. I examine the prevailing hierarchy between the international and places like North Korea (an extreme as well as a peculiar case), achieved by mobilizing visual binaries that rest upon a subject/object axis (e.g. over here/over there; seer/seen; actor/acted upon; benefactor/beneficiary). I do so through an engagement with photography of North Korean suffering in international circulation which helps us to interrogate visually – which I argue is a method of political thinking that foregrounds issues of relations – the prevailing assumption that suffering exists unambiguously in all spaces, bodies and subjectivities that constitute 'North Korea', an assumption that sustains the notion that suffering simply demands alleviation by outside intervention. Three differently styled photo books published in the early 2000s are examined for this purpose: Choi, Soon-ho's *Defectors*, which produces an abject North Korea through defector images and stories; Ri, Man-geun's *Landscape of the Everyday North*, which surreptitiously records rural everyday life in North Korea; and Philippe Chancel's *North Korea*, which pictures suffering in the official sites that the North Korean state promotes to outsiders.

As pointed out by postcolonial, feminist and poststructuralist thinkers, what needs interrogation is how the state or analogous body of authority (e.g. the international community) is perennially seen as a protector of naturally endowed rights, but all the while certain people – those who most often and urgently need to invoke their status as subjects of human rights and humanitarianism – must continually remain in that compromised position *under* their protector (see Spivak 2004; Orford 2003; Browne 2002; Bhambra and Shilliam 2009). In the case of human rights, those seeking the protection of human rights are always *under* the benevolent protection of those with the power to grant and protect such rights – an asymmetry that violates the very concept of global and universally applicable human rights. Analogously, in a humanitarian framework, the conception of poverty that places the biological as its definitive condition renders poverty as something that agents outside it, i.e. wealthier subjects, must correct (e.g. Edkins 2000; Campbell 2007).

Since the 1990s, discussions of North Korean poverty – an object of humanitarian concern – have occurred most crucially in terms of famine and food shortage, i.e. how much cereal the population needs to survive. This has been a central point of contention in scholarly debates on the North Korean famine, which I would argue misleadingly reduces famine and poverty to matters of bodily deterioration and bare survival (see Haggard and Noland 2007: 47; Haggard and Noland 2008: 203–15; Smith 2008; Ireson 2006: 13). Chapter 3, on photographic encounters with North Korean suffering, seeks to intervene in these human rights and humanitarian/famine debates which create a naturalized dichotomy of 'us' (a knowledgeable international community led by modern societies) and 'them' (starving North Koreans in a society stuck in the past). Conventional approaches construct and position the category of 'poverty' and famine (and to a lesser but important extent, political oppression) as realities that exist only in parts of the world outside advanced industrialized democratic societies. This hints at how the conventional conception of the Third World is firmly a perspective of those who think they are not part of that world which is poor, oppressed, suffering (i.e. those spaces with populations that do not possess 'normal' biological and bodily statistics, which are then equated with 'abnormal' political, material and economic living conditions). It is also a perspective from a position of power concerned with controlling, managing and containing the 'Third World'.

Chapter 4, 'I love you. Do you love me? Conflict, melodrama and reconciliation, South Korean blockbuster style', continues the critical examination of the hierarchical positioning of the international and North Korea by turning to how it gains articulation in South Korean narratives – namely, in the tropes of national reconciliation and unification. Building on previous critical readings of South Korean blockbuster films, the chapter examines the action/thriller film *Typhoon* and tearjerker melodrama *Over the Border*. I examine South Korean filmic stagings of the national division (*bundan*), which refers to the period since the Korean War that produced the two sovereign Koreas, South and North. I argue that 'I love you. Do you love me?' is the main question that South Korean films are asking, demanding reciprocity and mirroring from the North Korean Other. I also argue that it is a South Korean question that is simultaneously posed not just to North Korea but to the world. Relatedly, I interrogate the particular overture of sadness that pervades in the Korean national narratives of togetherness and the way *han*, an emotion of anguished lamentation that is supposedly unique to Korean cultural history, structures these narratives. Again, important to register here is how postcolonialism is a failed historicity, which demands that we work fully, and in the Korean context, with humility, with complexity of relations between the past and present. The Korean story of national division offers an example of how this failure to grasp produces a wealth of creative, strategic, bank-breaking modern projects that seek to move a certain constellation of 'us' forward, upwards and beyond. I ask, at what cost and for whom?

The concerns in Chapter 4 involving love and its intersections with the staging of the Korean conflict is part of a longstanding feminist argument that the problems of war, conflict, development and state repression look, feel and are solved differently when gender is taken as a central category of analysis. As observed by Christine Sylvester (2002: 161), in mainstream IR theory 'there seems to be a structuring-out of women and their activities and an implicit structuring-in of men and their activities'. This is significant because it is linked to the conception of who acts, how the world works, and how security, justice and equality look from subordinated positions and activities. Lene Hansen (2000) also powerfully illustrates in the case of conventional security studies that the way 'security' is defined renders the security of particular social groups illegitimate and unimportant as a subject matter for IR. Consequently, issues such as violence against women are relegated as 'less deserving' than issues such as national security. When we turn to South Korean narratives of the Korean conflict, we see how women, foreign bodies and foreign landscape become domesticated and are turned into instruments for the various male protagonists to achieve national and personal togetherness. While the centrality of love in South Korean popular imagination brings domestic relations and spaces into how we frame and narrate conflict, security and division, these domestic and everyday enactments do not necessarily disrupt the masculinist and heteronormative national imaginings of security, justice and equality. In short, how we define our terms really matters, but how thoroughly we question and learn to intervene in the commonsense everyday and domestic narratives such as romantic and familial love also seriously matter. I want us to attend to what goes into constructing narratives we tell about ourselves and the world, i.e. to our desires and anxieties.

The final analytical chapter, 'Objecting objects: be(com)ing North Koreans in an affective world', addresses head on an implicit argument that has run throughout the book on intercultural dimensions of global affairs – a commitment to activating the political agency of the Other. The main preoccupation that structures this chapter is with the limits as well as the possibilities for agency of the Other and intercultural communication. It turns to memoirs and autobiography as a collective site that is structured comprehensively by conventions of authenticity and self-representation, which powerfully constrains how Other-oriented knowledge production and meetings can occur. It examines North Korean defector memoirs in two different styles: Kang, Cholhwan's *The Aquariums of Pyongyang*, which tells a survival tale of his labour camp experience; and Hwang, Jang-yop's *The Memoir of Hwang Jang-yop*, which narrates his past as part of the North Korean elite class and his defection to take action for Korean unification. Both stories seek to deliver redemption to the people they left behind in North Korea by telling their own personal stories of survival and redemption – stories which crucially rest upon the authors' innocence and victimhood. The argument in this chapter is that such narratives of recovery and redemption are structured by placing empathy as the main objective of intercultural communications, which constrains how stories of survival can transform the intercultural sites in which they work.

In sum, what is problematized in challenging the fiction of North Korea is a politics of identity/difference that each of us, in our various positions, practice as we relate to and participate in the world. We establish difference at many crucial junctures, which also functions to constitute each of our identities. Under critique is the dominant articulation of identity/difference that works to exclude wherein the self is privileged over its supposed 'Others' and rigidifies differences (and the privileged identity) by producing and reproducing difference. Useful is how Campbell (1992) maps out the pervasiveness of the self/Other logic by differentiation of foreign policy and Foreign Policy. The term 'foreign policy' concerns all forms of exclusionary practice that constitute identity/difference, while 'Foreign Policy' refers more narrowly to the conventional use of the term in reference to diplomatic and inter-state relations. Historically and presently, this has involved establishing inside versus outside and self versus Other, which privileges the former through a series of binary oppositions of good/bad, civilized/barbaric, normal/abnormal, pure/impure, masculine/feminine. Considered in the North Korea case, the argument is that the consensus on North Korea as a problem is reached and reachable only through the continuous production of difference and Otherness that privileges those doing the constructing ('us' in the West) and subordinates the Other (an objectified North Korea). Just as attempts to secure a stable identity of privilege that is radically opposed to the 'problem' of North Korea *require* the production of differences to maintain the illusion of security, attempts to secure North Korea as self-reliant, functional and a victim of US imperialism also *require* the production of differences. I stress in this book that variously positioned North Koreans – the DPRK officials, North Korean defectors – crucially participate in, mediate or oppose this construction to secure a version of reality that sustains their various identity/difference positionings. However, no identity and reality are ever secure, nor do they even exist prior to the production of, and encounter with, difference. How do we escape this vicious cycle?

We do not. The politics of identity/difference is inescapable in constructing reality, and perhaps violence, too, is unavoidable. However, inescapability does not mean violence and exclusion are acceptable or accepted by, for instance, those intimately affected by these practices. My critical analysis that traces how and to what effect North Korea becomes an object of international action has an eye on articulating alternatives, which compose the final sections of Chapters 2 to 5. I turn to these chapter sections next.

Alternatives

In conceptualizing alternatives, Michael Shapiro (1999: 81) writes, 'the performers must of necessity be ready to be afflicted by the performance of the other', and similarly – or so it might seem – Sara Ahmed (2000: 5) argues that the problem of ethical encounter is not a problem of how we face 'the other' and be ethical in the face of alterity, but a problem of how alterity (embodied in the figure of the stranger) inhibits us from taking the crucial step of engaging in an encounter without predetermining or judging the form of alterity. While the quotations from Shapiro and Ahmed promote more open, ethical encounters with other and alterity, a survey of their productions that stem from their commitments to Otherness/alterity significantly differ in where and how the emphasis is placed, i.e. who acts and how agency is conceived in ethical encounters. They also crucially differ on their capacities to imagine Other worlds in *particular* forms. I return to this point in the chapters that follow, through the concept of positionality.

Positionality is a conceptual language that allows us to problematize the role of 'I' in how political transformation and agency are understood. In the Conclusion chapter I ask how we transform the way in which political change occurs if the very conception of transformation as something that *we* bring about for the rest of the world is what needs transformation. What strategies for decentring the self and activating the agency of the Other are available to us? These are questions that stem from a preoccupation with the complicity of the 'I' in the power/knowledge/reality production and is an articulation of how the different ways we are positioned and position ourselves require thorough reflexive engagement. Put differently, we cannot abandon who we are and we cannot escape from participating in the construction of identity/difference but we can be mindful of the specificity of our position.

Most prominently interrogated in Chapter 1, which sets the stage for a repetitive return to this theme, is the problem of knowledge production wherein how ethics as articulated by diverging critical thinkers foregrounds *our* action and ruminates (albeit self-consciously) *within or in close proximity to* an 'us' and 'our' approaches to intercultural encounters. My position is that we need a more pluralistic understanding of ethics, politics and the social, as well as a greater commitment to heterogenizing the sources, spaces, modes and processes of change.

Chapter 2, on the detective eye/I, contains efforts to make visible how alternative forms of translation, seeing and encountering 'mystery' are possible by exploring complex encounters with North Korea articulated in Oh, Young-jin's graphic novel, *Pyongyang Project*, and Kwon, Lee's metaphysical detective novel, *Left-handed Mr Lee*. We observe in these productions from South Korea subversions of generic resources and patterns that make objectification of North Korean bodies and landscapes too easy. They also offer a messier picture of what it means to translate the world(s) we encounter. Translation is not about clarity in intercultural communication but about getting lost in the mazes and games we construct which keeps afloat optimisms about ourselves and our power.

Chapter 3, on photographic encounters with suffering North Korea, considers how visuality that photography mediates can be useful when we move beyond looking for visible documentary evidence of suffering and instead explore how the encounter through photography can foreground the contingency and plurality of suffering (and visibility). It affirms the broad consensus that photography has the capacity to mobilize the tactile, mobile and emotive dimensions of intercultural encounters and to explore critically what suffering demands of spectators. At the same time, re-encountering North Korea and suffering has nothing to do with photographic images. It is about rethinking the very idea that sees responsibility and response in the visible, active form that fails to acknowledge how responsibility can also take less tangible, action-oriented forms. I explore this concept through Trinh Minhha's idea of voiding. This exploration begins with my chance encounter with Area Park's image of North Korean teenage boys in Seoul.

I attend to alternatives in Chapter 4, on love and inter-Korean relations, by turning to a story that arises from the division of the Korean peninsula which occurs in Japan to interrupt the easy narratives of togetherness that centre South Korea. Yang, Yonghi's filmic engagements in the form of two documentaries (*Dear Pyongyang* and *Goodbye Pyongyang*), and a feature film and a memoir both titled *Our Homeland*, are useful resources for working through the stickiness of love and nation and how we might outlive our desires to belong. Part of outliving our desires to belong and to possess the Other in the name of love is to attend to the ambiguous and shifting relationship between emotions of love and hate. This concern with belonging and reconciliation also extends to Chapter 5, on self-representation of North Korean defectors. If the previously examined memoirs remain squarely within the narrative of redemption, Choi, Jin-yee's *The Woman who Crossed the Border Thrice* is a disruptive translation of experiences of suffering which turns one's experiences of suffering into something else, which in turn forms the basis of the agency as a North Korean in South Korea. 'As a North Korean' is a deeply problematic perspective and positioning which requires negotiation with the difficulty that having been an object of privileged subject positions' action poses to efforts that seek to articulate and amplify one's subject position. Agency gained from the position of 'as a North Korean' mobilizes the very referential term that imprisons one to the object position. In other words, given that North Korean defectors gain agency through the mobilization of the public that requires them to *become* North Koreans, the hierarchic terms of their translation of suffering into something else – their recovery from trauma – perennially constrain how they survive and communicate with the world. Alternative intercultural communication through sites of self-representation must amplify the agency of the North Korean Other that shifts the terms of intercultural communication. Through a juxtaposition of Trinh Minh-ha and Gayatri Spivak, the concluding chapter begins to articulate more fully the implications of this book's position that heterogenizing and pluralizing sources, spaces and terms of knowledge and agency must crucially privilege the agency of the Other.

In sum, the interrogation of alternatives through culture in this book presents diverse and numerous resources for rethinking the existing approaches to the 'North Korea problem' and ways of responding in encounters with Otherness. Engaging politically with culture and popular culture gives us access to insights tied to the technologies, forms and conventions particular to specific cultural productions (e.g. photography's visual narrative or imaginaries invoked by music in films), which can point to alternative ways of understanding, imagining and responding to the world that the technologies of academic writing and systematic research cannot offer (Lisle 2003; Sylvester 2002; Shapiro 1997; Bleiker 2009; Connolly 2002). We gain access to narratives and images of, from, or contaminated by perspectives and lives that we would not otherwise have if we were just to focus on policy documents and 'official' activities, or if we were only to look at lives and experiences produced through social scientific methods. These are important resources to help us to think through and imagine alternative terms of intercultural encounters.

To be clear, one of the main arguments about alternatives in this book is that no new set of alternative images would unambiguously and necessarily be disruptive and transformative. Potency of image and meaning are always inescapably contextual and are productions that signify and produce effects through interpretation. Interpretation is an intercultural, intersubjective process which seeks to ascertain what comes after the interpretive act, moment, space. Because of this I believe 'what comes after' understanding North Korea in the world as an intercultural issue crucially involves deconstructing *and* reconstructing the North Korean Other.

Turning to North Korean defector memoirs in international circulation is just a small ground-clearing step towards thinking about encounters that reconstruct. Here, too, the important question is what comes after self-representation rather than what the substance is of self-representation per se. Spivak calls for developing an entirely different agenda around encounters in subaltern spaces which rejects the idea of reporting back, analysis, knowledge accumulation. I believe this is worth serious consideration in IR, a discipline that prides itself on studying the international, the global, the world. Let me repeat: this interest in the agency of the North Korea Other is not to side with the engagement policy camp in the current debate on how we must respond to the North Korea problem. Arguments for engagement and learning more *about* inside North Korea have their own politics and hierarchies. I want to cut through this hierarchy.

Problematizing the international in the 'North Korea problem'

Studies of North Korea that look *inside* North Korea are hot these days. If studies that focused on North Korea's external action and nuclear problem for the US strategic concerns proliferated in the past, there is a growing sense that North Korea observers are now – finally – interested in learning about not only the North Korean institutions but also about ordinary North Korean people's lives, culture and so on. In his article 'Trends in the Study of North Korea', Charles Armstrong celebrates, 'The most original and challenging recent studies of the DPRK have tried to penetrate the notorious opacity of that society and explicate everyday life, ordinary people, and popular mentalities in North Korea' (Armstrong 2011: 358; also see Kang 2011/12). Reviewed, most notably, are: Andrei Lankov's *The Real North Korea: Life and Politics in Failed Stalinist Utopia* (2013); Patrick McEachern's *Inside the Red Box: North Korea's Post-totalitarian Politics* (2010); and Kim, Suk-young's *Illusive Utopia: Theatre, Film and Everyday Performances in North Korea* (2010). These excellently titled studies do exactly what their titles suggest: they seek to look *inside the real everyday* DPRK/North Korea to give us a good sense of how North Koreans themselves perceive their world and what has been unfolding in a place called North Korea. These studies are part of an alternative turn in North Korea research which promotes engaging with North Korea, as attested by a steady and growing stream of books by heavyweight North Korea observers, such as: Stephen Haggard and Marcus Noland's *Engaging North Korea: The Role of Economic Statecraft* (2011); Sung-chull Kim and David Kang's edited book *Engagement with North Korea: A Viable Alternative* (2009); or even earlier, Hazel Smith's edited book *Reconstituting Korean Security: A Policy Primer* (2007).

My interest in alternatives and the everyday significantly diverges from the literature on engagement and alternatives mentioned above. While I am personally curious about inside North Korea, I stay at the level of relations and encounters in my research because I do not think that knowing more about North Korea is going to solve the 'North Korea problem'. Ascertaining the meaning of North Korea and keeping North Korea in the object position have always concerned North Korea observers. I argue in this book that the subject-object binary that structures our imaginations of North Korea is what fundamentally needs rethinking. So, I begin by critically examining the (observant) international in the North Korea problem, i.e. how the international community (including researchers) pursues knowledge about North Korea and the terms and order of the encounter. For me, alternatives and re-imaginings of North Korea involve exploring how the terms and order of our encounters with North Korea can be altered. To be clear, this is not to take the side, in the debate on the cause of and solutions to the North Korea problem, of scholars who argue that external factors produced problems like North Korean famine, belligerence, government clamp-down on mobility of people, products and ideas and so on. I am instead arguing that the either/or framework (belligerent/peaceful, manipulative/genuine, mad/rational, unknowable/knowable) and a mix-of-both approach have a way of producing the impasse that has constrained the study of North Korea. In this final section of the Introduction, I sketch out some key issue areas in the study of North Korea to provide more context to the larger field of North Korea studies of which this book is a part.

Nuclear North Korea: engage or contain?

Since the inception of the North Korean state in the wake of the ceasefire of the Korean War in 1953, security and strategic studies have dominated academic productions of North Korea. For this and the reason that they are home to militaristic thinking, security and strategic studies form a good starting point for unpacking the previous and ongoing debates in the study of North Korea. The North Korean security problem has largely been a concern that North Korea would 'lash out' under a multitude of internal and external circumstances where 'belligerent "lashing out" is the best and only policy' for this small, isolated, failing state that is geopolitically positioned in a dense area of interest for regional powers (Cha 2002b: 221). As Samuel Kim helpfully explains, by region, this crucially includes the USA as 'the extra-territorial, lone superpower' (Kim 2002: 4). One way to enter the debate on the North Korean security problem is by examining how opinions differ on North Korean intentions and goals for acquiring nuclear technology.

First, though, a brief background on this topic, which is often dubbed the 'North Korean nuclear crises'. Analyses focus on two periods: the first crisis of 1992–93, when North Korea withdrew from the Non-Proliferation Treaty (NPT); and the second crisis, which 'began' in 2002 and was meant to be resolved through the multilateral communication of the Six-Party Talks. The common international narrative on the recurring crises is that the first nuclear crisis 'began' when the USA confronted North Korea about its 'suspicious activities' uncovered by US satellite intelligence (which it had known about since 1982), and 'ended' with former US President Jimmy Carter's visit which eventually led to the signing of the Agreed Framework (see Oberdorfer 1997: 249–368; Downs 1999; Sigal 1999; Noland 2000). Within the framework, the North Korean officials consented to freezing the plutonium-based nuclear programme, which involved rejoining the NPT and submitting to International Atomic Energy Agency (IAEA) inspections in exchange for fuel supplies and the construction of two light-water reactors (LWRs), which were to be overseen through the Korea Peninsula Energy Development Organization (KEDO), based in New York. The second nuclear crisis, of 2002, is largely seen to have followed a US confrontation followed by a North Korean confession about the secret nuclear weapons programme through a different method from the first (highly enriched uranium technology – HEU) (see Bleiker 2007: 219–20; Cha and Kang 2003: 130–33; Moon and Bae 2003). The confrontation immediately stopped further shipments of heavy fuel oil and KEDO activities. North Korea withdrew from the NPT again and the LWR programme has been suspended since 2003. The first of the Six-Party Talks, designed to resolve the North Korean nuclear problem through 'increased transparency, increased communication and coordinated negotiation', began in 2003 with China playing the convenor and hosting high-ranking diplomatic teams from North Korea, South Korea, the USA, Japan and Russia.

Revolving around whether the malign North Korean intentions of the Cold War era have changed in the present post-Cold War world, the different positions on nuclear North Korea are constructed along a pessimist/optimist divide. Debate in the literature focuses on why North Korea is developing nuclear technology, i.e. if it is really due to security concerns (and if so, whether these are defensive or offensive), or if North Korea's nuclear technology is actually for North Korea's brinkmanship diplomacy (for securing economic aid to ensure the survival of the regime). The ultimate question for the analysts involved in this debate is whether North Korea could be made to give up its nuclear ambition if the right proposition were formulated, or an acceptable international context created, for its leadership. I argue that this pessimist/optimist divide shows how the diverging opinions actually share a lot in common – that is, much of the scholarship mainly has as its focal point the desire to *contain* North Korea.

For pessimists like Victor Cha, given that North Korea's military capability remains potent and its political ideology remains hostile – both assessments in principal reference to North Korean nuclear ambitions – we should not so easily dismiss the idea that North Korea intends to use its military force if it becomes a viable option. Beginning from the premise that North Korea as a state actor has always been hostile, Cha notes that we have no new evidence that refutes the hypothesis informed by history that North Korea harbours a deep-seated hostility towards the rest of the world (Cha and Kang 2003: 81–86; also see Downs 2001; Yun 2004: 37–39). This idea that North Korea's fundamental and belligerent attitude explains all its actions more recently gained articulation in Jonathan Pollack's book, *No Exit: North Korea, Nuclear Weapons and International Security* (2011). Pollack writes that North Korea's pursuit and recent 'attainment' of nuclear status is a deep and long-entrenched part of the country, and that nothing that the USA or its neighbours offer or do would make North Korea forego nuclear weapons. For Pollack (2011: 184), the term 'North Korean nuclear issue' is a 'misnomer'; it is the history of North Korea that is the source of the North Korea problem. The pessimistic argument rests on an insistence that continuity can be traced from North Korea's inception to the present, i.e. state actors can change, but not by much if they are like North Korea. To be concise, for these scholars, '[a] rogue is a rogue is a rogue' (Bleiker 2005: ix).

The optimistic position, however, is that North Korean intentions have significantly altered in the post-Cold War era and can be further encouraged to change. In fact, David Kang, in a book written with Victor Cha, thinks that North Korea no longer harbours aggressive intentions towards the external world, nor retains the military capability to cause a full-blown war on the peninsula (Cha and Kang 2003: 46–54). Kang further notes that North Korea is genuinely pursuing domestic economic and social reforms that involve opening up to the outside world, which, in turn, makes military aggression undesirable. Moreover, Samuel Kim argues that North Korea's foreign policy in the post-Cold War era has been constrained and shaped most significantly by the hard-line US policies that have repeatedly escalated hostility and, in contrast, regional actors have successfully de-escalated tensions through avenues like the Six-Party Talks (Kim 2007: esp. 11–14; also see Suh 2004; Sigal 1999; Moon and Bae 2003; Bleiker 2005: 48–52; Armstrong 2004, 2005). Specifically on the issue of North Korean nuclear capability, Kang (in Cha and Kang 2003), together with Feffer (2003: 69–70, 156–57) and Sigal (1999: 6, 138–42), argues that enough evidence is available to conclude that the intention behind nuclear development, while ambiguous, is largely a deterrence measure in response to US hostility. The optimistic position is that diplomacy works; the North Korean threat is a resolvable diplomatic and technical problem that comes with the recognition that the present-day North Korea is not like the North Korea of its initial inception and subsequent years during the Cold War.

Thus, the two sides of the debate mirror each other in their opposition. North Korea is either hostile or cooperative, manipulative or genuine, unrepentant or reformist. It is either a threatening, weak state that can be influenced by the international community, or a state immune to international pressures or norms. Given that the stakes are so high, pessimists like Victor Cha argue for a cautionary assessment that accounts for the worst case scenario, and advise 'hawkish' engagement to stabilize the volatile North Korea and learn more about this rogue state's intentions (Cha and Kang 2003: 100; Pollack 2011: 209). Parenthetically, in his latest book, *The Impossible State: North Korea, Past and Future*, Cha (2012) goes further and corrects his earlier inconclusive position about North Korean nuclear intentions which advised hawkish engagement: North Korea is impossible to engage. For pessimists, the mantra is realist in that it takes domination in inter-state relations as a given wherein the idea is to presume the Other is guilty (a threat) until proven innocent (an ally). On the other hand, a neoliberal-institutionalist argument frames the optimistic approach: states (including North Korea) are rationally driven to cooperate, and cooperation increases the cost of reverting on reforms and resorting back to power politics. Ultimately, this 'rational' form of cooperation will lead to 'peace'.

My point is that while the two sides of the debate present themselves as significantly different, and in direct opposition, the optimists and the pessimists have a lot in common which together is illustrative of what is at stake in the North Korea security debate. The debate on North Korean intentions and

goals focuses on the genuine identity of the North Korean state and is por-
trayed as a case of either being with us or against us, where there is no possibility of neither or both. Both the pessimist and optimist camps accept
'threats', 'threat perceptions' and 'state intentions' as discernible fundaments
of the international reality as sanctioned by neorealism and neoliberalism.
They work within the 'objective' either/or matrices of order/disorder, hostile/
friendly and so on wherein North Korea *must* be assessed as either an ally or
an enemy at any given time. This produces the two sides of the debate, with
pessimists saying that North Korea still fears the outside world so it is still a
threat, and optimists saying, yes, but not in the same way as before and only
because we're sending mixed signals!

From this point of convergence, both positions take an instrumental
approach to engagement that comes with specific, pre-set goals: to disarm
North Korea and make the present politico-social, cultural and economic
system in North Korea a *relic* of the past that the USA and the liberal world
have triumphantly won and put behind, i.e. the Cold War. The pessimistic
position articulated by Victor Cha wants to talk to North Korea but wants
'normalized relations' (e.g. normal diplomatic relations and assistance in
reforms) to be dependent on solving the military problem first. Meanwhile,
optimists like David Kang want to use 'normalized relations' now as an
instrument for solving the military problem. My point is that, contrary to the
mantra that a containment strategy is no longer pursued in a post-Cold War
era, engagement here is already foreclosed by what it wants to achieve, i.e.
transform North Korea as we see fit either by coercion or incentive. This idea
that North Korea must reform is to argue that North Korean Otherness
(embodied in its political and economic systems) must be re-formed in our
image *and* its military disarmed as a two-pronged security measure against
irreconcilable differences. It is a way of containing, managing and disciplining
North Korean Otherness that equates Otherness with disorder and violence.

Broadened security narratives: a failed state problem

The idea of roguery powerfully renders North Korea as a deviant outlier state
in security debates wherein the scholarly concern is with the fundamental
incompatibility of North Korean ideology, economy and governance structures
with those of the dominant Western states (see Ahn and Paik 1999: 80–81;
Cha and Kang 2003: 78–80; Hassig and Oh 2000; Bermudez 2006; Park 2007;
Dalton *et al.* 2012). This image of North Korea crucially rests on the idea
that there is something sinister about what is going on inside the country.

The failed state literature on North Korea, composed using a wide array of
diagnostic frameworks, namely human rights, humanitarianism and development, systematically pursues this. Here, North Korea is a case of a 'hard'
failed state that 'has repeatedly shown a willingness to allow its population to
suffer extreme deprivation' (Haggard and Noland 2005: 9). Scott Snyder
makes this same point by way of comparison. He writes, 'Unlike the "failed

states" of Africa, where political chaos has led to systemic breakdowns, the North Korean leadership has used totalitarian methods of political mobilization to maintain control despite the breakdown of the economic system' (Snyder 2000: 533). In short, if it were not for the draconian social control mechanisms reinforced by official propaganda, we would unambiguously observe the usual indicators of political chaos and systemic breakdowns observed in other failed states. North Korea is a 'peculiar' failed state in the sense that it is a failed state in every way – economically, politically, socially and ideologically – but its belligerent iron-fisted regime hinders transparent assessments of the situation and our implementation of existing international programmes that accompany our diagnoses.

A rogue is 'a creature that is born different ... incapable of mingling with the herd, it keeps to itself, and it can attack at any time, without warning' (Derrida, in Dillon and Reid 2009: 141). *If* so, an important dimension of the problem of rogues is that they scare (and fascinate) us not only because they are deviant but more so because this deviance is thought to be inborn and incorrigible. The formulation of North Korea as a problem of *rogue* failed state seems actually to preclude 'genuinely' successful reform and integration of North Korea into the international community. In different ways, scholars have made the argument that the designation 'rogue' denotes a systematic and rationalized response to a North Korea that exhibits an ability to pursue a foreign policy that can disrupt 'the new world order' under US hegemony (e.g. Bleiker 2005: 52–55, 2003; Gordy and Lee 2009; Homolar 2010). In other words, fear of rogues is fear of small state actors with 'unknown' and unregulated capacities to unleash disorder. Failed state narratives of North Korea and its economic, human rights and humanitarian problem contribute to and stem from this fear/fascination with outliers, which is intimately linked to the post-Cold War juncture of the present postcolonial global context.

I ask here how rogue failed states can be reformed if what becomes seen as roguery and failure are attributes that this state under interrogation deems essential for its system. In other words, what are our possible responses to fundamentally incommensurable worldviews that contest the very basis of our moral, economic and political judgements of the rogue failed state? The only options seem to be that either we can keep our terms of debate that define difference as roguery, deviance and threat, or we can explore ways that operate beyond our somehow unshakable sense that we are right and our judgements are sound. Debates that gain articulation within the first sensibility include: contentions about the causes of North Korean famine of the 1990s; assessments of North Korean economy; the extent of the regime's ability to introduce reform; the role that the international community should play in the marketization and opening up of North Korean economy and society; (im)possible North Korean human rights policies for international stakeholders; and finally, debate on whether cooperation or isolation of the North Korean government (which works towards regime change) works in inducing change inside North Korea.

The importance of nature and normalcy – that is, the idea that difference is an abnormality and that sameness/difference is somehow inborn and natural – in the construction of the North Korea failed state problem is plainly visible in the diagnosis and prescription of the poor performance of North Korea's economy. Marcus Noland, an economist, writes, 'One way to get a sense of how North Korea might look as a "normal" country is to use a standard "gravity" model of bilateral trade to simulate its post-reform trade pattern' (Noland 2000: 262). Noland uses his 'standard "gravity" model' to generate what he calls 'North Korea's "natural" pattern of trade' (ibid.: 262), and thus is able to show that if North Korea were to reform to become a 'normal' economy (i.e. liberal capitalist) and trade with countries like Japan, South Korea and China, then its 'natural' share would be greater than its current one as an unnatural economy that is largely closed. The idea here is that North Korea's current trade share is a 'distorted' percentage due to its self-reliant economic policy. Elsewhere, Noland further argues that this problem could be fixed if North Korea were to utilize its comparative advantage and trade with its 'natural' trade partners (Noland *et al.* 2000: 1773, Table 4). In this jointly written piece, Noland and his co-writers argue that the 'North Korean international trade share (exports plus imports) is around 12% of GDP [gross domestic product], which is well below the 50–55% observed in South Korea and a fraction of the trade share that North Korea would exhibit if it were a "normal" country of its size and structure' (ibid.: 1768). Furthermore, its military economy is seen to 'distort labour and factor mobilisation', which must be addressed if the North Korean economy is to open up and take advantage of its 'natural trade shares' (ibid.: 1774; Noland 2000: 261). Noland sums up the sentiment among observers of the North Korean economy when he concludes, 'North Korea is the most distorted economy in the world' (Noland 2000: 282). In Noland's later collaboration with political scientist Stephan Haggard, the pair argue that the North Korean regime's rogue policies are at fault: 'With effective [global] institutions and adequate [global] physical supplies, the occurrence of famine increasingly signals not lack of food or capacity, but some fundamental political or governance failure [of the country]' (Haggard and Noland 2005: 9). Only with political change would the resources and technical assistance from the international community be effective (Haggard and Noland 2007: 219; Scalapino 2007; Eberstadt 2007: 4–13). Humanitarian aid becomes a deep problem for these scholars because it does not get to the 'root' of the issue and, in fact, even worsens the problem by keeping in power those responsible for the famine. Haggard and Noland again articulate this poignantly:

Should the international community provide assistance even if it means prolonging the life of a despotic regime? Does aid prolong the very policies that led to the famine in the first place? Should donors provide assistance even if some portion of that assistance is diverted to undeserving groups, including the military and party cadre? If the decision is made to provide assistance, how can donors guarantee that food aid reaches vulnerable groups and achieves other objectives, such as inducing economic reforms or empowering new social groups?

(Haggard and Noland 2005: 10)

Haggard and Noland (2005: 37) recommend that unless the government policy that resists monitoring changes, 'scarce resources [of the international community] must be better deployed elsewhere [outside North Korea]'.

Hazel Smith (2008) criticizes Haggard and Noland in particular for creating 'fairy tales' about the 'wicked witch of the East' with their view that the regime is starving its population intentionally and prioritizing the military. In contrast to the above concerns, Smith has long argued for a cooperative approach to responding to North Korea's poverty and the opacity of the regime's workings. For instance, on the issue of monitoring humanitarian aid, which has been a contentious issue that led to the withdrawal of many Western nongovernmental organizations (NGOs) and agencies from North Korea in 2001/02, Smith (2005: 134) argues for 'practical solutions' within the existing humanitarian approaches, such as greater compromise by both the North Korean officials and the humanitarian workers. In Smith's view, North Korean officials should comply with the basic operational norms of transparency, accountability and efficiency to uphold the international humanitarian principle that aid go to the most vulnerable groups in a systematic and neutral manner (see also Reed 2004, 2005). In turn, the aid workers should be more patient and understanding that building trust takes time in North Korea (Smith 2005: 105).

What I am pointing to here is that hierarchic posturing that targets a changing cast of North Korean referents from a distance and from above is the unquestioned, but incredibly dubious, starting point for scientific productions of North Korea. They variously and devastatingly retain hierarchy, security and self-referentiality as promising ways of relating in contact zones. Put more pointedly, academic engagements with North Korea are overdetermined by the various selves – the international community, the USA, the academic discipline and the academic – and operate squarely within a hierarchic mode of encounter that seeks to contain and master the other and otherness. Rather than treat North Korea as an object of study, my suggestion is that we understand North Korea as a complex site of power relations in the post-Cold War era. This means thoroughly challenging the subject/object binary that variously structures how encounters involving 'North Korea' occur. Most problematic is the scientific productions of 'hard' failed state which depict the state, economy, human condition and society in law-like language as if we were talking about the natural world. Working within a static and homogenized understanding of the natural world, they claim that comparisons between states, economies, societies and populations can be made in 'natural' and 'neutral' terms because they are supposedly backed up by complex theoretical models and reasoning. Here, science turns all that it touches – nature, realities in North Korea, economic and bodily processes, possible futures, relations – into static, two-dimensional objects to be managed and acted upon.

Finally, I ask, how else can we respond to and be responsible for the problem of suffering, violence and oppression in ways that attend to incommensurable differences? How can we speak out against violence and atrocities that at the same attend to issues of intercultural differences which refuse to mobilize existing hierarchies (international/North Korea, normal/deviant, fortunate/unfortunate) in our favour? How do we act ethically while recognizing the continual deference of objective reality and position?

Critical and cultural approaches to the 'North Korea problem'

Historians Bruce Cumings (2004) and Charles Armstrong (2004, 2005) have long criticized how pervasively the 'Otherness' of North Korea – as backwards and unfit or as somehow an inferior mirror-image of the South Korean self – structures popular sentiment and policy towards North Korea in the USA. Cultural and communications scholars also document the politics of Other in the citizenship/identity discourses in South Korea (see Sung 2009, 2010; Jager 2002; Hughes 2008). From the discipline of IR, Jae-Jung Suh illustrates this point by explaining how the US–South Korea military alliance crucially depends on 'the extent to which South Korea and the United States see North Korea's identity eye to eye' as an Other (Suh 2007: 173). In similar critical spirit, Roland Bleiker (2005) focuses on relations and argues for an ethics of difference that fundamentally questions the prevailing problem-solving premise that reductively posits the international and South Korea as sources of solutions and redemption. IR scholars such as Bleiker (2005) and Suh (2007), as well as political scientists like Koo (2006, 2007), have begun reconceptualizing traditional IR/security frameworks. These scholars challenge the conventional security framework by showing how the 'North Korea threat' is a problem produced by states. While offering different accounts of how this has occurred, Bleiker, Suh and Koo converge on the premise that all the states involved – not just North Korea – need to change if we are to address the security concerns of the Korean people (in the North and South) rather than the security of privileged states such as the USA and Japan.

In my opinion, Bleiker (2005) pushes conventional wisdom the furthest when he insists that the 'North Korean threat' is one which requires a solution that promotes reconciliation by forgiveness and transforms the root of the antagonism through everyday, face-to-face experiences. For Bleiker, what lies at the heart of the problem is antagonistic identities rooted in Cold War geopolitics and the institutionalized memory of the Korean War produced by states in the name of 'national security'. Both Suh (2007) and Koo (2006) offer analyses that are narrower in scope and remain mostly concerned with restructuring the military. For instance, Koo turns to the transformative potential of a 'peace-state' identity, which he envisions as a political system driven by peace rather than security which necessarily entails a reduction of armed forces as a key structural change. The idea here is that if one Korea adopts a 'peace-state' identity, then the two Koreas would truly be on their way towards the kind of reconciliation and unification that best ensures human security.[5] These reformulations highlight how the culture of (in)security in the region must be altered to 'solve' the North Korea security problem but do so in a way that remains state-centric. One major premise that prevails in this strand of thought is that states can be made more benign at the international level by mending their exclusionary national identities (i.e. from antagonistic to 'shared' or 'reconciled') and redefining national goals and priorities (i.e. from 'security' to 'peace'). The assumption here is that states as actors can be altered to pursue more benign goals and enact more benign identities by simply 'fixing' the problematic components of the state.

In the chapters that follow, I want to trouble two things: the retention of the state as a political unit, and how the goal of Korean unification remains the main way in which the North Korean problem is engaged. I believe the two retentions from a traditional security framework – the (nation)-state as a unit of analysis and national unification as a political goal – are related, in that they are mutually reinforcing and similarly problematic. What alternative forms of political community remain unexplored in keeping the idea of a nation-state? Is Korean unification and the recognition of a singular national identity of Korea the only answer to peace on the peninsula? What kind of peace is enabled (and what kind of peace is silenced) by insisting on a single national identity of Korean-ness for all subjects we call Koreans? Is tolerance and acceptance of difference of North and South Korea(ns) – the ethics of difference that Bleiker prescribes – the answer to the North Korea problem, or is there a more complex ethics of difference that could apply to the North Korean case?

While Bleiker and Koo differ considerably in what the idea of 'one Korea' means (which inevitably leads to differences of opinion on the definition of 'peaceful unification'), all *solely* work within the idea of 'one Korea state'.[6] In Bleiker's defence, he does justify his framing by pointing to the 'strong myth' of insider/outsider and Korean/foreigner that exists in both Koreas and the particular kind of nationalism that dominates both societies. However, my contention here is that the idea of insider/outsider in Korean nationalism is a modern myth (Han 2007; Shin 2006), and while Bleiker is right to position contemporary nationalism as a powerful discourse, we might want to look at less-dominant versions of nationalism or alternative discourses of political community to explore how the insecurity problems on the Korean peninsula can be framed and solved. My point is that a heterogeneous reconceptualization of political identities, values and projects with respect to the North Korea/South Korea/international community nexus is important *because* the myth of a homogenous society is so strong in the dominant Korean discourse. Silence on these questions about alternative formulations of political community and peace occurs because an assumption prevails that because the divided status of the peninsula is a major source of insecurity, then it must mean that solutions lie mainly in reunification. Maybe so, but this should not mean national unification becomes the *main* site to work on, or that we must conceive of reunification in a reductive or homogenous way.

Similar questions and concerns can be raised about seeking alternatives through the concept of human security in Koo and Bleiker. In chapters that follow, I trace how broadening the concept of security to 'human security' to encompass other human pursuits such as peace, freedom, equality and justice, and to involve the wider referent of humans, 'securitizes' these human pursuits and creates the illusion that 'security' can encompass all humans. On the former point of securitizing other human pursuits (i.e. universalizing the practice of 'making something and oneself secure' in all spheres), one might ask whether the concept of secure freedom, secure equality, or secure justice best 'secures' these social aspirations, or whether these aspirations are even securable. For instance, would not securitizing these aspirations necessarily depoliticize the violent process of 'administering' justice, equality, freedom and peace, given that desiring them in secure forms requires understanding them as stable, pre-determinable objects? Similarly, on the latter point of widening the security referent, one could question whether broadening security out to include all humans eschews the exclusionary and violent production of difference involved in the underlying logic of state security at work in 'human security'. It is hard to say that it does, since in defining their 'inclusive' formulation – who and what is 'human' – enacts its own exclusions and violence and thus echoes my earlier concerns about closure in retaining the idea of state.

Interestingly, security, nation-state and national rhetoric of reconciliation and unification that seemed to constrain political imagination open out to a different world in Ryang and Lie's critical research from the field site of Japan (Ryang and Lie 2009; Ryang 2000, 2009a; Lie 2008). Anthropological and historical in their emphasis, this body of work already begins from the field of everyday, and in this sense already distinguishes itself from Bleiker, who seeks to take IR there (and spends much of his time trying to get there), or Suh and Koo, who do not explicitly locate their imagination/concern anywhere in particular and are unapologetically engrossed in the elite world of 'decision makers'. Moreover, while not completely unfettered by the international narratives about the 'North Korea problem', their agenda extends far beyond correcting proclamations about North Korea as a rogue failed state and a totalitarian society. As Ryang put it:

> We are told, time and again, that North Koreans are loyal to their leader, that they would do anything, even die, for him, and that they are fiercely proud and nationalistic. But, equally, we are told that they are oppressed, suffering, and ready to rise against the evil dictator. What do we know beyond or between these opposing assumptions? We do not even know why and how they are like that and, indeed, even if they *are* like that. We

are not equipped with the conceptual tools that could lead us beyond the current securitization of our discourses on North Korea.

(Ryang 2009b: 5, emphasis in original)

I share their interest in developing alternative perspectives on North Korea but I diverge from this body of research in at least one important way. As stated earlier, I am not interested in knowing *about* North Korea, even if it is a better or more ethical form. The main concern, as further elaborated in the next chapter, is to remain in the realm of relations to critically *and* culturally explore the international dimension of how North Korea gets constructed. I stay attuned to issues of aesthetics, emotion and desire, which displaces the problematic emphasis on rational and institutional dimensions or grand societal-level processes in much of the research about North Korea. I am interested in an intimate, contingent rethinking of the Korean conflict and North Korea in international relations attuned to everyday practices and performances. As I prepare to publish my research, critical research on North Korea that rigorously engages the themes of representation and culture has begun to emerge (e.g. Kim 2010; Gelézeau *et al.* 2013; Shim 2013). I am excited and I celebrate their flamboyant claims that they each tell us something new in relation to North Korea. However, I also ask, including myself, how does foregrounding issues of representation and culture matter in ushering in political transformation for those who are most intimately entangled, marked and constrained by the cultural politics of international imagination?

Notes

1 'Other' is consistently capitalized in this book because 'the Other' has become so iconic in its usage and meaning that it seems to demand a proper noun status. It is also capitalized, rather contradictorily perhaps, to accentuate the theoretical commitment of this thesis that seeks to recognize the agency, plurality and presence of what is deemed the Other.
2 The timeframe in this research begins from the late 1990s, during which period we see a growth in cultural representations of North Korea in mainstream cultures. Cultural engagements on the theme of divided Korea in South Korean popular culture date back much further and are important as related discourses (see Lee 2000; Standish 1992). However, my focus is on how this theme of divided Korea feeds into the constructions of North Korea from the late 1990s and 2000s.
3 While productions in other languages abound (e.g. French and Japanese), they are often translated and their cultural imaginings are circulated in Korean and/or English languages. This is not to say that the focus solely on English and Korean language productions does not have its limits with respect to the heterogeneity and multiplicity of cultural and political imaginations. The hope is that this focus on English and Korean representations serves as a useful beginning for further interrogations of the intermixing and translation between the different language productions.
4 Alternatively, Gloria Anzaldua (1987) terms this space 'borderland' and emphasizes the alternative 'emancipatory' consciousness that emerges in this space. Anzaldua's formulation of space of encounters with otherness offers a different way

in which contact zones can be conceptualized and explored. Unfortunately, the full implications of this alternative formulation remain mostly unexplored in this book.
  5 For Koo, a 'peace state' is a process rather than an attribute, so adopting a 'peace-state' identity does not immediately mean the complete rejection of arms and the idea of national defence, but rather indicates a move towards the reduction and reprioritizing of defence in state policy. However, the mechanism by which one country's 'peace-state' identity changes another is complex (Koo 2006: 39–41; Koo 2007: 37–80, 225–39).
  6 Suh's analysis remains strictly on military alliance systems, institutional alliances and state identity, and thus contributes little to these larger questions.

Bibliography

Agathangelou, Anna and Ling, L.H.M. (2009) *Transforming World Politics: From Empire to Multiple Worlds*, London: Routledge.

Ahmed, Sara (2000) *Strange Encounter: Embodied Others in Post-coloniality*, London: Routledge.

Ahn, Byung-Joon and Paik, Jin-Hyun (1999) 'North Korean Communism in the Post-communist World: House of Kim or House of Cards?' in Jin-Young Suh and Chanrok, Soh (eds) *The World After the Cold War*, Seoul: Graduate School of International Studies, Korea University.

Anzaldua, Gloria (1987) *Borderlands/La Frontera: The New Mestiza*, San Francisco, CA: Aunt Lute Books.

Armstrong, Charles (2004) 'Inter-Korean Relations: A North Korean Perspective', in Samuel S. Kim (ed.) *Inter-Korean Relations: Problems and Prospects*, Basingstoke: Palgrave Macmillan.

——(2005) 'Inter-Korean Relations in Historical Perspective', *International Journal of Korean Unification Studies* 14 (2): 1–20, www.kinu.or.kr/upload/neoboard/DATA03/Vol.14,%20No.2_Charles%20K.%20Armstrong.pdf (accessed March 2012).

——(2011) 'Trends in the Study of North Korea', *Journal of Asian Studies* 70 (2): 357–71.

Ashley, Richard K. (1988) 'Untying the Sovereign State: A Double Reading of the Anarchy Problematique', *Millennium: Journal of International Studies* 17: 227–62.

Bermudez, Joseph S. Jr (2006) *North Korea's Strategic Culture*, SAIC, www.dtra.mil/documents/asco/publications/comparitive_strategic_cultures_curriculum/case%20stud ies/North%20Korea%20(Bermudez)%20final%201%20Nov%2006.pdf (accessed May 2009).

Bhabha, Homi (1994) *The Location of Culture*, London: Routledge.

Bhambra, Gurminder and Shilliam, Robbie (eds) (2009) *Silencing Human Rights: Critical Engagements with a Contested Project*, Basingstoke: Palgrave Macmillan.

Biersteker, Thomas J. and Weber, Cynthia (eds) (1996) *State Sovereignty as Social Construct*, Cambridge: Cambridge University Press.

Bleiker, Roland (2003) 'A Rogue is a Rogue is a Rogue: US Foreign Policy and the Korean Nuclear Crisis', *International Affairs* 79 (4): 719–37.

——(2005) *Divided Korea: Toward a Culture of Reconciliation*, Minneapolis: University of Minnesota Press.

——(2007) 'Dealing with a Nuclear North Korea: Conventional and Alternative Security Scenarios', in Anthony Burke and Matt Mcdonald (eds) *Critical Security in the Asia-Pacific*, Manchester: Manchester University Press.

——(2009) *Aesthetics and World Politics: Rethinking Peace and Conflict Studies*, Basingstoke: Palgrave Macmillan.

Browne, M. Anne (2002) *Human Rights and the Borders of Suffering: The Promotion of Human Rights in International Politics*, Manchester: Manchester University Press.

Campbell, David (1992) *Writing Security: United States Foreign Policy and the Politics of Identity*, Minneapolis: University of Minnesota Press.

——(2007) 'Geopolitics and Visuality: Sighting the Darfur Conflict', *Political Geography* 26: 357–82.

Cha, Victor (2002a) 'North Korea's Weapons of Mass Destruction: Badges, Shields, or Swords?', *Political Science Quarterly* 117 (2): 209–30.

——(2002b) 'Assessing the North Korean Threat: The Logic of Pre-emption, Prevention, and Engagement', in Samuel S. Kim and Tai Hwan Lee (eds) *North Korea and Northeast Asia*, Lanham, MD: Rowman and Littlefield.

——(2012) *The Impossible State: North Korea, Past and Future*, New York: Harper Collins.

Cha, Victor and Kang, David (2003) *Nuclear North Korea: A Debate on Engagement Strategies*, New York: Columbia University Press.

Chow, Rey (1995) *Primitive Passions: Visuality, Sexuality, Ethnography and Contemporary Chinese Cinema*, New York: Columbia University Press.

Chowdhry, Geeta and Nair, Sheila (eds) (2002) *Power, Postcolonialism, and International Relations: Reading Race, Gender and Class*, London: Routledge.

Connolly, William E. (2002) *Neuropolitics: Thinking, Culture, Speed*, Minneapolis: University of Minnesota Press.

Cumings, Bruce (2004) *North Korea: Another Country*, New York: New Press.

Dalton, Toby and Lewis, Jeffrey, with Lee, Sung-yoon and Pollack, Jonathan D. (2012) 'Book Review Roundtable', *Asian Policy* 13: 167–90.

Dillon, Michael and Reid, Julian (2009) *The Liberal Way of War: Killing to Make Life Live*, London: Routledge.

Doty, Roxanne L. (1996) *Imperial Encounters: The Politics of Representation in North-South Relations*, Minneapolis: University of Minnesota Press.

Downs, Chuck (1999) *Over the Line: North Korea's Negotiating Strategy*, Washington, DC: The AEI Press.

——(2001) 'Discerning North Korea's Intentions', in Nicholas Eberstadt and Richard J. Ellings (eds) *Korea's Future and the Great Powers*, London: The National Bureau of Asian Research in association with University of Washington Press.

Eberstadt, Nicholas (2000) 'Disparities in Socioeconomic Development in Divided Korea', *Asian Survey* 40 (6): 867–93.

——(2007) *The North Korean Economy: Between Crisis and Catastrophe*, London: Transaction.

Eberstadt, Nicholas and Banister, Judith (1992) 'Divided Korea: Demographic and Socioeconomic Issues for Reunification', *Population and Development Review* 18 (3): 505–31.

Edkins, Jenny (2000) *Whose Hunger? Concepts of Famine, Practices of Aid*, Minneapolis: University of Minnesota Press.

——(2006) 'The Local, the Global and the Trouble', *Critical Review of International Social and Political Philosophy* 9 (4): 488–511.

Edkins, Jenny and Pin-Fat, Veronique and Shapiro, Michael (eds) (2004) *Sovereign Lives: Power in Global Politics*, London: Routledge.

Feffer, John (2003) *North Korea South Korea: U.S. Policy at a Time of Crisis*, New York: Seven Stories Press.

Gelézeau, Valérie, de Ceuster, Koen and Delissen, Alain (eds) (2013) *De-Bordering Korea: Tangible and Intangible Legacies of the Sunshine Policy*, Abingdon: Routledge.

Gordy, Katherine and Lee, Jee Sun E. (2009) 'Rogue Specters: Cuba and North Korea at the Limits of US Hegemony', *Alternatives: Global, Local, Political* 34: 229–48.

Haggard, Stephan and Noland, Marcus (2005) *Hunger and Human Rights: The Politics of Famine in North Korea*, Washington, DC: US Committee for Human Rights in North Korea.

——(2007) *Famine in North Korea: Markets, Aid, and Reform*, New York: Columbia University Press.

——(2008) 'Authors' Response: Famine in North Korea – A Reprise', *Asia Policy* 5: 203–21, Book Review Roundtable, asiapolicy.nbr.org (accessed June 2009).

——(2011) *Engaging North Korea: The Role of Economic Statecraft*, Honolulu, HI: East-West Center, www.eastwestcenter.org/sites/default/files/private/ps059_0.pdf (accessed April 2014).

Han, Kyung-Koo (2007) 'The Archaeology of the Ethnically Homogeneous Nation-state and Multiculturalism in Korea', *Korea Journal*, Winter: 8–31.

Hansen, Lene (2000) 'The Little Mermaid's Silent Security Dilemma and the Absence of Gender in the Copenhagen School', *Millennium: Journal of International Studies* 29 (2): 285–306.

Hassig, Ralph C. and Oh, Kongdan (2000) *North Korea through the Looking Glass*, Washington, DC: Brookings Institution.

Homolar, Alexandra. (2010) 'Rebels without a Conscience: The Evolution of the Rogue States Narrative in US Security Policy', *European Journal of International Relations* 17 (4): 705–27.

Hughes, Theodore (2008) '"North Koreans" and Other Virtual Subjects: Kim Yong-ha, Hwang Seok-yeong and National Division in the Age of Posthumanism', *The Review of Korean Studies* 11 (1): 99–117.

Hwang, Eui-gak (1993) *The Korean Economies: A Comparison of North and South*, Oxford: Clarendon Press.

Inayatullah, Naeem and Blaney, David L. (2004) *International Relations and the Problem of Difference*, London: Routledge.

Ireson, Randall (2006) 'Food Security in North Korea: Designing Realistic Possibilities', Shorenstein APARC, shrenstein.stanford.edu (accessed July 2009).

Jager, Sheila Miyoshi (2002) 'Monumental Histories: Manliness, the Military, and the War Memorial', *Public Culture* 14 (2): 387–409.

Kang, C.S. Eliot (2001) 'North Korea and the U.S. Grand Security Strategy', *Comparative Strategy* 20: 25–43.

Kang, David (1998) 'North Korea: Deterrence through Danger', in Muthiah Alagappa (ed.) *Asian Security Practice: Material and Ideational Influences*, Stanford, CA: Stanford University Press.

——(2003) 'International Relations Theory and the Second Korean War', *International Studies Quarterly* 47 (3): 301–24.

——(2011/12) 'They Think they're Normal: Enduring Questions and New Research on North Korea – A Review Essay', *International Security* 36: 142–71.

Kim, Byung-Yeon, Kim, Suk Jin and Lee, Keun (2007) 'Assessing the Economic Performance of North Korea, 1954–89: Estimates and Growth Accounting Analysis', *Journal of Comparative Economics* 35: 564–82.

Kim, Samuel S. (2002) 'North Korea and Northeast Asia in World Politics', in Samuel S. Kim and Tai Hwan Lee (eds) *North Korea and Northeast Asia*, Lanham, MD: Rowman and Littlefield.

——(2004) 'Introduction: Managing the Korean Conflict', in Samuel S. Kim (ed.) *Inter-Korean Relations: Problems and Prospects*, New York: Palgrave Macmillan.

——(2007) *North Korean Foreign Relations in the Post-Cold War World*, Strategic Studies Institute, US Army War College, www.strategicstudiesinstitute.army.mil/pubs/display.cgm?PubID=772 (accessed January 2009).

Kim, Samuel S. and Lee, Tai Hwan (eds) (2002) *North Korea and Northeast Asia*, New York: Rowman and Littlefield.

Kim, Suk-young (2010) *Illusive Utopia: Theatre, Film and Everyday Performances in North Korea*, Ann Arbor: Michigan University Press.

Kim, Sung-chull and Kang, David (eds) (2009) *Engagement with North Korea: A Viable Alternative*, Albany, NY: SUNY Press.

Koo, Kap-woo (2006) 'The System of Division on the Korean Peninsula and Building a "Peace State"', *Korea Journal* Autumn: 11–48.

——(2007) *Critical Peace Studies and the Korean Peninsula (Bipanjeok Pyeonghwa-Yeongu-wa Hanbando)*, Seoul: Humanitas.

Krishna, Sankaran (1999) *Postcolonial Insecurities: India, Sri Lanka and the Question of Nationhood*, Minneapolis: University of Minnesota Press.

Lankov, Andrei (2013) *The Real North Korea: Life and Politics in the Failed Stalinist Utopia*, Oxford: Oxford University Press.

Lee, Hyangjin (2000) *Contemporary Korean Cinema: Identity, Culture and Politics*, Manchester: Manchester University Press.

Lie, John (2008) *Zainichi (Koreans in Japan): Diasporic Nationalism and Postcolonial Identity*, Berkeley, CA: Global, Area, and International Archive, University of California.

Lisle, Debbie (2003) 'Screening Global Politics', *International Feminist Journal of Politics* 5 (1): 134–41.

——(2006) *Global Politics of Contemporary Travel Writing*, New York: Cambridge University Press.

Manning, Robert A. (1997) 'The United States and the Endgame in Korea: Assessment, Scenarios, and Implications', *Asian Survey* 37 (7): 597–608.

McEachern, Patrick (2010) *Inside the Red Box: North Korea's Post-totalitarian Politics*, New York: Columbia University Press.

Moon, Chung-in (2002) 'The Sunshine Policy and the Korean Summit: Assessments and Prospects', in Tsuneo Akaha (ed.) *The Future of North Korea*, London: Routledge.

Moon, Chung-in and Bae, J.Y. (2003) 'The Bush Doctrine and the North Korean Nuclear Crisis', *Asian Perspectives* 27 (4): 9–45.

Moon, Chung-in and Kim, Yongho (2001) 'The Future of the North Korean System', in Samuel S. Kim (ed.) *The North Korean System in the Post-Cold War Era*, New York: Palgrave.

Noland, Marcus (1997) 'Why North Korea will Muddle Through', *Foreign Affairs* 76, 4: 105–18.

——(2000) *Avoiding the Apocalypse: The Future of Two Koreas*, Washington, DC: Institute for International Economics.

Noland, Marcus, Robinson, Sherman and Wang, Tao (2000) 'Rigorous Speculation: The Collapse and Revival of the North Korean Economy', *World Development* 28 (10): 1767–87.

Oberdorfer, Don (1997) *The Two Koreas: A Contemporary History*, London: Little, Brown and Co.

O'Hanlon, Michael and Mochizuki, Michael (2003) *Crisis on the Korean Peninsula: How to Deal with a Nuclear North Korea*, New York: McGraw-Hill.

Orford, Anne (2003) *Reading Humanitarian Intervention: Human Rights and the Use of Force in International Law*, Cambridge: Cambridge University Press.

Pak, Sunyoung (2004) 'The Biological Standard of Living in the Two Koreas', *Economics and Human Biology* 2: 511–21.

Park, Han S. (2007) 'Military-first Politics (Songun): Understanding Kim Jong-il's North Korea', *Korea Economic Institute Academic Paper Series* 2 (7): 1–9, keia.org/publication/military-first-politics-songun-understanding-kim-jong-ils-north-korea.

Pollack, Jonathan D. (2011) *No Exit: North Korea, Nuclear Weapons and International Security*, London and Abingdon: International Institute for Strategic Studies and Routledge.

Pollack, Jonathan D. and Lee, Chung Min (1999) *Preparing for Korean Unification: Scenarios and Implications*, Washington, DC: Rand Corporation, Arroyo Center.

Pratt, Mary Louise (1992) *Imperial Eyes: Travel Writing and Transculturation*, London: Routledge.

Pritchard, Charles L. (2007) *Failed Diplomacy: The Tragic Story of how North Korea got the Bomb*, Washington, DC: Brookings Institution Press.

Reed, Edward (2004) 'Unlikely Partners: Humanitarian Aid Agencies and North Korea', in Choong-yong Ahn, Nicholas Eberstadt and Young-sun Lee (eds) *A New International Engagement Framework for North Korea? Contending Perspectives*, Washington, DC: Korea Economic Institute.

——(2005) 'The Role of International Aid Organizations in the Development of North Korea: Experience and Prospects', *Asian Perspective* 29 (3): 51–72.

Ryang, Sonia (ed.) (2000) *Koreans in Japan: Critical Voices from the Margin*, London: Routledge.

——(ed.) (2009a) *North Korea: Toward a Better Understanding*, Plymouth: Lexington Books.

——(2009b) 'Introduction: North Korea – Going beyond Security and Enemy Rhetoric', in Sonia Ryang (ed.) *North Korea: Toward a Better Understanding*, Plymouth: Lexington Books.

Ryang, Sonia and Lie, John (eds) (2009) *Diaspora without Homeland: Being Korean in Japan*, Berkeley, CA: Global, Area and International Archive and University of California.

Scalapino, Robert A. (2007) 'North Korea – Challenge for the Major Powers', *Asian Security* 3 (1): 2–11.

Schwekendiek, Daniel (2008) 'Determinants of Well-being in North Korea: Evidence from the Post-famine Period', *Economics and Human Biology* 6: 446–54.

Scobell, Andrew (2006) 'Kim Jong Il and North Korea: The Leader and the System', *Strategic Studies Institute*, www.strategicstudiesinstitute.army.mil/pubs/display.cfm?PubID=644 (accessed July 2009).

Shapiro, Michael J. (1997) *Violent Cartographies: Mapping Cultures of War*, Minneapolis, MN: University of Minnesota Press.

——(1999) *Cinematic Political Thought: Narrating Race, Nation and Gender*, Edinburgh: Edinburgh University Press.

Shih, Shu-mei and Lionnet, Françoise (eds) (2005) *Minor Transnationalism*, Durham, NC: Duke University Press.

Shim, David (2013) *Visual Politics and North Korea: Seeing is Believing*, Abingdon: Routledge.

Shin, Gi-Wook (2006) *Ethnic Nationalism in Korea: Genealogy, Politics, and Legacy*, Stanford, CA: Stanford University Press.

Sigal, Leon V. (1999) *Disarming Strangers: Nuclear Diplomacy with North Korea*, Princeton, NJ: Princeton University Press.

Smith, Hazel (2000) 'Bad, Mad, Sad or Rational Actor? Why the "Securitization" Paradigm Makes for Poor Policy Analysis of North Korea', *International Affairs* 76 (3): 593–617.

——(2005) *Hungry for Peace: International Security, Humanitarian Assistance and Social Change in North Korea*, Washington, DC: United States Institute for Peace.

——(2007) *Reconstituting Korean Security: A Policy Primer*, Tokyo: United Nations University Press.

——(2008) 'North Korea as the Wicked Witch of the East: Social Science as Fairy Tale', *Asia Policy* 5: 197–203, Book Review Roundtable, asiapolicy.nbr.org (accessed July 2009).

Snyder, Scott (2000) 'North Korea's Challenge of Regime Survival: Internal Problems and Implications for the Future', *Pacific Affairs* 73 (4): 517–33.

Son, Key-young (2006) *South Korean Engagement Policies and North Korea: Identities, Norms and the Sunshine Policy*, London: Routledge.

Song, Jiyoung (2011) *Human Rights Discourse in North Korea: Post-Colonial, Marxist and Confucian Perspectives*, Abingdon: Routledge.

Spivak, Gayatri C. (2004) 'Right Wrongs', *The South Atlantic Quarterly* 103 (2/3): 523–81.

Standish, Isolde (1992) 'United in Han: Korean Cinema and the "New Wave"', *Korea Journal* 32 (4): 109–18.

Suh, Jae-jung (2004) 'Bound to Last? The U.S.-Korea Alliance and Analytical Eclecticism', in J.J. Suh, Peter Katzenstein and Allen Carlson (eds) *Rethinking Security in East Asia*, Stanford, CA: Stanford University Press.

——(2007) *Power, Interest and Identity in Military Alliances*, New York: Palgrave.

Sung, Minjyu (2009) 'The "Truth Politics" of Anti-North Koreanism: The Post-ideological Cultural Representation of North Korea and the Cultural Criticisms of Korean Nationalism', *Inter-Asia Cultural Studies* 10 (3): 439–59.

——(2010) 'The Psychiatric Power of Neo-liberal Citizenship: The North Korean Human Rights Crisis, North Korean Settlers, and Incompetent Citizens', *Citizenship Studies* 14 (2): 127–44.

Sylvester, Christine (2002) *Feminist International Relations: An Unfinished Journey*, New York: Cambridge University Press.

Weber, Cynthia (2006) *Imagining America at War: Morality, Politics and Film*, London: Routledge.

Weldes, Jutta (2003) 'Popular Culture, Science Fiction, and World Politics', in Jutta Weldes (ed.) *To Seek Out New Worlds: Exploring Links between Science Fiction and World Politics*, Basingstoke: Palgrave Macmillan.

Woo-Cumings, Meredith (2002) 'The Political Ecology of Famine: The North Korean Catastrophe and its Lessons', *Research Paper Series*, Asian Development Bank Institute, www.adbi.org/research%20paper/2002/01/01/115.political.ecology/ (accessed January 2011).

Yun, Duk-min (2004) 'North Korean Long-range Missiles: Development, Deployment, and Proliferation', *East Asian Review* 16 (3): 17–40.

1 International relations, interrupted

Issues of positionality and intercultural relations

Introduction

What lies behind claims of expertise and possession of a good grasp of a place and a problem like North Korea? Their benefits are widely assumed but what are the consequences of such knowledge claims? Who bears the cost and who benefits when North Korea can be 'packaged up' and 'known'? How does reality come to be rendered as a static, singular object that can be known? This chapter questions the very basis of such judgements.

If North Korea – a term with an ever-changing referent – has largely become a numbing reality, it is not because we have exhausted all that we can know about North Korea under the tight censorship of that state. If the North Korean state feels predictably belligerent and barbaric, and its society unknowable but at the same time mappable, this sense of familiarity is not a mere reflection of reality. Knowing North Korea (or to be more precise, our positions of knowingness) arises from the over-determined way various bodies, sites and representations associated with North Korea are imagined using our binary constructions of good/bad, better/worse off, normal/deviant and benign/malign that prevail in international imagination. Put differently, the way frameworks, theoretical concepts and scientific methodologies are deployed, prop up a privileged and idealized image of the international community wittingly and unwittingly, that necessitates the numbing repetitive production of an 'Other'. They are caricatures, which in themselves are not bad, but they are caricatures that not only hinder our understanding and efforts to solve the problem of North Korea in any meaningful sense but create the problem of a deviant North Korea, which in turn produces things such as international crises and international conundrums.

The main argument in this chapter is that the postcolonial recasting of 'international problems' as 'intercultural problems' has fundamental, reverberating implications on how we go about encountering, engaging with, intervening in, worrying about and imagining politics, the international and a problem like North Korea. As mentioned in the Introduction, intercultural refashioning means attending to international politics as a series of encounters between bodies that are differently inscribed by power and cultural mediation. While Inayatullah and Blaney (2004: 14–15) value culture for how it highlights the constructed order of reality (and explain this by pointing out how culture is different from nature), I shift the focus slightly and value culture for highlighting how *specific, situated* cultural resources get mobilized by differently mediated intersubjective positions in reality and sense-making practices. Seeing international problems as instances of intercultural encounters is to insist that there is no objective reality or neutral position from which to compel solutions to problems of war, conflict, instability and violence, nor is there a morally defensible or harmonious way of resolving tensions and conflicts. I argue that the perennial problems of violence, conflict and domination are fundamentally problems of difference, identity and power that are mediated by and mediate culture as well as the movement between cultures. To be clear, cultures themselves only exist as 'units' through reification of differences and the continual maintenance of the power asymmetries that make this reification of cultures possible. My primary concern in this chapter is to lay a theoretical foundation for the cultural turn taken in this book.

The chapter begins by interrogating how critical traditions in IR have gone about problematizing the prevailing approaches to international relations that see social, political and ethical problems solely or primarily as policy problems requiring the production of the most accurate facts and the most sophisticated assessments. While appreciative that poststructuralist, postcolonial and feminist traditions reflexively question truth claims about sovereignty, anarchy, security and so on, the chapter seeks to push the debate further by examining how they face up to and debate the issue of positionality. In other words, it asks how fully these critical traditions face up to, question or displace their different positions and practices of complicity that sustain the current contours of power. Archiving alternative terms of intercultural relations, locating shifts in power asymmetries and creating alternative presents and futures – these are major and recurring concerns in this chapter and this book. I introduce the metaphor of translation to articulate the idea that alternative terms of intercultural encounter do not exist outside power or culture but exist somewhere between 'inside' and 'outside' culture, power and our imagination. The latter half of the chapter juxtaposes arguments made by Donna Haraway and Trinh Minh-ha with those made by critical IR scholars who have spoken explicitly on the question of displacing the prevailing hierarchies and ushering in alternatives. Trinh Minh-ha engages political events and issues of responsibility, social change and justice from a position that radically rethinks the relationship between culture and politics. Focusing on Trinh's concepts of 'speaking nearby' and 'non-knowingness', I argue that her various aesthetic, lyrical and poetic compositions help to make explicit the intimate problems of identity, difference, culture, knowledge and language. Trinh helps to foreground how critical engagements with international/intercultural relations require multilayered, multi-directional interpretative interventions that profoundly respect the mediatory dimensions of politics. Self-reflexive interrogation of critical interventions is not optional but formative to this project.

Dissent

In writing about North Korea, I am not interested in the knowledge agendas grounded in Western science that take an accumulative, instrumental approach to knowledge. I am invested in shifts away that understand knowing in relational ways. I try to flesh out this commitment throughout the book. Many IR scholars have made this book's shift from problem solving to critical engagements possible by working to denaturalize and decentre mainstream versions of realism and liberalism. Tactics range from Ashley's (1984, 1988) philosophical deconstruction, to Sylvester's (1995) and Tickner's (1992, 1997) deployment of feminist theory, and to Inayatullah and Blaney's (1996, 2004) efforts to bring postcolonial historicity into IR theory. As a collection, they offer critical examinations of the philosophical, theoretical and scientific roots of the claims that 'the international' is a distinct sphere or level of analysis best characterized using the concept of anarchy and as a realm composed mainly by rational, isomorphic states. These critical interventions question the universalizing effects of the idealized image of the 'West' and 'Man', and challenge mainstream IR dependence on positivist, structuralist and statist assumptions to prop up their positions. (Neo)realism and (neo)liberalism are particular views that privilege Eurocentric, patriarchal, masculinist and colonialist positions that have gained prominence through structuralism and positivism. Relying on structuralism and positivism for authority (and assuming that this position is politically neutral and value-free) confuses particular and deeply problematic cultural beliefs for universal scientific truths and unmediated, incontestable facts.

The thrust of these dissentions lie in their argument that IR's inability to respond adequately to critiques of Eurocentrism, sexism, intolerance of difference (or indeed, the manner in which IR assimilates these critiques in order to neuter them) is symptomatic of the positivist commitments of the discipline. For instance, Richard Ashley notes how in the face of a specific historical problem (i.e. the post-World War II era of America's growing international ambition), the discipline made 'an ideological move toward the economization of politics' (Ashley 1984: 279; also see Tickner 1997: 618–19). Here Ashley points to the ways in which mainstream IR sought to depoliticize international practices that are inherently ambiguous, contentious and contingent by relying on the reductive and technical treatment offered by positivism and structuralism. Christine Sylvester (1996) expresses an opinion shared by many others when she points out how Eurocentric and masculinist logics embedded in mainstream IR's foundational concepts remain intact in 'new' conceptual developments; that is, 'new' conceptual frameworks use the same technical and theoretical assumptions whilst claiming to achieve a clean break from colonialism and patriarchy. In their effort to expose these problematic logics, critical IR scholars have scrutinized directly theoretical frameworks such as development, good governance, human rights, strategic asymmetry, regional stability and so on.[1]

The above convergence of critical positions is not an entirely harmonious affair and perhaps rightly so. The early 1990s dispute between Sankaran Krishna and James Der Derian in the pages of the journal *Alternatives: Global, Local, Political* remains an illustrative example of the tensions between different critical IR positions. Underlying Krishna's original review article of the poststructuralist and postmodernist IR writers is the idea that these writers are out of touch with the realities of international politics from their insulated positions of privilege as Western academics.[2] Krishna argues that the focus on representation, the self and the rejection of modernist politics works against and appears limited and delimiting from a postcolonial perspective attentive to the continuing domination of the world by the West. In response, Der Derian argues that Krishna has misrepresented the postmodern/poststructuralist approach, and moreover, the accusation that postmodernist international theory works to depoliticize global politics is an expression of intolerance by Krishna. Der Derian argues that productive styles of political engagement come in many forms, and attempts to turn this debate with Krishna into an occasion for 'dialogical reasoning' (Der Derian 1994: 13). Moreover, Der Derian and those sympathetic to his 'indulgent' endeavours would point out that personal and expressive explorations are especially important at this historical juncture when 'the heroic myth' of intellectuals uncovering truth 'to an attentive public which thus "enabled" can change the course of history for the better' no longer holds true. For Der Derian, there is an ever greater need to 'break through the logjam of social scientific discourse' (ibid.: 137, 139).

Partly because of the indirect way in which Krishna goes about his criticism, his contention that postmodern/poststructuralist IR is 'out of touch' and a product of privileged Western academia that can be politically disabling, remains unaddressed by Der Derian. In response to Krishna's impatience for his kind of critically engaged research, Der Derian retorts, 'That none of us [IR poststructuralist writers] have written the book Krishna would have is of little concern to me; that others should do so is' (Der Derian 1994: 134). In other words, Der Derian does not see anything theoretically and politically problematic about poststructural theory as articulated in his writing. This debate between Krishna and Der Derian is useful for my exploration of the theoretical underpinnings of the cultural turn at work in this book. Put very simply, I think Der Derian's response has missed the point and the valuable ideas behind Krishna's criticism, and especially the significance of *positionality* in IR.

Positionality

Feminist IR scholars like Cynthia Enloe (1990, 1993, 1996, 2000, 2003) and Ann Tickner (1992, 1997, 2001) have persistently raised this issue of positionality in relation to gender and women. They argue that occupants of the centres, which admittedly are difficult to define but all the while exist, have a hard time 'hear[ing] the hopes, fears, and explanations of those on the margins, not because of physical distance ... but because it takes resources and access to be "heard" when and where it matters' (Enloe 1996: 186). While I think that their conceptualization of power in relation to positionality requires further complication, the point I wish to emphasize is that an *adequate* recognition of one's position in the circulation of power as an issue of difference requires something more than Der Derian's kind of retort to Krishna. Centring requires a lot of work – active, conscious, habitual, ingrained and ingraining – which at the same time involves keeping some Others away from the centre, in the margins and on the bottom rung. My guess is that undoing this is equally a lot of work. Much feminist research and criticism, most certainly works by Enloe and Tickner, has been directed at mainstream IR, especially the canon of (neo)realist and (neo)liberal thinking, but the thrust of their argument can also be directed at critical and poststructural IR. In short, all approaches – no matter how critical – must adequately face up to the challenge of positionality. However, seeing the value of these arguments does not necessarily mean we also have to commit to a rigid model of political research; indeed, a single model for political empowerment and power would simplify the objects of our study.

Where Der Derian disappoints is that his dialogic model still privileges the masculine, white, erudite self, not only in how research is conducted and written, but also in how political change is pursued. For instance, in his more recent publication, *Virtuous War* (2001), Der Derian sees himself as a lone traveller making a journey into the world of military-industrial-media-entertainment network where agents of international relations remain little changed from those envisioned by mainstream IR. In short, the focus on 'men' as the doers and the absence of 'women' and 'others' in global politics remains completely unaddressed. Even after decades of feminist IR criticism, Der Derian does not even ask the most obvious reflexive questions – for example, what is it about his subject position in the network that gives him access to the discourse circulating among US military officers, Pentagon staff and other high-ranking security strategist types? Nor does he ask historicized and contextualized questions about virtuality and technological warfare – for instance, what are the different consequences of technology for subjectivities that are differently positioned by gender, class, ethnicity and religion, to name only the most obvious? While Der Derian (2001: 199, 202) at times relies on insights by feminists like Haraway and Elshtain to further a particular argument about virtuous war and virtuality, he does not consider the larger feminist concerns about gender (and here I would add race, ethnicity, postcoloniality) in considering issues of power, mimetic mediations, military-technoscientific authorities and violence in global politics. I am here returning to an observation by feminists: 'Some men want to appear to acknowledge and accept feminist arguments without actually giving up any of their conventional androcentric beliefs and the practices that seem to follow so reasonably from such beliefs' (Haraway 1991: 154; see also Sylvester 1996: 255).

This is not an idiosyncrasy particular to Der Derian but a widespread problem in the critical tradition in IR and beyond; it works by them acknowledging that gender and feminist scholarship matter but proceeds without seriously reflecting on what this means in their own intellectual work and habits. An adequate recognition of positionality would involve not only giving up some common and 'instinctual' beliefs and practices with regards to the pursuit of research, but also engaging with arguments from 'the margins' and reflecting this shift and engagement in how knowledge is produced.

These disputes and dissent among critical IR scholars illustrate that while all are equally committed to the transformation of IR as a discipline and practice, their conception of how this transformation can take place (as well as their roles as 'intellectuals' in this process) differ considerably. Scholars like Krishna and Enloe do, of course, see that their research concerns are as much issues of the domination of bodies, territories and materiality as they are issues of imagination and subjectivities. Feminist and postcolonial scholars do not deny the importance of language, culture and representation, and all acknowledge the role culture plays in transforming international relations (e.g. Gruffydd Jones 2006: 2; Chowdhry and Nair 2002b: 15–17). Here, Krishna, for instance, gives his analytical attention to the traditional social scientific realms such as the public sphere, governmental activities and state building. In other words, the traditional realm of state-bound 'sovereign' activities holds over in defining not only what is political, but also how and where transformation of the political might occur. In the case of Enloe, her feminist vision that sees the personal as inextricably political (and vice versa) means that she escapes privileging the public and the state as the primary space of politics. Her structural version of socialist feminism, however, means that change is equated with redeeming woman, femininity and other oppressed groups and values from their derogated places. For instance, Enloe writes:

> If we expose their dependence on feminizing women, we can show that this world system is also dependent on artificial notions of masculinity: this seemingly overwhelming world system may be more fragile and open to radical change than we have been led to imagine.
>
> (Enloe 1990: 17)

Enloe is not interested in interrogating concepts like 'woman' and the 'standpoint of the oppressed' for their contested and constructed nature, nor does she specify or legislate what kind of radical change will emerge from exposing the artifice of masculinity in world politics. For Enloe, the privileging of 'women', 'exposing artifice' and radical change arise because without them as objects, objectives and/or subjects of socialist feminist knowledge, scholarly productions that can aid emancipatory movements would be difficult. In short, Enloe's work needs a stable referent (e.g. woman, the Other) and faith in the ability of revolutionary upheavals to bring about visible change to lend moral and political authority to her 'socialist feminist causes'. Here, though, I take a breath and pause to wonder … what if efforts to create solidarity between 'standpoint' positions such as woman and the Other in order to further an emancipatory political project are actually a hindrance to 'real change', given the diffused way that power works in today's global context? What if listening to the margins – as anthropologists, socialist scholars and activists do wherein they rely on some version of the idea that their task is as gatekeepers of the authentic stories – produces its own divisions, hierarchies and politics of inclusion and exclusion?

These questions point to how the issue of positionality is much more complicated than some postcolonial and feminist scholars assume, and their conception of how and where transformative politics occur might be too narrow, as there is no way out of complicity and failures of communication, authenticity and truth. In highlighting such limitations, I want to gesture towards alternative trajectories in which a more complicated reflection on positionality might gain articulation. In other words, a more complex and nuanced account of positionality – which avoids the 'convenience' of essentialism and referentiality – can produce a profound kind of transformative politics. Recognizing complexity and the critical value of positionality in transformative politics means we have to re-examine and reconsider the hegemonic language and culture in which positionality and transformative politics inescapably gain attention. This is not to let off the hook critical engagements that privilege the same traditional actors (e.g. states, statesmen, the public sphere) and offer an obligatory acknowledgement of one's position (e.g. white, male, elite). It is not a call to celebrate differences, embrace relativism or stay self-centred given the inescapability of the self and importance of expressive knowledge production. On the contrary, I think a more complicated treatment of positionality and identity/difference is necessary to incite responses and encounters that could prove transformative.

New concerns from this created space

From these new spaces where mainstream theories are denaturalized and decentred, it becomes possible to formulate alternative IR research agendas. We can now re-imagine what the 'problem' in international relations is, what kinds of questions or issues IR can concern itself with, and what our 'objects of analysis' can be. The questions in this book arise from this critical space and thus begin with the notion that an international problem is one of difference wherein intolerance for difference lies at the heart of the diplomatic tensions, humanitarian and human rights crises and international instability. These international problems cannot be 'solved' by ascertaining the wrongdoers or the root of the problem – that is, by determining the facts and causes and seeking technical solutions within the accepted definitions of diplomacy, human rights, humanity and stability. Rather, these international problems require attention to issues of translation, mediation and power relations that diplomatic tensions, humanitarian and human rights crises and international instability signify. I am thus interested in exploring intercultural differences that are produced and negotiated in moments of cross-cultural contact ushered in by prevailing frameworks of international problems.

While Inayatullah and Blaney (2004) and Chowdhry and Nair (2002a) do not frame the problem of difference in these exact terms, their critique of mainstream theoretical frameworks expressly recognizes the need for cultural translation in international politics. These postcolonial writers argue that privileging 'sameness' and 'integration' in the face of difference is to construct the world according to an idealized image of the self that is violent, unethical and self-contradictory. Differences between East and West, North and South, the historically colonized and colonizing subjects, and the plurality of genders, religions and cultures demand a reformulation of how the world of politics is conceived. By framing international relations as instances of intercultural encounters, I am drawing attention to the need for, among other things, translation that privileges mediation as a process and as an act of transmission. It is to use translation and other culture-specific language to conceptualize denial, exclusion, domination or assimilation that predominantly characterize international/intercultural relations. The point here is that while translation can be a form of mediation that seeks to deny, exclude, dominate and assimilate, it is a form of mediation that is self-conscious of its function of mediation, i.e. of passing something onwards. I believe an explicit emphasis on mediation and transmission is important if differences and plurality are to shape politics in our world(s) more prominently.

By translation, I mean the necessary and power-laden process of mediation that accompanies all moments of recognition and enactments of difference. Drawing specifically on Rey Chow's work, I argue that all intercultural contacts require explicit negotiations with this process of mediation and with the question of how alterations of the process and the bodies involved can occur (Chow 1995: 177–79). It is important to stress that the concept of translation at work here is not an argument in favour of a transparent transfer of meaning. Rather, what translation must stay 'faithful' to is itself, i.e. the process of translation, not the content or the form. The process of translation helps to articulate the act of transferring, the transmission rather than a depth of meaning or faithfulness to the original. The function of translation is to serve 'the passages that head not toward the "original" that is the West or the East but toward survival in the postcolonial world' (Chow 1995: 202). In other words, translation is concerned with the continuation of life in *this* world, which for the bodies inscribed as 'cultural Others', intimately involves remaining in circulation in various contradictory and contingent ways, including those ways that can come under criticism for 'yapping and nibbling at the heels of imperialism' (Saurin 2006: 41, n.35). The idea is that through this process of translation, rather than mere continued circulation, something 'new' is created and brought into circulation that changes the terms of translation, circulation, life.

Chow's main concern is that intercultural encounters (she uses the adjective 'postcolonial') are inescapably constrained by power asymmetry along observer/observed, producer/consumer, self/Other and other binaries which render the latter of the two coordinates as people, culture, places and subjectivities that come after and as a supplement to the former. For the bodies inscribed as 'cultural Others' to remain in circulation *and* shift these binary terms that subordinate them, the process of mediation itself is what requires negotiation. In other words, this concept of translation is about negotiating with the mediated nature of intervention, mitigation and transformation in a postcolonial world. Conceptualizing the process of negotiation involved in shifting the hierarchic terms of intercultural encounter as a process of translation is to attend to the contaminating and contaminated condition of creating a shift in hierarchical relations in the postcolonial world. In short, while power relations and 'co-optation' in mediation are inescapable, these conditions that structure intercultural encounter and mediation can be altered through the entangled and contaminating process of mediation rather than seeking some pure, uncontaminated, unmediated position to reach or return.

Seeking out something completely new or returning to a tradition that is supposedly free from and uncontaminated by power relations simply fails to make sense in a world that is always already steeped in self/Other, West/East, seer/seen binaries. Concepts such as authenticity, essence, culture-as-units and differences-as-absolutes that privilege a 'radical' break or a 'return' to the past require searches for something or somebody else in which we place all our hopes. These fantasies always involve an imagined and displaced Other – rather than what is in front and on the surface – which comes to be seen as the key to a better understanding, a more desirable situation, a resolution. Privileging of an achievable 'depth', an identifiable 'authenticity' and indeed an originary 'meaning', allows the *perpetual postponement* of facing differences and facing the embodied particular Other in intercultural encounters (Chow 1995: 198–201). By recognizing both the futility of seeking authenticity and our complicity with the global hierarchy, Chow argues that intercultural contacts must be about negotiations with what is present and what stands in front of us. Our contacts must be 'literal', 'superficial' and 'coeval' (ibid.: 184–86, 194).

I return to elaborate on Chow's formulation of translation in the next chapter, but for now, my larger point is that a 'good' cultural translation is not an instance of the authentic, honest or faithful transfer of meaning, nor is it an instrument that enables a clear, uncomplicated or transparent communication. A 'good' translation enables the continued circulation of representation significant in intercultural relations as a way to ensure that bodies in the encounter remain open to difference, present to the moment and attend to the mediation process that they engage and are engaged by. This means departing from the literal meaning of an original experience and creating, through the process of translation itself, a new space where the conventional division between form and content breaks down. Put in the language of translation, the 'original' is used to create something that is neither new nor the same as the 'original', and in this sense, the process of translation is a re-creation, or creating anew in a different medium and for a different end (for examples of this idea in translation studies, see Bassnett and Triveli 1999; Spivak 2000; Simon and St-Pierre 2000; Davis 2001; Tymoczko 2007). This movement, as those with some experience in translation might be familiar with, is a repetitious process of departing from and returning to the 'original text': with each repetition, the movement changes in texture, speed and feel. In other words, because translating the 'original' requires changing 'the form' to express 'the content', it is a process that makes the distinction between content and form, original and secondary, 'over here' and 'over there' impossible (Trinh 1999: 60). As a result, we have changed the terms of mediation and have in effect entered a different realm – what Chow (1995: 192–95) calls 'the Third Term', and Trinh variously refers to as 'in-betweeness', 'the interval', 'the void' – spaces of mediation that recognize the mediating and mediated condition that produces 'the third scenario' (see for instance, Trinh 1991: 112–45). For Trinh (1999: 61), 'Translation leads us ... to the fictive nature of language and image'.

Interruption

One of the central concerns motivating this book is that even the most careful juggling of postcolonial, poststructural and feminist claims, or even the most intricate concepts seeking to reflect the tensions between these claims, might not enable transformative praxis. In part, this is a suspicion about the institutional homes of these theories within established academia. This feeling of suspicion does not arise from a view that academia is more complicit than other homes, or that it is more corrupt and contaminated than other sites of knowledge production (indeed, where does corruption and contamination *not* occur?). Rather, it stems from a sense that academic conventions and practices perpetuate the prevailing hierarchy of reality/culture production. Cultural and aesthetic spaces and modes are relegated as peripheral and/or epiphenomenal to international politics 'proper' (see Danchev and Lisle 2009; Bleiker 2009; Moore and Shepherd 2010). Moreover, even when studied as legitimate objects of analysis, they are disciplined by academic conventions that not only foreclose the form that the analysis takes but also the content.

It is in this context that I ask how we can discuss the critical issues that this research project shares with other academic works without giving rise to the idea, no matter how impressionistic or momentary, that the theoretical, political and ethical concerns of this book can be summed up and framed entirely within existing academic debates. Is not this containment a way of allowing IR to discipline what questions get asked and how ideas are thought out? In other words, does not this containment in effect parse, polish and discard ideas in ways that privilege academic conventions and discourse over many other ideas, forces, representations and ways of seeing that have shaped this research? What I am troubled by is that if dissident/critical IR is about challenging and disrupting the knowledge/power nexus exemplified so clearly by mainstream positivist-inspired IR research, then discussing the concerns of this book within the existing academic debates – even the intra-critical debates – feels as if it is a way of allowing a reincorporation of critical voices rather than disrupting the nexus. The presence of a 'critical turn' in IR could be seen as just another space for reifying and enabling the smooth operation of the hierarchic terms of culture/knowledge production. It can be a space of complacency and self-survival rather than a site of disruptive production that reinvigorates 'the thinking space' committed to shifting the terms of politics (Jim George, in Bleiker 1997: 60).

One way to think about this nagging problem is to shift the reference of Bleiker's question – 'How is one to proceed in the face of [the academic discipline's] disciplinary power?' – from orthodox IR to critical IR itself, and ask how to proceed not entirely *inside* critical IR and, by extension, the academic conventions it reproduces (Bleiker 1997: 65). Bleiker's original question was raised in the face of positivist language used by the gatekeepers of IR that made critical engagements sound 'unintelligible'. Bleiker argues that this policing, in fact, makes resistive methodologies, such as poetry, images and aphorisms, necessary in trying to displace the orthodox foundations of IR as well as its academic practices of gatekeeping. His point is that one must not face the gatekeepers on their own terms (that is, as scary and forbidding creatures), but rather forget them in the Nietzschean sense (that is, by re-casting their 'scary' features as something else entirely by remembering and forging ahead differently; ibid.: 58–60). When we raise the issue of disciplinary effects of academia in general, and critical IR more specifically, we must be concerned with how our efforts to give form to alternatives are always disciplined by our positionality, for instance by our academic institutional homes and the conventions that this space generates. In other words, we need to address more explicitly the limitations of critical IR itself and the academic conventions it continues to use. We might consider what it means to disrupt, displace or challenge when academics discuss and construct alternatives, or even how one might question, trouble and transgress these limits, orthodoxies and horizons of knowledge. I raise this issue of limitation not to turn away from the focus on language (i.e. the labelling of something as 'Other'), but rather to scrutinize further our notions of critical intervention, resistance and alternatives, which, we cannot deny, are inescapably a question of language. In other words, when Bleiker calls for dissident scholarship to 'incinerate the dry grass of orthodox IR prairies', we need to ask to whom this incineration is important, and which parts of our conventions, practices and beliefs need to be set ablaze (ibid.: 79). I think this issue of disruption and transgression must be considered not only as an issue of disciplinary effect within academia but also as part of the larger context of reality/knowledge production in a postcolonial, late-capitalist, elitist, patriarchal world.

Donna Haraway's 'socialist-feminist culture and theory in a postmodernist and non-naturalist mode' is useful in articulating this question (Haraway 1991: 150). Haraway is concerned with the entrance of formerly excluded subjects into social areas of power such as science, technology and the university. These middle-class professional jobs are significant for their relation to reality production, reproduction and communication. It is important to examine how these professionals are involved in structuring the conditions of what can be real, possible or present in an age that is 'living through a movement from an organic, industrial society to a polymorphous, information system' (ibid.: 161). This is not to contradict the insights from feminism and cultural studies that the production of reality is not only by producers but also in daily lived practices. Haraway's point is that there is a division of labour in the production of reality wherein the structuring of the rough contours of how and what gets constructed, spoken and written is still asymmetrical in favour of a white, Western, male, heterosexual, bourgeois consciousness.

While not a focal point of Haraway's work, the global nature of this division of labour as well as the professionalization process is not lost on Rey Chow. In discussing the production of diasporic intellectuals, Chow writes:

> What happens eventually is that this 'third world' that is produced, circulated, and purchased by 'third world' intellectuals in the cosmopolitan diasporic space will be exported 'back home' in the form of values – intangible goods – in such a way as to obstruct the development of the native industry.
> (Chow 1993: 118–19; also see Miyoshi 2000: especially 37–50)

However, recognition of this imbalance is not to argue that the problem can be solved simply with the inclusion of more groups (i.e. diversity), or by building up and multiplying the 'native' industry. Certainly the fact that formerly excluded or discriminated groups can increasingly enter spheres that were once closed off to them is politically significant; however, there is nothing necessarily *transformative* about gendered, sexed or racialized bodies entering these spheres, or in redistributing capital to economically marginalized groups. Haraway's point is that while spheres such as science and higher education have become occupied by a more diverse mix of social bodies, and thus appear more inclusive, the entire process of inclusion still occurs on the terms of those in power. In short, the norms and processes are maintained rather than transformed through seemingly inclusionary practices. Chow's point is that this hegemonic relation of production is not escaped by claiming that there is something emancipatory or progressive in postcolonial space of intellectual production, since these productions must circulate within an already established system. What writers like Haraway and Chow highlight is the need for transformation at the very basic level of knowledge/culture/reality production. Haraway sums up what is at stake when she asks how we enable the presence of new groups in the production of knowledge and imagination in such a way that the varied personal preferences and cultural tendencies of these groups converge with feminist-transnational-socialism so as to contribute to progressive politics (Haraway 1991: 169). To put it another way, in what sense can 'Others' resist reincorporation into a centre that is already determined?

Haraway's question expresses the need for a new consciousness and imagination in three important ways. First, we need to populate this new imagination with theoretical, linguistic and cultural productions which incorporate the experiences, histories and feelings of these new entrants (i.e. the marginal standpoints). In the context of technology and science, Haraway (1997: 16) argues: 'What we need is to make a difference in material-semiotic apparatuses, to diffract the rays of technoscience so that we get the most promising interference patterns on the recording films of our lives and bodies in the world.' By using the optical metaphor of diffraction, Haraway stresses that 'incorporation' into the project of constructing a new critical consciousness means divergence and fragmentation as well as absorption and merging. This is similar to the function of cultural translation in intercultural relations discussed earlier, where the technology of translation – the repetitive movement back and forth between the 'original' and the 'copy' – brings newness into the relationship and perhaps even a shift in the terms of intercultural encounters.

Second, Haraway highlights who, or better yet *what*, needs changing: the professional, white, middle-class, Western, heterosexual *mentality* and *way of life*. Articulating the target of transformation in social identity terms brings into focus that the question of *who* needs to be transformed is a difficult one; that is, the object of critical theory *is* and *is not* a specific social group. Transformation is directed more generally at the pervasive mentality that finds a home in whomever and whatever it touches regardless of race, nationality, class, sex, gender, institution, heritage and so on. It is a mentality and a way of life driven by a desire to assume *the* uncontested position as a given, i.e. as the norm, the neutral, the universal. However, it is also directed at a specific 'social group' in the sense that what needs transformation is 'us' – those who occupy positions of privilege in 'the informatics of domination' (Haraway 1991: 161). Lastly, Haraway's work makes visible why it is so urgent and important to question the limitations of academic critical engagements that do not actively disturb the hierarchies of academic convention as well as the hierarchy in knowledge/reality production. This means the privileged academic conventions and interventions that are used for the purposes of critical intervention must also be subject to scrutiny, interrogation and transformation. To put it simply, practices of diffraction in academia mean we cannot only be concerned with *what* we are critiquing; we must also be concerned with *how* we perform that critique.

However, just as 'new entrants' have limited transformative effects, there is a gap between claims that creative innovations for transformative ends are effective, and the extent of effectiveness of these innovative turns. In other words, making knowledge claims in creative and innovative ways (i.e. through fiction, poetry, paintings, etc.) is effective only to an ambiguous extent in shifting the terms of knowledge production and reality making more broadly.

Haraway is important here because she takes seriously the issues of positionality, relationality and the limitations of inclusion (whether this be social groups or innovative technology), and calls for the use of diffractive strategies and situated knowledges. I share Haraway's concerns and raise two additional questions with respect to re-casting the North Korean case as an intercultural problem. I ask what kinds of critical strategies, transgressions and resources are necessary when the problem is so centrally a product of scholarship in collaboration with other cultural and political elites, and how we can produce alternatives when neither the scholarship nor the cultural and political centres hold the key to undo the problem as it is constructed, or unmake reductive cultural products. In other words, is there hope in examining culture as a site for politics and theory even when the realm of culture (especially dominant scientific, modern and Western cultures) are so central in constituting the 'North Korea problem'?

Cultural and aesthetic sites do not hold the key to the limitations that academic or scientific approaches exhibit in how they articulate or mediate issues of international/intercultural relations; that is, culture does not and will not provide a 'resolution' to the 'North Korean problem' as it is constructed. However, attending to the cultural realm as a site of significant intercultural encounters is still productive, not least because it allows a heterogeneity of modes of knowing wherein scientific or academic conventions are only two modes amongst many others. It is to engage sites of cultural production for how they can potentially open up alternative spaces, terms and processes. Here, though, we have to be mindful of how the dominant modes, processes and sites of intercultural relations can unravel in manners that require us to develop new ways of knowing and exploring. This is not just because the realm of culture has only recently been intimately explored as a site of international politics, but also because what the cultural site might accentuate is how inescapably unknowable processes such as unravelling, unmaking and transformation could be.

Turning to culture for alternatives

The turn to culture as explored in this book has at least three main connotations. The first is methodological: fiction, art, images and creative writing are useful precisely for their power to displace, forget and resist the restrictive academic conventions upon which both mainstream and critical IR rely. The second is theoretical: approaching international relations as an issue of intercultural encounter in which incommensurable positions are always in relation means that these tensions can never be *resolved* through dialogue or through privileging diversity. Interculturality means recognizing diversity, complexity and differences without seeking resolutions. The third is political: we cannot simply opt out of exploring the idea that we need shifts, an inducement of newness and an acknowledgement of positionality in how political re-imagination is practised. Of course, new consciousness and imagination do not arise out of thin air, and are in fact 'new' only in the sense that existing cultural resources and processes are used and juxtaposed in different ways, and accessed in different modes, strategies and political agendas. For this reason, the idea of translation and in-betweeness are central to how change and newness are conceived.

Agathangelou and Ling (2009) best exemplify such a multifaceted turn in IR with their introduction of the term 'worldism'. The idea of 'worldism' recognizes the importance of a new theoretical language that speaks explicitly about postcolonial, race, gender, sex and class realities. They address the need for such an approach by introducing a new theoretical framework that is attentive to the fact that colonial history has not only shaped and affected social identities differently, but has given rise to entwined multiple worlds and trans-subjectivities that have not erased colonial relations but rather (re)constructed them. While Agathangelou and Ling understand that the self/Other binary that besets world politics is relational (and therefore always contingent, agonistic and ambivalent, making it difficult to formulate any collective form of resistance), they argue that historical and identity-related materialities such as race, class and gender are significant and necessary when considering alternatives (ibid.: 1–7, 85–92). Worldism is understood as a syncretic engagement with two simultaneous processes of describing and analysing: first, capturing what is going on in world politics understood as daily lived experiences (describing); and second, simultaneously analysing the extent to which world politics can 'disrupt strategies of empire or other forms of hegemony to ensure emancipatory reconstructions even as we recover new, less violent worlds' (ibid.: 6). Fiction and poetry, according to Agathangelou and Ling, provide the necessary spaces to critique and materialize new relations of multiple worlds in the global arena (ibid.: 99–117).

While sharing the larger themes articulated by Agathangelou and Ling, I again differ from their research on how culture is critically and creatively engaged for politics. My interest most crucially differs in where the emphases are placed when critical studies of international politics look towards culture. When these writers' efforts are read in conjunction with the concerns I have raised through Bleiker and Haraway, their academic/social scientific incorporation of the multiple worlds that emerge from subordinated socio-cultural sites become apparent as limitations. To begin, their reverential reading of fiction, poetry and the arts has a way of putting limits on the terms through which alternatives can emerge. Agathangelou and Ling offer illustrative readings of fiction (e.g. a multi-authored ancient Chinese novel, *Honglou meng*, which tells tales of a stone's travel) and even an original piece of creative writing (a play script, 'Othello's Journeys', which re-scripts the Shakespeare play). In their various illustrative readings and re-scripting, the lessons about multiple worlds are explained in each example and how multi- and trans-subjectivity is to be found in various stories, poems and social contexts from the margins. The lessons are listed and summed up as guidelines in various chapters: pluralize the self, acquire wisdom and experience from marginalized subjectivities, build communities and make history on a daily basis, mobilize multi- and trans-subjectivities through innovation, adaptations and learning (see for instance, Agathangelou and Ling 2009: 6, 102–5, 128–31, 136–37).

For me, this emphasis on illustrating and providing guidelines and lessons prompts more questions than offer a viable trajectory for further critical foray into culture. At this theoretical juncture where we feel an increasing need to attend to issues of positionality, relations and heterogeneity, is what we need instructions, recipes and guidelines? *If* lessons and instructions are productive in engaging in some quarters and as one component of 'worldism', are there other ways of articulating them than as recipes that assume if we just follow these clearly delineated steps, we can produce what we want? What other formulations and articulations of a new theoretical language are possible which speak explicitly about postcolonial, race, gender, sex and class realities but do not foreclose what this new theoretical articulation produces because of our efficient research methods? I think, rather than 'worldism' as unpacked by Agathangelou and Ling which places emphasis on clear illustrations and readings of fiction, poetry, etc. for singular lessons (about multiple worlds), what the new theoretical language needs is an unpacking of a different order to support the writers' claim about transformative effects. These scholars wish to make the effects of their engagement with multiple worlds too clear; that is, they subsume the subject of their analyses under an analytical eye which polishes the unruly or fleeting effects of their reading, and arranges the unclassifiable, ambivalent and contingent moments in their 'objects of analysis' into neat concepts. What I am pointing to is a need for a theoretical engagement that unpacks what fiction, poetry and creative writing do or can do in intercultural relations, and how multiple worlds can be articulated and recognized. This means thinking about how we might register the need for a more pervasive and serious attention to issues of positionality, relations, heterogeneous worlds and historical acuity. I believe a sustained interrogation of, and thinking about alternatives to, the mode of articulation that these authors prefer is a productive place to begin.

Disrupting the culture of science

Trinh Minh-ha, a feminist filmmaker and political theorist, interrogates power through culture which crucially involves interrogating the tools and resources she uses for her own filmic and textual productions. Trinh's engagements are marked by her attempt to recognize the cultural order that constrains all productions of reality, including her own. One place to begin reading Trinh's critical effort is by looking at how she brings into focus the need to interrogate social scientific conventions and displace science from its privileged position in the social realm. Her critique of science calls attention to the favoured role of the analytical intellectual and 'his' activities of problem solving for social change. The critique is meant to broaden out the accepted conception of how we can know, what knowing the world means, and what the relationship could be between knowing and inducing change in the social and political world. Science here is viewed as an attitude or a way of thinking, desiring and dreaming rather than a set of methods or a body of knowledge.

In other words, Trinh takes issue with science *as culture* that encompasses all of the practices and processes that use, keep alive and fortify prevailing ideas of facticity and realism; that is, the amassing of data, evidence and 'facts' to make objective knowledge claims. Facticity and realism are predicated on a desire to bypass inter-subjectivities or relational encounters, and what Trinh shows us is how 'Reality runs away, reality denies reality' (Trinh 1990a: 90). Differently put, Trinh is interested in critiquing the oppositional binaries that legitimize scientific approaches – e.g. subject/object, fact/value, real/fiction – that are produced by a mentality, an attitude, i.e. something that is extra-logical and thus better understood as a culture.

Critically examining the *culture* of science most centrally involves disrupting scientific modes of ordering, disciplining and constituting reality in a way that displaces rather than replicates the instrumental and dominating impulse driving these scientific modes of knowing. Trinh's strategy of critique is meant to offer alternative approaches to knowing which question the subject-object distinction in which the scientist-producer assumes he can know and speak *about* some*thing* as an outsider, and that what is uttered is separate from the act of speaking and knowing. Trinh writes:

> ['Speaking about'] places a semantic distance between oneself and the work; oneself (the maker) and the receiver; oneself and the other. It secures for the speaker a position of mastery: I am in the midst of a knowing, acquiring, deploying world – I appropriate, own, and demarcate my sovereign territory as I advance – while the 'other' remains in the sphere of acquisition. Truth is the instrument of a mastery which I exert over areas of the unknown as I gather them within the fold of the known.
>
> (Trinh 1990b: 327)

Instead of 'speaking for or about' objects of analysis, Trinh thinks it is important to 'speak near by or together with' as a way of disrupting the subject-object distinction (Trinh 1986–87: 33). She disrupts the binary not through familiar academic conventions, but rather through poetry, lyricism, mixed-medium expressions and aphorisms that accentuate the positive value of 'not knowing' in conceptualizing what is politically enabling. To 'speak nearby' is to respect the excesses of an 'object of analysis' as well as the excesses of itself as a 'method'; it is to place the non-containment of all things – ideas, reality, experiences, method, logic – at the forefront of critical engagement. Thus, to respect the concept for how it exceeds its own representability in textual articulation, Trinh's own dancing around her concept of 'speaking nearby' is useful:

> Going beyond logic to experience what is large in what is small
> Clear, simple, irreducibly complex in its simplicity.
>
> (Trinh 1992: 39)

Their names I know not,
But every weed has
Its tender flower.

(Sampu, in Trinh 1990b: 26)

Reassemblage. From silences to silences, the fragile essence of each fragment speaks across the screen, subsides, and takes flight. Almost there
half named.

(Trinh 1989: 118)

For me, key words in relation to the above quotes are irreducibility, non-
knowing, contradictions, fragments without whole. The contexts in which
Trinh composes these fragmentary thoughts – in Senegal, travelling between
dwelling spaces and through a filmic contemplation in *Naked Spaces: Living
is Round* – viscerally convey how speaking nearby not only brings into frame
the issue of identity/difference but also encourages us to let go of the view that
intelligibility is the only form that critical intervention can take. Trinh's
strategy of speaking nearby moves away from the focus on making intelligible
what one witnesses (which inevitably reproduces a speaking witness and an
object that is spoken about), and focuses instead on the difficulty, heterogeneity
and aesthetics of acts of speaking.

By replacing 'speaking about' as an ideal in knowledge production with the
notion of 'speaking nearby', we might begin to produce complex, ambivalent
and ultimately open-ended encounters that are not easily appropriated by, or
used to facilitate, authoritative ordering practices that seek to control, contain
or eradicate cultural Otherness. In short, it is necessary to rethink how we
might come to 'know' or understand social and political realities. The first
step is to abandon the possibility of 'speaking' (with exhaustive completeness)
and listening (with ears that have strong filters that jump to grasp rather than
hear). Trinh accentuates two incongruous ideas involved in a critical engagement: *speaking*, which is necessary in order to re-appropriate meaning in ways
that resist dominant notions of propriety over Others; and *not-speaking*,
which is a way of resisting the desire that speaking will always produce a
better, clearer, more complex understanding. For Trinh, speaking must occur
'without' occurring, just as listening and attending to marginalization,
inequities and injustice must take place without knowing.

Doing political theory differently

Trinh's distinct mode of critical intervention introduces the need for a *non-
knowing approach* to political theory rather than a *new* or *better* normative
theory of world politics that claims to produce transformative ends. In her
various enactments and articulations of this approach, Trinh emphasizes how
critical theoretical engagements must address the subject that is part of the
circulation of power, i.e. the subject that says, 'Everything must hold together.

In my craving for logic of being, i [sic] cannot help but loathe the threats of interruptions, disseminations, and suspensions' (Trinh 1986–87: 27). In this sense, Trinh not only problematizes notions of a unitary identity whose decipherable 'essence' is threatened by interruptions and a lack of closure, but also critiques all subject positions that analyse, think and write with the express desire for coherence, clarity and closure. It is in this context that Trinh talks about 'strategies of displacement' as acts of wandering and wondering into 'an empty, "no-baggage" moment in which passion traverses the non-knowing (not ignorant) subject' (Trinh 1990b: 333). An empty non-baggage moment does not mean relying on 'natural forces' and 'chaos' that stem from natural/cultural, order/disorder binaries; it is instead an approach to knowing and encountering that values strategies of grafting and play.

We see a performative instance of grafting and play in her film *Surname Viet, Given name Nam*, in which Trinh carefully stages interview scenes with Vietnamese women using Vietnamese-American women as actors, which is then interwoven with 'on-site' interviews with the same women in their 'real-life' contexts (for descriptions, reflections and explanations of the film, see Trinh 1992: 49–91, 137–210). Trinh grafts different storylines into one film and one theme (Vietnam) by playing with the true, the fictive, the staged, the real, the 'over there' (in the past, in Vietnam) and 'over here' (in the present, the USA). While scripted (in parts) and carefully planned out (e.g. lighting, location, themes), Trinh explains how once the filming begins she lets the situations unfold and lets the problems that arise in the process of filming layer and change the pre-production preparation. Analogous practices that displace the subject position of the filmmaker are also at work in the editing process. The grafting/play that is embodied in Trinh's non-knowing approach incites a mixture of spiritual, meditative and critical modes of knowing so that analytical thinking and writing are not positioned antithetically to mystical, spiritual or emotional forms (Trinh 1992: 140–41, 89, 1989: 39–44, 49).

Trinh can be read as making a case for incorporating new components (e.g. aesthetics, fiction, culture) into IR, which would be in step with what many critical IR scholars have done (e.g. Shapiro 1997, 1999; Bleiker 2000, 2009; Weber 2006), but she can also be read as making a case for her radical displacing of science in the study of social and political worlds which problematizes any neat distinction between theory (the framework) and art/culture (object of analysis). What makes Trinh's work interesting is that her theoretical (academic) claims are worked out in the cultural realm through films that she makes and installations she designs. Her cultural work (filmmaking, visual art) expresses her theoretical and academic concerns. In Trinh's work, aesthetics becomes both an object of analysis *and* a method of inquiry, and in this sense, it functions as a particular kind of transformative politics. By combining aesthetics and analysis, Trinh offers a far-reaching and layered disruption to the easy, common-sense, business-as-usual assumptions about what counts as politically relevant. In the process, she raises concerns about how a desirable life for some is only possible at the cost of Others who are continually less valued. Reading Trinh also tells us that transformative politics must, whether we like it or not, embrace the invisibility of 'results', acknowledge that presence is at work in 'absence', and begin from and make use of the contradictions and unacceptability of 'methods', 'logic' and 'reality'.

To sum up, Trinh's strategies intimately reconsider the relationship between culture and politics, and I believe this is important in the politics of international/ intercultural relation. Her strategies of disruption and displacement (e.g. grafting, non-knowing, speaking nearby) give us a conception of transformation that distinctly refuses to work with total conceptions, absolutes and complete understanding. In other words, while transformation is possible and indeed considered the primary goal of politics, this political agenda is conceived without assuming the need to commit to the idea that emancipation is absolute and definable universally or presently with existing concepts like freedom, progress and equality. Moreover, these concepts are valued for how they enable the constant displacement of power by their constant and contradictory impulses to move, roam and displace. The movement that these concepts propel gives rise to occasions for another grafting, juxtaposition and translation of changing bodies in their specificities.[3] It is for this reason that Haraway's cautionary but attentive treatment of constructing alternative consciousness and culture is important. However, being attentive, here, does not mean following suit. Trinh herself practises theory with little concern for caution and with a strong conviction that the issue of effectiveness matters little (since she embraces invisibility and absence as positive modes of knowing).

My position, however, is that Trinh's insistence on specificity and positionality cautions against celebratory attitudes about 'new' constructions of consciousness and imagination. By choosing to remain with Trinh's strategies in their fragmented forms, I am not saying there is anything conceptually wrong with the 'new' theoretical constructs such as Haraway's (1997) cyborg and OncoMouse, or Anzaldua's (1987) 'la Coatlicue state'.[4] I am instead pointing out that no 'new' theoretical construct seems to have the cascading transformative effect it claims for itself, and thus it can never transcend the limits from which it operates. In other words, new imagination from critical engagements attentive to hybridity, complicity, gender, class and race still seem transformative only insofar as they produce resistance within already constructed limits. Presently, the intercultural contact exemplified by these movements of resistance only occurs in select spheres of privilege: so what is the cause for hope? For me, Trinh's elaboration of displacement and resistance is more useful for how it suggests that it is more fruitful to work from an in-between place to displace hegemonic discourses continually and contextually rather than attempting to create a new consciousness for transformative ends.

Conclusion

The focus on North Korea solely as a policy issue in IR has meant that the larger questions about transforming 'the international' and the culture that produces a problem like North Korea remains unexplored. However, applying critical IR to the North Korean case is not the answer either. I have argued in this chapter that critical IR is not without its limitations. While it is curious that critical traditions in IR have produced very little *specifically* about North Korea, my point is not to proclaim, 'There must be more attention to small countries in critical IR'. That would merely brush the surface of the issue and produce its own problems of hierarchy, power asymmetry, imperialism. I want to maintain a critical relation to critical IR as I do with the widespread tendency to objectify North Korea as an international problem for us to solve. In this chapter, I have suggested that 'speaking nearby' the 'North Korea problem' – by grafting and playing – might produce a more fruitful engagement. The theoretical approach here is not aimed at producing an 'improved' template of knowledge that seeks to know North Korea better but has as its goal alternative modes, processes and terms of engagement with 'North Korea'. I have argued that the alternative modes of knowing North Korea are established not only in reference to the privileged hierarchies of self/Other, subject/object, inside/outside that frame intercultural encounters with 'North Korea', but also in reference to Eurocentric, analytical and critical traditions in IR which, consciously or not, prevent many alternative scenarios from emerging.

Trinh, as well as other poststructural, postcolonial, feminist writers, demonstrates how displacement of Western, patriarchal and logocentric ideas through fiction, poetry, new social groups or new worlds is never a simple story of redemption. There is no final escape from our positions in (the dominant) culture. This does not render critical engagements useless, but rather, it urges us to be attentive to these limitations through a continual insistence on being reflexive about our positions, relations and how our specific locations are just one of heterogeneous many. Translation is a useful concept and metaphor to think through how newness can emerge as well as how the terms of intercultural encounters can shift. Processes and practices of translation bring into view the importance of movement, repetition and the privileging of what stands in front of us (rather than an originary 'deep' and singular meaning) in our efforts to conceptualize change. These practices blur the distinction of original/copy, here/there, content/form, and produce an in-betweeness through which something *else* emerges. Trinh offers particularly potent ways of remaining attentive to the process and space of mediation. Not only does Trinh acknowledge the excesses, fluidity and incompleteness, but her *mode* of attentiveness and acknowledgement exemplified in her conceptual language of 'speaking nearby' and 'non-knowingness' produces another layer of disruption. The next four chapters unpack and extend many of the ideas introduced here – translation, non-knowing theory, in-betweeness, survival in a postcolonial world – in specific cultural representations in order to interrogate and displace the international/North Korea hierarchy.

Notes

1 For instance, Inayatullah and Blaney (2004) tell us that development is part of modernization theory that temporally sequences and spatially demarcates self and other by recourse to a Eurocentric norm. Moreover, this modernization theory is recycled in other contemporary IR theories such as liberal peace, global civil society and a pluralistic global community that merely moves from the level of state to the global while retaining the pernicious Othering logic (ibid.: 116–23). Sylvester (1999, 2002: 85–105) and Edkins (2000) focus on development and humanitarianism to question the cost of development and humanitarian assistance on 'the beneficiaries' that goes uncounted in conventional theories. Peterson (1990), Nair (2002), Orford (2003) and Browne (2002) write that human rights frameworks are deeply entrenched in liberal, neocolonial, patriarchal discourses. Klein (1994) and Campbell (1992) are just two among many who have problematized conventional security and strategic approaches. This is but one brush stroke in a larger painting of critical IR which has created space for my kind of engagement in IR.
2 This is a paraphrasing of the multiple theory-based arguments in Krishna's piece in light of his later publication that more poignantly articulates his views in terms of irony and aesthetics in politics (Krishna 1999: xxii–xxxiii).
3 For example, Trinh (1999: 25) writes: 'As women gain agency and move into a position of power, being able to make themselves heard through their own voices, we can't simply occupy that subject position at the centre, for this is what we have also been consistently fighting against in our struggle. So we would have to open up that position again, to remark and unmark it anew. What seems very recognizable at first is necessarily displaced with the steps we take as we affirm difference through repetition'.
   This is akin to Foucault's point that 'Liberation opens up new relationships of power, which have to be controlled by practices of liberty' (Foucault, in Trinh 1991: 19). Critics might argue that emancipatory transformation is something that too often engenders the idea of a desirable future without acknowledging that we always occupy and write from the present, but Trinh, and indeed Foucault, are saying that concepts such as emancipation and liberation are necessary tools to keep the constant, repetitious process of displacement going.
4 Cyborg, OncoMouse and la Coatlicue state are constructions of these theorists to give their political theories expressive, ontological forms. While Haraway turns to hybridity that accentuates the effect of technology and science, Anzaldua draws from Mexican and Indian heritage to construct the hybrid state that 'disrupts the smooth flow (complacency) of life' (Anzaldua 1987: 46).

Bibliography

Agathangelou, Anna and Ling, L.H.M. (2009) *Transforming World Politics: From Empire to Multiple Worlds*, London: Routledge.

Anzaldua, Gloria (1987) *Borderlands/La Frontera: The New Mestiza*, San Francisco, CA: Aunt Lute Books.

Ashley, Richard K. (1984) 'The Poverty of Neorealism', *International Organization* 38 (2): 225–86.

——(1988) 'Untying the Sovereign State: A Double Reading of the Anarchy Problematique', *Millennium: Journal of International Studies* 17: 227–62.

Bassnett, Susan and Triveli, Harish (eds) (1999) *Postcolonial Translation: Theory and Practice*, London: Routledge.

Bleiker, Roland (1997) 'Forget IR Theory', *Alternatives: Global, Local, Political* 22: 57–85.

——(2000) 'Stroll through the Wall: Everyday Poetics of Cold War Politics', *Alternatives: Global, Local, Political* 25 (3): 391–408.

——(2009) *Aesthetics and World Politics: Rethinking Peace and Conflict Studies*, Basingstoke: Palgrave Macmillan.

Browne, M. Anne (2002) *Human Rights and the Borders of Suffering: The Promotion of Human Rights in International Politics*, Manchester: Manchester University Press.

Campbell, David (1992) *Writing Security: United States Foreign Policy and the Politics of Identity*, Minneapolis: University of Minnesota Press.

Chow, Rey (1993) *Writing Diaspora: Tactics of Intervention in Contemporary Cultural Studies*, Bloomington, IN: Indiana University Press.

——(1995) *Primitive Passions: Visuality, Sexuality, Ethnography and Contemporary Chinese Cinema*, New York: Columbia University Press.

Chowdhry, Geeta and Nair, Sheila (eds) (2002a) *Power, Postcolonialism, and International Relations: Reading Race, Gender and Class*, London: Routledge.

——(2002b) 'Introduction', in Geeta Chowdhry and Sheila Nair (eds) *Power, Postcolonialism, and International Relations: Reading Race, Gender and Class*, London: Routledge.

Danchev, Alex and Lisle, Debbie (2009) 'Introduction: Art, Politics, Purpose', *Review of International Studies* 35: 775–79.

Davis, Kathleen (2001) *Deconstruction and Translation*, Manchester: St Jerome.

Der Derian, James (1994) 'The Pen, the Sword, and the Smart Bomb: Criticism in the Age of Video', *Alternatives: Global, Local, Political* 19: 133–40.

——(2001) *Virtuous War: Mapping the Military-Industrial-Media-Entertainment Network*, Boulder, Co: Westview Press.

Edkins, Jenny (2000) *Whose Hunger? Concepts of Famine, Practices of Aid*, Minneapolis: University of Minnesota Press.

Enloe, Cynthia (1990) *Bananas, Beaches and Bases: Making Feminist Sense of International Politics*, Berkeley, CA: University of California Press.

——(1993) *The Morning After: Sexual Politics at the End of the Cold War*, Berkeley, CA: University of California Press.

——(1996) 'Margins, Silence and Bottom Rungs: How to Overcome the Underestimation of Power in the Study of International Relations', in Steve Smith, Kenneth Booth and Marysia Zalewski (eds) *International Theory: Positivism and Beyond*, New York: Cambridge University Press.

——(2000) *Manoeuvres: The International Politics of Militarizing Women's Lives*, Berkeley, CA: University of California Press.

——(2003) *Curious Feminist: Searching for Women in a New Age of Empire*, Berkeley, CA: University of California Press.

Gowman, Philip (2008) 'Pyongyang – The View from Europe', *London Korean Links*, 13 February, londonkoreanlinks.net/2008/02/13/pyongyang-the-view-from-europe/ (accessed April 2012).

Gruffydd Jones, Branwen (ed.) (2006) *Decolonizing International Relations*, Lanham, MD: Rowman and Littlefield.

Haraway, Donna (1991) *Simians, Cyborgs and Women: The Reinvention of Nature*, New York: Routledge.

——(1997) *Modest_Witness@Second_Millennium.FemaleMan©_Meets_OncoMouse^{TM}: Feminism and Technoscience*, London: Routledge.

Inayatullah, Naeem and Blaney, David L. (1996) 'Knowing Encounters: Beyond Parochialism in International Relations Theory', in Yosef Lapid and Friedrich Kratochwil (eds) *The Return of Culture and Identity in IR Theory*, London: Lynne Rienner.

——(2004) *International Relations and the Problem of Difference*, London: Routledge.

Klein, Bradley S. (1994) *Strategic Studies and World Order*, Cambridge: Cambridge University Press.

Krishna, Sankaran (1999) *Postcolonial Insecurities: India, Sri Lanka and the Question of Nationhood*, Minneapolis: University of Minnesota Press.

Miyoshi, Masao (2000) 'Ivory Tower in Escrow', *Boundary* 2 (27): 7–50.

Moore, Cerwyn and Shepherd, Laura J. (2010) 'Aesthetics and International Relations: Towards a Global Politics', *Global Society* 24 (3): 299–309.

Nair, Sheila (2002) 'Human Rights and Postcoloniality: Representing Burma', in Geeta Chowdhry and Sheila Nair (eds) *Power, Postcolonialism, and International Relations: Reading Race, Gender, and Class*, Florence, KY: Routledge.

Orford, Anne (2003) *Reading Humanitarian Intervention: Human Rights and the Use of Force in International Law*, Cambridge: Cambridge University Press.

Peterson, V.S. (1990) 'Whose Rights? A Critique of the "Givens" in Human Rights Discourse', *Alternatives: Global, Local, Political* 15: 303–44.

Saurin, Julian (2006) 'International Relations as the Imperial Illusion; or, the Need to Decolonize IR', in Branwen Gruffydd Jones (ed.) *Decolonizing International Relations*, Lanham, MD: Rowman and Littlefield.

Shapiro, Michael J. (ed.) (1997) *Violent Cartographies: Mapping Cultures of War*, Minneapolis: University of Minnesota Press.

——(1999) *Cinematic Political Thought: Narrating Race, Nation and Gender*, Edinburgh: Edinburgh University Press.

Simon, Sherry and St-Pierre, Paul (eds) (2000) *Changing the Terms: Translating in the Postcolonial Era*, Ontario: University of Ottawa.

Spivak, Gayatri C. (2000) 'Translation as Culture', *Parallax* 6 (1): 13–24.

Sylvester, Christine (1995) *Feminist Theory and International Relations in a Postmodern Era*, New York: Cambridge University Press.

——(1996) 'The Contributions of Feminist Theory to International Relations', in Steve Smith, Kenneth Booth and Marysia Zalewski (eds) *International Theory: Positivism and Beyond*, New York: Cambridge University Press.

——(1999) 'Development Studies and Postcolonial Studies: Disparate Tales of the "Third World"', *Third World Quarterly* 20 (4): 703–21.

——(2002) *Feminist International Relations: An Unfinished Journey*, New York: Cambridge University Press.

Tickner, J. Ann (1992) *Gender in International Relations: Feminist Perspectives on Global Security*, New York: Columbia University Press.

——(1997) 'You Just Don't Understand: Troubled Engagements between Feminist and IR Theorists', *International Studies Quarterly* 41: 611–32.

——(2005) 'Gendering a Discipline: Some Feminist Methodological Contributions to International Relations', *Signs* 30 (4): 2173–90.

Trinh, T. Minh-ha (1986–87) 'Difference: "A Special Third World Women Issue"', *Discourse* 8: 10–35.

——(1989) *Woman, Native, Other: Writing Postcoloniality and Feminism*, Bloomington and Indianapolis: Indiana University Press.

——(1990a) 'Documentary/is/not a Name', *October* 52: 76–98.

——(1990b) 'Cotton and Iron', in Russell Ferguson, Martha Gever, Trinh Minh-ha and Cornel West (eds) *Out There: Marginalization and Contemporary Cultures*, New York and London: The New Museum of Contemporary Art and the MIT Press.

——(1991) *When the Moon Waxes Red: Representation, Gender and Cultural Politics*, London: Routledge.

——(1992) *Framer Framed*, London: Routledge.

——(1999) *Cinema Interval*, London: Routledge.

Tymoczko, Maria (2007) *Enlarging Translation, Empowering Translators*, Manchester: St Jerome.

Weber, Cynthia (2006) *Imagining America at War: Morality, Politics and Film*, London: Routledge.

2 Displacing the detective eye/I
Seeing translation and mediation

DAVIES: You know, I can imagine some people listening to the story that might be thinking, well, this is certainly very unfortunate but an American journalist captured in North Korea has to know that sooner or later they're going to get to come home, that they're going to be a pawn in some diplomatic game but they're not going to get sent to a labor camp ...

Ms. LAURA LING: Well, I did try to maintain hope throughout most of that time. And, as you said, you know, I didn't know if they would in fact send us to a camp. But North Korea is also one of the most unpredictable countries in the world with a history of duplicity and everybody you speak to is very vehement about their, speaks very vehemently about their anger toward the United States.

(Fresh Air 2010)

Introduction

The above epigraph is an excerpt from a radio interview with Laura Ling, one of the two Asian-American journalists who were detained by North Korean authorities and released after Bill Clinton's visit. It was an interview on the occasion of the publication of her memoir, co-written with her celebrity sister Lisa Ling, titled *Somewhere Inside: One Sister's Captivity in North Korea and the Other's Fight to Bring her Home* (2010).[1] As the interview excerpt hints, Ling highlights the duplicitous and baffling nature of North Korea and positions herself as a victim of North Korea's irrationality and a survivor of a traumatic event. The 'capture' became another occasion to rehearse the script of North Korean human rights abuses, the fragile and precarious security problem of its nuclear armament and its extortionary brinkmanship in international diplomatic negotiations (see *American Morning* 2009; *Anderson Cooper* 2009; Choe 2009). We see another element of the occasion come more clearly into view in the above survivor interview exchange in 2010, that there is, of course, no reason to fret and surely an American cannot be sent to a labour camp – that is. American exceptionalism as the most powerful country in the world. Surely a weakling like North

Korea cannot detain and punish citizens of the United States of America. I wonder what Kenneth Bae, another Asian-American still in North Korean custody, would make of the exchange. Bae was arrested by the North Korean authorities in November 2012, sentenced to 15 years of hard labour and is currently serving his sentence in a North Korean labour camp. In a recent interview with a Swedish diplomat, Bae assured his family, 'I have not lost hope and have not given up anything' (Mullen 2014). That Bae's case remains unresolved contributes to our bafflement about North Korea and adds to the mix of bizarre events that makes the international headline: Dennis Rodman's visit to North Korea to play basketball on the occasion of Kim Jong-un's birthday; news that steadily trickles out about the Japanese kidnappings which North Korea vehemently denies; scandals, idiosyncrasies and exposed secrets involving the Kim dynasty (e.g. a trip to Disneyland in 2001 by Kim Jongnam and the late Kim Jong-il's love for movies and whiskey).

The argument made in this chapter is that the 'baffling' North Korea that we want to demystify must primarily be understood as an effect of 'our' attempts to solve international problems like North Korea. In other words, practices engaged in solving the 'North Korea problem' – for instance, documentary projects about the trafficking of North Korean women, diplomatic engagements to release foreigners imprisoned in North Korea or cultural exchanges that engage North Korea – construct North Korea as a mystery that needs to be solved, cracked and unveiled for what it 'really' is. This demystification/construction of North Korea assumes that the object under scrutiny is other than it appears, and that ascertaining and discovering this other truer and more authentic version is the first step towards a resolution. I argue that this is an over-determined way of encountering North Korea, which, as Rey Chow writes in a US context, occurs through the self-referentiality in production:

> As long as knowledge is produced in this self-referential manner, as a circuit of targeting or *getting* the other that ultimately consolidates the omnipotence and omnipresence of the sovereign 'self'/'eye' – the 'I' – that is the United States, the other will have no choice but remain just that – a target whose existence justifies only one thing, its destruction by the bomber.
>
> (Chow 2006: 41, emphasis in original)

What needs loosening is the grip that self/eye/I has on the terms of international/intercultural relations. Chow's point is not that this self-referential circuit succeeds in eradicating and erasing the targeted Other, but that its 'strategic logic' confines, ghettoizes, postpones and discriminates in an attempt ultimately to exclude (Chow 2006: 41; see also Chow 2002b). The hierarchy in intercultural encounters cannot simply be overthrown and replaced with more equal or anti-hierarchical terms of interaction. Rather, a loosening of the grip that the self/eye/I has on the terms of intercultural encounter must be pursued to open out this encounter to allow heterogeneous narratives and happenings to emerge.

This chapter is divided into three sections. The first section argues that mystery/detective fiction and graphic travelogues converge on how they privilege a particular kind of seeing, which I term a 'mode of detection'. It is an observant, evaluative mode of encountering North Korea that constructs it as a mystery that needs to be solved. I bring the concept of translation and visuality together to argue that seeing is an act of creation and less that of discovery, and that to see and create is to *translate*, i.e. to turn what one encounters into something else for the purpose of transmission. Building on the discussion in my previous chapter, I argue that altering the hierarchic terms of intercultural encounter depends on how this creative, translative, mediated-and-mediating visuality is explored.

The second section examines the mode of detection in two different genres that share much in common: the Inspector O mystery series that takes place in North Korea written by a former Western intelligence officer, James Church (a pseudonym), and a graphic novel, *Pyongyang: Journey in North Korea* (2005) by Guy Delisle. I illustrate how efforts to demystify North Korea through detection construct a binary North Korea that aligns with prevailing images of the country in international politics. More specifically, I focus on how seeing as an act of creation and creativity is delimited by mono-culturalism and self-referentiality in intercultural encounters. The third section focuses on how shifts away from this fixation on demystifying North Korea through detective work can and do occur in more heterogeneous modes and narratives. The discussion here is organized around Oh, Young-jin's graphic novel *Pyongyang Project: Oh, Kong-shik's Wishy-washy Tale of North Korea* (2007), based on the author's travel experience, and Kwon, Lee's novel, *Left-handed Mr Lee* (2007), which turns demystification on its head in the story of a dysfunctional family in Seoul and their lodger, Mr Lee, a North Korean 'resettler'.

Travelling and translating with a detective eye/I

Mystery fiction and graphic travelogues are genres of popular culture that revolve around detection – an evaluative reading and looking that deploys 'our powers of observation and of reason' to demystify and unravel puzzles (Allen and Chacko 1974: 77). Detection is centrally a mental activity that engages with the material world by subsuming the latter under an intellectual project of answering a question devised for the assertion of the mind.[2] Mysteries and puzzles in these genres are objects to be revealed for what they really are – as events and occurrences that, with enough time and uninhibited access, can be explained. Demystification, then, is an attempt to turn the 'unknown' into a 'known' through the application of our mental and physical faculties. It assumes that mysteries, which are inescapably detection's construct, exist out there and that by solving them, we arrive at a better place. It is a rehearsal of the mantra, 'Truth shall make you free' (Miller 1988: 34). In terming 'adventure in search of a hidden truth' an activity of the detective eye/I, I am stressing the act of seeing and the role of sight – visuality – in how detection mediates and is mediated (Chandler, in Malmgren 2001: 93).

In the section that follows, I show how detection is predominantly an activity that conflates investigatory adventures in search of truth with the observant/seeing self. In other words, what defines the identity of the 'person' doing the detecting is his/her identity as a truth see(k)er and an observant collector of information with pressing questions to answer. My argument in this section is that this 'I' engaged in a truth-finding adventure is a self that positions the eye/I above whatever lies in its line of vision, which it attempts to constrain, dominate and gain control over. The detective eye/I is a hier-archical way of securing the self in the face of the Otherness that a journey to 'far away places' like North Korea supposedly incites.

The travelling mode of detection

The mode of detection is widespread and is part of a larger visual culture especially prevalent in intercultural contexts. Illustrative here is how travelo-gues and mysteries share the same archetype of a protagonist – whether he/she is a lone traveller or a brooding detective – who solves problems with active roaming eyes and mind and itchy feet. Lewis (2009: 145) makes a similar argument that the 'solitary traveller' is central to the iconic detective's heroic status. Her larger point is that this solitary traveller-heroic detective can be mitigated by 'horizontal ethics' and 'egalitarian relationships', which differs from my argument here.

My focus is on how the singular, unidirectional mode of seeing pervades narratives of detection (and thus remains problematic), regardless of whether the detective eye/I has a family network or egalitarian ethics. The protagonist is engaged in documentation, verification, revelation *and* conquering of an unknown truth, land, psyche and people. The act of detection requires the positioning of, and travelling to, a place of difference, i.e. to 'cordoned-off' physical and psychological worlds such as the extraordinary site of violence, the world's hotspots, the criminal mind and so on. This protagonist is an observant, introspective inspector, the brain and the intellectual who sees his/her surrounding as an object requiring subjection, subordination and order.

An image from one of the graphic novels examined in the chapter helps to illustrate this generic convergence. In Guy Delisle's first travelogue *Shenzhen: A Travelogue from China* (2006), we see the author's sketch of himself as Tintin, the 'boy reporter' protagonist of Hergé's famous comic about the detective reporter who travels the world over to 'reveal the occult forces at work and the interests they serve silently' (Denis 2007: 117; see Figure 2.1).[3] In this transposition of Delisle into Tintin, with a banner of large Chinese characters in the foreground (read: exotic, foreign), the fantasies of detective fiction and of foreign adventure overlap. We have here a figure of the world-travelling

Figure 2.1 Guy Delisle, the author as Tintin, *Shenzhen*

detective reporter heroically fighting crimes, which takes him to far-flung places, positioning him to create an 'inventory of the world' (Denis 2007: 117). While Delisle does not closely mimic the heroism in the Tintin adventures, Delisle, like Tintin, is engaged in the documentation, verification and revelation of 'the world'.

My larger point is that the detective figure easily merges with figures of other professional or literary genres such as the traveller, the journalist, the scientist and the explorer because detection is a common and popular mode of seeing and inhabiting the world. I am echoing the argument others have made that Eurocentrism, neocolonialism, masculinism and even racism operate in such seeing practices under the guise of scientific, ethnographic, journalistic conventions among others (see Pratt 1992: 15–37; Mills 1991; Lisle 2006: 38–40; Holland and Huggan 2000: 12–19). The detective figure is not limited to a single profession, i.e. the detective; rather, the figure of the detective is merely an economical way of conjuring up ideal vocations of 'the expert in the field, the man who can read clues and find solutions', or even an 'artist hero – solitary, studious, given to wandering the city streets by night, and above all a thinker whose ratiocinative powers have been honed on higher things than murder' (Allen and Chacko 1974: 77; Porter 1981: 25). In short, the aura of a discerning, clever and worldly traveller/detective invites readers to participate in the fantasy that the entire world – especially the most exotic or crime-ridden parts – can be deciphered and evaluated to solve problems and overcome Otherness. Thus, the world that the mode of detection assumes is chaotic and anarchic, much like the international realm in IR, which the protagonist must order and make rational.

What is perhaps most significant is the *desire* to order, control and master. It is this desire that undergirds the mode of detection, enacting a unidirectional and hierarchical way of seeing and encountering the world. Detection is unidirectional because the act of seeing is treated as a one-directional occurrence where one observes but one is not seen, and thus is not interrupted. It is hierarchical because this attempt to tame the landscape, the encounter and the event relies on and reifies asymmetrical power relations. In the context of crime fiction, Simon Dentith focuses on knowingness afforded to the detective by detection and delivered in the narrative by the 'hard-boiled' writing style. Dentith writes, '[the hard-boiled] style provides knowingness rather than knowledge', which is an 'attitude', in combination with other generic traits, that constitutes 'a way of negotiating with city life … a way of getting through the day with your self-esteem intact' (Dentith 1990: 26). In other words, the mode of detection is an effort to attain the position of being in the know, to know what is going on so as to control how it unfolds. While Dentith (1990: 20) celebrates this mode as potentially politicizing for how it can inflect a 'radical or leftward direction' when the detective figure aligns with the minority/marginalized subjectivities (echoing note 3), I am pointing to how this potential 'move leftward' is necessarily hierarchical. At the heart of the problem is how the detective mode of seeing that travels to a 'geographical elsewhere' stays within the equation 'home-safe-same' in opposition to 'world-dangerous-different'. Here, 'foreign' explorations become activities that reify the self as civilized, ordered and safe, and produce the (third) world as dangerous, barbaric and disintegrating (see Breu 2005; Pearson and Singer 2009; Pepper 2000; Holland and Huggan 2000; Lisle 2006; Huggan 2009; Adams 2003). Taking an inventory of the world in the detective mode closely accompanies scripting it in the moral language of good/bad, civilized/barbaric, with us/against us. The moral language of the inventory of the world also privileges sameness over difference wherein sameness means to accord with the self. As later illustrated in the analysis of the Inspector O mysteries, not only is this supposedly exotic foreign society reductively rendered and subordinated under an idealized image of the self (which goes undetected due to its universalized form), some elements of that exotic culture get hand-picked (i.e. the ancient) as that which can save the otherwise decrepit, decaying world in which the mystery plot takes place.

In short, the *self* in mystery literature that travels to an elsewhere to solve a puzzle or crime (i.e. the travelling detective eye/I) gets privileged over and against the Other in various ways. The 'pleasurable' experience derived from cultural productions that enable this travel is problematic because it is a highly controlled and self-preserving way of experiencing the foreign and the unknown that requires the production of an Other. It predetermines the encounter with the foreign, the unfamiliar and the unknown by relying on one's preferred knowledge and cultural resources to subordinate the Other and Otherness. My point is that the mode of detection, expressed most clearly in detective novels and travelogues, reifies, reproduces and secures existing geopolitical discourses that divide the world into good and evil, order and disorder, explicable and inexplicable, controllable and defeated. Literary critic John Cawelti (2004: 334–56) puts this idea slightly differently and argues that literature can be categorized as 'mystery' when the idea of good and evil (i.e. the quest to save the good from evil in its varying degrees and permutations) prevails through the play of explicability/inexplicability. Cawelti's point is that mystery in modern literature plays with the tension between explicability and inexplicability, which moreover occurs to move the religious question of good and evil to a secular terrain of order and disorder. Critics have also pointed out how the inerasable ambiguity embedded in genres' foundational dialectics means that productions from these generic sites can be examined for how they potentially open up opportunities to foreground and benefit from the said founding complexity. Critics of detective/mystery fiction, for instance, find grounds to be optimistic about the genre and argue that fiction which plays with the idea of mystery can effectively put the very idea of demystifying an unknown under question (see Cawelti 2004: 341; Knight 1990, 2004: 195–208; Pearson and Singer 2009).

I do not share the above focus on the mystery genre and its generic traits in thinking about alternative terms of engaging with Otherness. Rather than make generic sites the focal point in critical re-imagination, I begin by attending to what *specifically* is constructed as an Other and an 'unknown' that must be turned into a 'known' by the scrutiny of the detective eye/I. In other words, I begin by asking what a 'geographic elsewhere' is doing in a mystery fiction and travelogue. When the *specific* Other (in our case, North Korea as the location where the narratives unfold) is used as the focal point for a given critical intervention, a serious play with mystery solving and the binaries that get mobilized by it feels inadequate. What *also* needs a serious play are the foundational binaries that get mobilized in travelling to 'foreign' lands like North Korea, namely modernity/ancient, past/present, authentic/inauthentic and pure/contaminated (see Lisle 2006: 260–78; Anand 2007; Huggan 2009: 68–71, 86–98). To disrupt a broader network of hierarchical delimiters on imagining and encountering North Korea, I turn to interrogate the 'mode of detection', i.e. what the self/Other and the seer/seen binaries are doing. The issue here is the convergence in how North Korea is imagined across different genres (i.e. the detective novel and graphic travelogue) *and* across various sites such as 'official' policy circles and academic and policy literatures. In all these prevailing representations of North Korea, the self is privileged through the figure of a seer who operates primarily through the mode of detection. Thus, the extent and manner in which this mode of seeing is disrupted and interrogated are of particular concern in exploring how alternative terms of encounter between North Korea and the 'outside world' are possible. This focus on the terms of engagement with North Korea includes examination of generic limitations and possibilities but it is intimately juxtaposed with questions about intercultural relations, i.e. to what extent and how the power asymmetry in intercultural encounters between the observing 'us' and the observed 'North Korea' can be complicated and disrupted.

Seeing translated

The significance of seeing in detection and interpretation comes to the fore when interpretation in general, and detection in particular, occurs in a visual medium such as the graphic novel.[4] Acts of seeing are mediated, and visuality occupies a defining and vitalizing position in how the world is mediated. The graphic form is especially interesting because its drawn and written form not only tells but *shows* a story that makes explicit its interpretative status as well as its style of interpretation and drawing. The editors of a special issue on the graphic narratives in *Modern Fiction Studies* try to capture this generic characteristic:

> Graphic narrative, through its most basic composition in frames and gutters – in which it is able to gesture at the pacing and rhythm of reading and looking through the various structures of each individual page – calls a reader's attention visually and spatially to the act, process, and duration of interpretation. Graphic narrative does the work of narration at least in part through drawing – making the question of style legible –

so it is a form that always refuses a problematic transparency, through an explicit awareness of its surfaces.

(Chute and DeKoven 2006: 767)

Chute and DeKoven are making two points. First, they identify what is particular about the genre: the grammar of the graphic form that they refer to as 'frames and gutters' (box panels in sequence called frames and the spaces between the panels called gutters), and the mixed medium form that plays with and foregrounds the relationship between images and words, among others. Second, they believe these characteristics mean that the graphic form is particularly conducive to a complex production of identity, truth and cultural differences that diverges from the dominant, conservative and conventional literary forms such as the novel (also see Whitlock 2006; Naghibi and O'Malley 2005; Tensuan 2006; Dodds 2007; Baetens 2001, 2008). Echoed in the *Modern Fiction Studies* special issue are references to Scott McCloud's argument that the gutters help open up readers' minds and create a 'limbo' and 'fracture both time and space, offering a jagged, staccato rhythm of unconnected moments'. This, in turn, requires the readers to do a lot of the interpretative work to create 'her own sense of closure' (McCloud, in Tensuan 2006: 950). While some are more reserved (e.g. Baetens 2008), the hybrid form and self-conscious playfulness of the graphic mediation is celebrated for how it opens up, disrupts and re-appropriates dominant narratives and images.

As I demonstrate later, the graphic form in the travel genre is indeed significant for how it allows us explicitly to register the interpretative work involved in faithfully reproducing what one saw in one's travels. However, I want to turn now to the interpretive work that gets foregrounded by visual representations from an *intercultural* framework. Like Chute and DeKoven, Rey Chow also places importance on visuality and the importance of acknowledging the interpretative dimension of identity, truth and cultural differences. Chow puts it more strongly and argues that seeing is a form of creation; moreover, seeing, i.e. visual creation in intercultural relations, is best understood through 'inescapability of stereotypes' (Chow 2002a: 54). Here, Chow is pointing to how exaggeration, essentialism and even stigmatization of some hand-picked characteristic of the Other is inevitable because it is an inescapable condition of intercultural relations. For Chow, intercultural relations is 'a matter of the outer edge of one group brushing against that of another, that it is *an encounter between surfaces rather than interiors*' (ibid.: 57, emphasis in original). Cultural differences are always productions that result from surface-level encounters wherein, through mobilization of power/ culture, groups '*insist on boundaries exactly at those points where in reality there are none*' (Dyers, in Chow 2002a: 59, emphasis in original).

What stereotypes (and in the graphic form, caricatures) help to register is that cultural differences are creations of superficial differences that emerge from arbitrary understandings of the Other that develop during an *observant* encounter. Stereotype-producing encounters (i.e. intercultural contexts) are encounters that are visually oriented and are managed through maintaining distance from the encountered. Drawn caricatures pictorially accentuate and exaggerate differences and distance from the encountered, which in turn makes the differences pronounced. However, Chow's point is that intercultural encounters are also encounters that are close enough, despite their distance and distancing effects, for the bodies to brush against each other and interact at the level of surfaces. In other words, the problem with caricatures and stereotypes is not that they are *superficial* creations (i.e. fictive and thus unfaithful reproductions), but rather that caricatures and stereotypes become problems because they often fail to induce change in the object that mobilized caricaturing and stereotyping in the first place and, at the same time, reify the power relations that produce such figurations. Thus, rather than attempt more 'genuine' encounters by seeking to get 'under the surface' upon which caricatures and stereotypes operate, we need to orient our critical ways of seeing to the surface level where intercultural interpretation and understanding inescapably stay and must stay. The critical issue here is that of creating and staying on the level of surfaces in ways that bring creativity and newness into intercultural relations. In other words, how can we see differently? How can we navigate interculturally the visual world that we inhabit and create?

What needs to be examined, then, are the multiple ways in which differentiated bodies brush against one another, and the effects of these surface-level encounters. The concept of cultural translation is useful in highlighting how the work of such encounters is a continual and incomplete process of mediation, circulation, creation and destruction. As introduced in Chapter 1, translation is a process of transmission, i.e. the transfer of (human, ideational, cultural) bodies from one space and time to another that denotes continuation, multiplicity and continued circulation. It simultaneously foregrounds the survival of the 'old' or 'original' through relocation, reinterpretation and repetition, *and* the loss and destruction of that original. This is to privilege all bodies that come into contact and as a result ensure the survival of those participating in the encounter, which the mode of detection presumed impossible by operating under the assumption that survival is the survival of one(self) *over* the Other (the unknown, the encountered). When the intercultural encounter is framed as translation or a practice of mediation, the survival of both interlocutors can be at the centre of the project, because while the relationship can very easily be adversarial, it does not have to be. Unlike, for instance, the conventional security framework that interprets difference as threat, one of the rationales for the intercultural processes are to defuse adversarial intents by speaking the Other's language. Moreover, the concept of translation is valued for making the surface-level work of this incomplete, creative and destructive process explicit. Translation creates stereotypes – imitations, inappropriate interpretations, caricatures from superficial encounters – in its movement between cultures. The point here is not to distinguish a 'good' stereotype from a 'bad' stereotype, but rather to enable relations of exteriors to be open to and possibly induce change in the terms of intercultural encounters, thereby loosening the grip that the dominant self has on the production and management of encounters. This chapter attends to this surface-level process of mediation, creation and circulation in intercultural encounters to examine what constrains as well as what is enabled in these encounters. More specifically, it is concerned with how translation can be a process of bringing newness into the intercultural context. Here, translation's practices of mediation and interpretation are profoundly issues of positionality and relationality, and thus identity/difference becomes central to the methods and aims of its practice.

North Korea detected

As already discussed, graphic novels and detective fiction that travel to 'the cultural and political black hole that is Kim Jong Il's North Korea' have a lot in common (Hart 2005: n.p.). On a basic level, both genres centrally involve practices of evaluation, observation and investigation that begin from the premise that a puzzle demands scrutiny and that successful scrutiny will lead to a solution (i.e. the revelation of truth). In this section, I examine how this mode of reading, seeing and using North Korea produces mysterious North Korean objects that reproduce, prop up and reify the international/North Korea hierarchy.

North Korea according to Inspector O

James Church's Inspector O mystery series revolve around a solitary, independent-minded North Korean police detective whom we know only by his job title (Inspector) and his last name (O). Each instalment follows Inspector O on mysterious and often trivial assignments (e.g. a surveillance assignment or an investigation of a bank robbery) which turn into multi-layered labyrinths of corruption, political sabotage and espionage.[5] By following where Inspector O goes, readers are given a close-up look into the 'inner workings' of power, the cordoned-off areas in North Korea (e.g. border towns), a decrepit nuclear facility that 'officially' does not exist and even the innermost chambers of important North Korean minds. For instance, the first novel, *A Corpse in the Koryo*, is a sprawling tale of multiple deaths (and corpses) and mysterious events, which ultimately maps out the geographic, psychological and cultural terrain of 'North Korea'. Illustrative is O's trip to the border town which begins with a detailed survey of the layout of the town, followed by an explanation of what the place is *really* about. Here a character more knowledgeable about the area tells Inspector O:

> You'd be amazed, Inspector. This is a border town. Lots of things here will amaze you. Actually, this isn't really Manpo. That's down the road a bit. It's crooked in its own way, but nothing like this. This is a new town, Sinmanpo. Lots of activity ... It doesn't exist, officially. There's no such

place in the administrative records. No official police presence. Everyone wants some of the action, especially the army. Every security
agency is watching every other agency to make sure no one gets too far
in front.

(Church 2006: 95, also 88–90)

The question driving these ruminations on North Korea is not only a straightfor-
ward question of 'whodunit' in detective fiction, or of 'what is *really* going on'
in a baffling series of events. Rather, what is driving these narratives is a much
more 'serious' question of 'What is really going on *inside North Korea*?' In
other words, because the Inspector O novels take place mainly in North
Korea, involve North Koreans or somehow make use of 'North Korea' (the
place, culture, the people), the text that interprets individuals, landscapes and
situations through the detective mode becomes a text that 'detects' North
Korea. As one book reviewer wrote, 'the real mystery that *Corpse* [*A Corpse
in the Koryo*] solves isn't who the killer is, but what daily life is like in one of
the world's most closed societies' (Wittig 2007: 27; see also *The New York
Times* 2009; Picker 2008). It is assumed here that the mystery that needs to be
solved, and enjoyed, is the mysterious world of North Korea that Inspector O
novels reveal for us to read.

The landscape that emerges is a North Korea where nothing works the way
it should. Nothing here ranges from minor things like a work-issued camera
and tea kettle, to major structural problems with the train, government institutions and its officials. The first novel of the series sets the stage for the way
North Korea is detected, and thus is the focus of my discussion. The mystery
in *A Corpse in the Koryo* unfolds around the criminal car-smuggling business
and corruption at the centre of power. Here, North Korea is described as a
worn-out, crumbling and desolate place that is corrupt to its core, but the
actual centre of power and corruption is always off the page and remains
an ominous and mysterious unknown, the effects of which, nevertheless, are
clearly felt. Illustrative is O's exchange with his estranged brother (a loyal
Party member) who warns him, 'Sit. Shut up and listen for once. Things are
happening, but you don't know what they are … Everything will move,
compass points will change' (Church 2006: 196). O responds dismissively,
to which his brother insists, 'No, this time is different'. This exchange is
illustrative of how at the same time that Inspector O 'demystifies' North
Korea for the reader (i.e. shows us what it is really like), the plotline also
creates a mysterious and ominous North Korea beyond the world to which a
'lowly' police detective in North Korea can have access. The looming presence
of inaccessible and invisible real movers of events lends tension to the
narrative.

Inspector O navigates this crumbling, corrupt North Korea through his
extraordinary power of detection. Inspector O's detective mode is established
early on in the first novel. Describing Kang, who turns out to be the main
villain of *A Corpse*, O makes the following prescient assessment:

The man's face was never going to give me a clue, so I moved my attention to his hands. 'I remember, I saw it in Prague.' It's hard for people not to react at all. If they keep their faces under control, they often do something with their hands. Just a finger lifting off the table, one thumb tapping the other, nothing you'd normally notice.

(Church 2006: 34)

The idea here is that the most perceptive detective eyes can extract 'telling' information about a person (what he/she wants, who he/she is) by closely observing and following a person's physical expressions. In this highly observant mode of seeing and interacting with the world, it is important always to attempt to 'read' and 'decode' the Other carefully. Inspector O's mode of detection is a way of being in control in a place that is out of control and chaotic; that is, this mode *orders* the world O inhabits. This ordering is aided by the hard-boiled descriptive style of 'flat and seemingly objective descriptions of events and circumstances in which the larger moral or emotional import of the events is left for the reader to deduce' (Breu 2005: 87). Dentith (1990: 25–26) makes this argument in relation to his protagonist and his protagonist's ability to secure a knowing position through the sparse, 'rational', 'deductive', in-control and distanced descriptions. Here I would like to stress how a knowing position is not necessarily about possessing knowledge but could also more crucially be about exhibiting knowingness through the character's mannerism, style and persona which aligns with what a knowledgeable persona looks, talks and thinks like. In other words, a knowing position could be not only about the substance of the description but also the descriptive style, thus making significant the ability to be in character with being in the know. The descriptive style of detective mode of seeing/narrating pulls together the fragments of stereotypes, emotional attachments and/or cultural ideals that lie underneath the carefully composed and seemingly neutral 'seeing' prose. To be more precise, Church's detective novels largely work within the generic demands of detective mystery which presuppose a world riddled with mystery, evil and disorder. This is crucially achieved by making use – in an established writing style – of the stereotypical image of North Korea as a place of danger, corruption and menacing secrets (e.g. a dangerous place with secret nuclear facilities and frequent inter-ministry assassination plots). Prevailing assumptions about North Korea (as mysterious, corrupt, backward, etc.) supposedly justify the detective's investigatory reading of both the landscape, which is unwelcoming, threatening and difficult to 'decode', and the other characters, who are automatically assumed to be suspicious (e.g. Church 2006: 3–5, 12–13). The familiar binaries of order/disorder and good/evil turn the world that the inspector inhabits into one continuous terrain to be discovered, decoded and rendered knowable.

What centrally mediates this real mystery of Church's novels (i.e. the 'real' North Korea) is that the protagonist Inspector O is a particular *kind* of North Korean. He is a reliable and intriguing protagonist who is, most importantly, a 'good' North Korean. This moralizing casting of Inspector O as 'good' is produced and secured through a further binary distinction between ancient Korea (which is pure and authentic) and modern North Korea (which is contaminated, corrupt, disorderly). Inspector O's deceased grandfather, a revered general who fought in the revolution against the Japanese and who disapproved of the newly independent North Korea under Kim Il-sung, performs an important function of establishing O as a 'good' North Korean by way of nostalgia. Here, the grandfather's role in the revolution against the Japanese colonial power establishes him (and his subsequent disapproval of the new regime when he was alive) as unambiguously 'good'.[6] Through the figure of the grandfather (who is painstakingly constructed in *A Corpse*), a layered nostalgia is produced so that both Inspector O and the reader yearn for a time before the communist North Korea, when humans were in a more 'natural' state. The figure of the grandfather also points to how the construction of what is good centrally involves a *longing* for an uncontaminated, distant Korea of the past in touch with nature and what is natural (read: human). Not only is General O dead when the novel begins (and thus exists only through a series of recollections, i.e. as a past), but he is a man who, when confronting the difficulties of his own present communist North Korea, stubbornly held onto an ancient past and retreated into nature.

What is particularly significant here is that Inspector O closely resembles his revolutionary grandfather not only in his distaste for the North Korean government and politics in general, but also in his solitude and, most notably, his retreat into woodwork. Just as General O turned to carpentry to cope with the 'new' North Korea established after fighting the Japanese, his grandson does the same to cope in the 'corrupt' modern North Korea. This love and attachment to wood, nature and carpentry are expressed in numerous ways in the novels. Insinuated in the various deployments of wood and carpentry that fill out Inspector O as a character is that Inspector O, like wood, remains untainted, natural, virtuous and even mystical in a corrupt, contaminated modern North Korea. Illustrative of the conflation of 'wood', 'nature' and the 'natural' with what is 'good' and 'pure' is his grandfather's soliloquy as retold by O: 'You can't shape people, just like you can't shape wood. You've got to find the heart and work from there. There's no such thing as scrap, not wood, not people' (Church 2006: 102). These words are recalled as the now deceased grandfather's criticism of what is wrong with the communist North Korea. This anchoring of what is 'good' in a past that supposedly existed before the present communist Korea is also powerfully deployed in the use of old Korean poetry as epigraphs in the first novel. One of them reads, 'At dawn, the hills wake from the mist, /one row, then another, /Beyond is loneliness/ Endless as the distant peaks' (O. Sung Hui 1327–58, in Church 2006: 3, also see 77, 176, 203, 253). These poems are attributed to poets from the distant past and depict an exotic landscape of mountains, open horizons and times of dawns and dusks. They work to create authentic (North) Korea as a mist-laden, melancholic, ancient place devoid of corruption and menace that is under threat of erasure by the corrupt, modern North Korea. In short, the 'good' North Korea is a stereotypical 'East' – primitive, ancient and exotic – and Inspector O, as the reincarnation of his grandfather, embodies, longs for and fights for this 'good'. There is a convergence between the generic conventions required by detective mysteries and the dominant stereotypical understanding of the 'real' contemporary North Korea.

What is interesting about the stories in Church's novels is how the good/bad binary that constructs a sinister North Korea in the present occurs by propping up a more authentic Korea in the past rather than by constructing a 'good' outside world (i.e. the West). In fact, the absence of redemption in the West is expressed numerous times by Inspector O. In *A Corpse*, for example, the problem with a moral binary of North Korea and the West is expressed as a passionate rebuttal to Western hegemony:

> So. We're not real ... If that's how we impress you, I must apologize. How rude of us, not to seem human to someone like you ... We're real, every one of us. Don't forget it. And yes, I have been overseas. Some things are good, some things aren't, same as here. Nothing is perfect. This god-forsaken country, as you call it, is where I live. This is my home ... I like it just fine.
>
> (Church 2006: 83–84)

Inspector O is saying that the whole of the modern world is the same; there is corruption everywhere and North Korea is no exception. Inspector O is 'at home' in the crumbling North Korea, just as he might be 'at home' in other cities such as New York or Geneva, where we see him travel on assignments. Everywhere he goes, he is a lone figure; indeed, modern comforts and display of wealth are not important, impressive or comforting to him. Not only are stereotypes of the present North Korea and Korea of the past mobilized, but stereotypes of the modern world (soulless, cold) and the authentic man (introspective, misanthropic), are pitted against each other to propel the narrative forward. While the outside modernity is not held up as an unambiguously better state than modern North Korea, the narrative still locates the authentic moral Korea in an elsewhere and continues to construct a mysterious North Korea through this deferment.

James Church's Inspector O mysteries have been widely praised for their realism. In reference to the first instalment, the director of a public policy research group praised the novel for being 'the best unclassified account of how North Korea works and why it has survived' (Hayes 2006). This praise is echoed by Barbara Slavin (2008), an experienced US foreign policy journalist who recommends that the novels be mandatory reading for US diplomats negotiating with North Korea. Value is placed on how they supposedly provide substantial, informative (i.e. practical) insight into international politics and foreign policy. In highlighting the constructed and mediated reality in the Inspector O novels, my contention has been that, though not in the same category as *The Expediter* by David Hagberg (2009), where a thriller plot unscrupulously supplants Pyongyang,[7] they nevertheless remain squarely within the mystery genre in terms of how they 'see' North Korea. The 'realism' of these novels is a realism constrained and even produced by generic conventions that rely on establishing differences between the good and the bad in a disordered world which must be ordered by explaining mysteries away while always retaining a dimension of inexplicability to propel the story forward. All this leads to an unquestioning acceptance of North Korea as a mysterious and sinister place.

Operating in the praise of the novels' realism is the fantastical assumption found in mystery and detective novels in general: that a perfect unleashing of the powers of observation and reason is possible if skilled detectives can enter inaccessible and cordoned-off areas. Given that North Korea is accessible only in severely limited form to many official observers with such skills (e.g. journalists, experts, researchers), the Inspector O novels function as the next best thing; that is, even though North Korea is rendered in 'fictional terms', this is an 'authentic' Korean perspective that will help outsiders access the 'real' North Korea. In endorsing James Church and his novels, North Korea experts, pundits and book critics alike operate with the idea that fiction can playfully fill the gaps in our knowledge for 'black box' cases like North Korea. This is especially obvious in the latest reincarnation of Inspector O in a newly launched website, 38north.org. Here, James Church regularly 'files' his 'interviews' with Inspector O and takes part in the website's larger goal of 'bring[ing] the best possible analysis to all those who work on North Korea for a living and those who are just interested in what happens there' (www.38north.org/about).[8] This internet project, supported by the US–Korea Institute at Johns Hopkins University's School of Advanced International Studies (SAIS), includes analyses of media coverage and expert reportage of key issue areas, namely human security, weapons of mass destruction (WMD), and North Korean domestic and foreign affairs. The 'interviews' with Inspector O appear under the author's pseudonym, James Church, and in a 'fictional mode', cover a wide range of issues similar to those that appear in the website's other categories.

In one instance, Church stages a secret meeting with O in the remote town of Yanji, where they surreptitiously exchange notes on the appearance of Kim Jong-il's young son, Kim Jong-un, as his successor (Church 2010). O tells Church why the succession should not be taken as a joke or evidence of instability: 'Our leadership is and always has been more practical than ideological. Our new leader's biggest challenge will not be ideology but a political system that gives him more power than is good for any one person' (ibid.). Inspector O sounds uncannily like an expert giving knowledgeable advice, which in his case derives from 'being an insider' although a mere fictional one. In the immediate aftermath of Kim Jong-il's death, James Church filed another story. This time Inspector O cannot be reached but the author closely dissects the elite personalities and what their public appearances and absences signify (Church 2012). On Kim Jong-un, Church writes, 'Anything worth noting in Kim Jong Un's first visit being to a military unit? Not hardly. Kim Jong Il often went to KPA [Korean People's Army] units for his first visit of the year. This will not raise any eyebrows in North Korea; if anything, it is familiar, business as usual, the machinery humming along' (ibid.). Peter Hayes seems not entirely satisfied with Church's analysis and in a rather familiar tone (Church's 'interviews' with Inspector O first appeared in the policy series of the think tank that Hayes heads), Hayes writes in the 'Reader Feedback':

> Anyway, what's the range of the young man's first possible audacious moves? We all know about the time afforded by the mourning rituals; and we hear all the time about a 3rd test threat (boring); *but what could he do that would actually surprise us?* Turn up in Seoul at March Nuclear Security Summit and invite everyone to emulate the DPRK's nuclear security procedures? What else?
>
> (emphasis added)

Hayes wants Church/Inspector O to tell us something he, as an expert and close follower of the North Korean security problem, does not already know. Knowing that Church is a pseudonym belonging to 'a former intelligence officer', Hayes's response can be interpreted as an expectation that Church, a seasoned expert, through the world of and mode of intellectual engagement with his character, Inspector O, will *think up* something that a conventional expert constrained by positivist conventions cannot *say*. In other words, the expectation is not that a detective fiction writer who, after all, is an outsider and a Westerner like other experts, knows more than the experts contributing to the other columns on 38 North and other public platforms. Rather, the expectation lies in Church's ability, as a master of detection, to produce a perspective that is different as a result of O's position as a fictional character. What Church is able to create and explore, which other experts cannot, is an *imaginary* realm that is informed and shaped by prevailing expertise on North Korea. Thus, the entrance of fiction in 38 North occurs by privileging intimate access into areas that are inaccessible through conventional social scientific methods.

It is this shared faith in the mode of detection in both detective fiction and social scientific convention that enabled this fictional encroachment into the expert community. Both detective fiction and social science exhibit the unquestioned need for knowledge and being (intimately) in the know. Fictional and 'real' investigation work together to satisfy *our* need to know, order and control North Korea. In short, Church and other 'relevant' professionals (e.g. journalists, North Korea experts) operate as if it is their responsibility and within their powers of observation to acquire and accumulate information that can solve the North Korean problem and mystery. In operation is the detective eye/I that enforces a hierarchical way of seeing and navigating the world. To return to an earlier point, while Inspector O in the novels does not reify an idealized image of the outside world (and instead relies on an idealized image of an ancient, pure Korea of the past), Church and O participate in constructing an idealized image of the outside expert community. This self-image is produced through the (re)production of the sinister, mysterious North Korea that sticks because of the fiction of 'insider protagonist' that lends authenticity to this construction. Here, the international community outside – an invested network of close observers with disaggregate methods and interests converging only on finding out the truth – is constructed as the collective problem solver that positions North Korea as an object upon which outside mystery/problem-solving efforts are enacted. This is a hierarchical terming of an intercultural encounter that not only fails to recognize the work of mediation and construction involved in 'investigating' North Korea, but the plurality of ways that the North Korean Other can be encountered. The playful inroad that the fiction of James Church/Inspector O seems to make into our serious quests for knowledge about North Korea is an instance of play that *contains* fiction.

The detective Guy (Delisle)

What becomes clearer in Guy Delisle's graphic travelogue, *Pyongyang: A Journey in North Korea* (2005), is how the detective mode of seeing is a one-directional and mono-cultural way of encountering difference. Like Church's detective mystery, Delisle's graphic travelogue is centrally organized by the detective eye/I, and it too has been widely praised for its insightful, 'generous' and 'good-humoured' portrayal of North Korea(ns) (Sacco 2008; Kay 2009; Drawn and Quarterly). Delisle's graphic novel is based on the author's two-month stay in Pyongyang to supervise an animation project for a French company in the studios of North Korea's SEK (Scientific Educational Korea). As Delisle explains in the preface to the (South) Korean edition, his interest lies in depicting 'the everyday lives of North Koreans that looked so other worldly' (Delisle 2004: preface, n.p., my translation). Parenthetically, the title of the Korean edition translates as *Pyongyang: A French Cartoonist's Crash-bang Journey in North Korea*, hinting to the violent *and* comical nature of the travel experience. The title of the Korean edition also identifies Delisle as a French writer, which would cause some confusion in readers familiar with Delisle's French-Canadian background. This short-hand of the Korean edition highlights the tricky territory of translation (and Emily Apter (2006) would add, 'transnation') that we have entered, where difference and sameness take on changing meanings.

To return to Delisle's interest more pointedly, the author does not believe in the official rhetoric that North Korea is a socialist paradise and therefore takes a critical approach to the everyday aspects of North Korean society. In a mental monologue, Delisle, the character in the graphic novel, asks: 'There's a question that has to be burning on the lips of all foreigners here … one cannot help asking yourself: Do they [the North Koreans] believe the bullshit that is being forced down their throats?' (Delisle 2005: 74). This monologue is followed by a short (and comic) history of North Korea and explanatory panels about its surveillance and policing system (ibid.: 72–73, 75–76).

Delisle here frames his critical attitude towards North Korea as a disgust with totalitarianism and love of freedom, which he expresses early on in his narrative by making references to George Orwell's dystopian novel, *Nineteen Eighty-Four*, which gives a harrowing account of life under a totalitarian regime wherein ideas that are valued (freedom, love, peace) are perverted to create a society that learns to detest completely what is 'essential' in these ideas. Drawing on Orwell's descriptions of Oceania, the fictional totalitarian society in the novel, Delisle portrays North Korea as a place of constant and pervasive surveillance and policing (see Delisle 2005: 22, 40). However, Delisle's disgust expands beyond its resemblance to Orwellian nightmare; he is also cynical about all things North Korean and complains about how North Korean restaurants and hotels are run, the way his North Korean animators work, the rules he must follow, and the bad movies, music, coffee and french toast he is subjected to in this strange land (e.g. ibid.: 20, 27–28, 35–36, 44, 67, 165, 173–74). Embodying a familiar 'difficult-to-please' traveller persona who is critical about local 'modernities', Delisle, perhaps unintentionally, constructs a pervasive sense of superiority over the North Koreans with whom he interacts, and over the everyday North Korea he encounters.

The hierarchic nature of Delisle's attitude to all things North Korean is exhibited in his response to illegibility in a place where he does not speak the language or understand its aesthetics. Delisle, like other travellers before and after him, treats the guides and translators assigned to him by the North Korean government as minders who hinder rather than assist. Yet, a local mediator is indispensable to Delisle, not only so he can communicate with his colleagues but also so he can turn illegibility into what he wants it to mean (totalitarianism). More to the point, the moments when the necessity of a mediator is felt are also the moments when illegibility, masked over in much of the travelogue, becomes visible. Most illustrative are sequences where Delisle's colleagues try to communicate with him on those rare occasions when Delisle's translators are not there. On such occasions, the word bubbles of North Koreans turn into incomprehensible symbols and Delisle has a conversation by himself (see Figure 2.2). The Korean words – the individual 'characters' and 'sentences' – are not readable as Korean language, but are instead visual illustration of illegibility. The word bubbles, in this instance, do not perform their usual function as a conveyor of texts but have become an instrument for graphic representation of illegibility. The (Korean) 'words', then, are graphic, i.e. illustrated interpretation of the author's illegible experience in North Korea, rather than a textual illustration of a cross-cultural exchange or learning.

My larger point is that Delisle's translators are indispensable to the initial inroads he makes into North Korea to make sense of what he sees. Delisle

Figure 2.2 A conversation with a colleague
Source: Delisle 2005.

never really accepts their explanatory leads but that is exactly the process that allows the construction of meaning. Analogous to the incomprehensible exchange with his colleagues without his translator, Delisle's encounter with 'everyday North Korea' is initially riddled with inaccessibility, distance and illegibility. For example, in his passing encounters with anonymous North Koreans, their activities bemuse him: locals painting a bridge or a circle of rocks; locals brushing the highway manually; locals cutting grass with a sickle; and little local students watering the public grass lawns with water from a decorative fountain. In the sequence in Figure 2.3, the process of meaning making is clear and linear: Delisle's reaction (puzzlement) → Delisle's sighting (cause of the puzzlement) → Delisle's subsequent action of asking his translator for an explanation.

While not all 'baffling' sightings are rendered in this clear unidirectional sequencing mediated by his translator(s), Delisle's various accounts of the

Figure 2.3 A view on a car ride
Source: Delisle 2005.

'mystifying' North Korea follow the sequential ordering of, 'This is what I saw, how could I not be perplexed?', followed by 'This is what they told me, how could I believe them?' Crucially, Delisle is able to transform his initial sense of disorientation and loss of meaning and feed it into his larger narrative of North Korea as an enigmatic totalitarian society primarily through his interactions with the mediators. It is by asking for an explanation from his guide as seen in the third panel in Figure 2.3 that the significance of the second panel becomes clear. Delisle's question here is poking fun at the same baffling explanation that his North Korean mediators give him for the various strange activities he sees – all these people are volunteering their time out of their love for the country. It is through the equally bemusing insistence of his North Korean mediators who stick rigidly to one ridiculous explanation that Delisle is able to translate these otherwise meaningless events to fit his larger narrative that something more sinister or coerced is behind this labour. Delisle communicates this to his readers towards the end of these episodes, using the figure of a wind-up doll preceded by a text panel that reads: 'With a six-day work week, one day of "volunteer" work and preparation for big events, the average citizen has almost no spare time. Body and soul serve the regime' (Delisle 2005: 59). Another illustrative visual translation of Delisle's scepticism of the mediator's 'official' story of volunteerism is a full-page close-up sketch of a few schoolgirls seated in rows playing the accordion (ibid.: 145). Their big uniform smiles and dilated eyes look unnatural, strained and lifeless. Not all of the girls appear in the picture in their entirety, suggesting there are more of these mechanized, identical North Koreans outside the frame. However, what makes the picture even eerier is that on close inspection, we see that the accordions are drawn in place of the torsos in the sketch. In short, the girls are uniformly drawn as mechanical, automated machines that appear human only because of our inattentive and fleeting glance. In sum, Delisle assumes that there is only one explanation (Orwellian) and one reaction (puzzled) to what he 'simply' encounters in Pyongyang. Delisle is perhaps one of those Westerners whom Inspector O cannot stand: a visitor who thinks North Korea is inauthentic and unreal.

In my opinion, many moments of meaninglessness, illegibility and bafflement in Delisle's journey have been translated mono-culturally through the instruments available to the graphic novel/travelogue form, for example through sequencing and drawing from the traveller/narrator's line of vision and viewpoint propped up by one's cultural references. 'Seeing' is always interpretive: it is mediated by the interpretive cultural resources available, accessed and created by the 'seer'. Delisle's interpretation seems mono-cultural in at least two ways. It fails to acknowledge his need for a translator or a translative language in these intercultural encounters and it fails to recognize that his interpretation is only one among many possible interpretations. While Delisle's own translations occur in a singular and unidirectional manner, these moments of illegibility, such as the episodes in Figures 2.2 and 2.3, actually point to the need for translation. The last panel in Figure 2.3 is telling: Delisle and his translator sit next to each other in embarrassed silence – an impasse. To clarify, my point is not that knowledge of the (North) Korean language and culture would have allowed a more 'correct' reading and reproduction of North Korea(ns), or that Delisle's concern for the effect of state control in North Korea is wrong. My issue with Delisle's concern is how he places (him) self outside the reach of the interpretive frame of George Orwell's thesis in *Nineteen Eighty-Four* in order to bring the mechanized North Korea(ns) into visual existence and reduce the question of responsibility to an issue of assigning blame, which for Delisle falls squarely on the North Korean regime.[9] I explore the question of responsibility in later chapters, but for now, I highlight how Delisle's experience points to the need for cross-cultural mediations and intermediaries. It was mediated not by the visitor's familiarity with the language or culture of the place he visited, but by his mono-cultural viewpoint and cultural skills in 'seeing' North Korea, and his unidirectional knowledge production. I wonder what a keen observer like Guy Delisle would have produced if intercultural acuity were also part of the story.

As we saw in the way Inspector O/James Church was positioned within the North Korean expert community, a detective mode of seeing and travelling in North Korea *eyes* the North Korean Other as a target, an object and a problem in need of solving while simultaneously positioning the eye/I radically outside that 'problem'. This mode of seeing creates a distance between the self and the Other, where the Other is evaluated from a higher moral position. Much as the demands of genre led to the construction of binary Koreas in the Inspector O novels, Delisle's *Pyongyang* would not have been possible without a clear vision that determined *beforehand* what he would 'see' (e.g. a population of automatons) and what he would ignore. Both the mystery series and the graphic travelogue produce North Korea in a self-referential manner; that is, they answer *our* questions, focus on *our* actions upon and towards North Korea, use *our* cultural references, and work to satiate *our* desire to know and tame North Korea. They fail to interrogate the mediatory resources and technologies themselves from an intercultural framework and fail to register a need for translation and intermediaries. However, my larger point is that because Delisle's *Pyongyang* operates in the travelogue genre, the narrative is 'about' *the encounters* themselves, which, as a result, unwittingly shows the need for translation and intermediaries. While this generic characteristic does not mean it is necessarily 'about' the encounter (and indeed, the genre itself can be deeply narcissistic; see Lisle 2006: 44–47; Holland and Huggan 2000: 11–12), it does mean that the encounter and the mode of encountering Otherness is at the forefront of the story. Broadly speaking, the plot of the travelogue is constructed around the protagonist's encounters with differences, strangers and unfamiliar landscape throughout his journey, and the stories are about meeting, reacting and interrogating various forms of Otherness as well as sameness.

This leads me to return to my earlier point that North Korean mediators are indispensable for Delisle despite his resistance to their mediation. Delisle's *Pyongyang* is partly a product of Delisle's faith in his own observational power, sanctioned by the prevailing figure of the independent traveller found in popular culture, but it is also partly a result of North Korean mediators' mediation that enacted the official narrative of North Korea. The guide and translators assigned to Delisle act as *knowledgeable* mediators between their guest and North Korea, wherein they simultaneously assume three things: first, that an authentic North Korea pre-exists their efforts at mediation; second that the mediators are the representatives of this pre-existing North Korea and are able to communicate it clearly to the guest; and lastly, that the guest is ignorant or has many misconceptions about North Korea which must be corrected. Put differently, an elusive 'real' North Korea becomes the 'original text', the mediator's explanations become the 'translation' and Delisle's 'world' becomes the 'receiving culture'. Thus, at the centre of the process of mediation is the monolithic and incontestable 'truth' (the 'original') which has supposedly undergone no construction and no mediation of its own. This sacred text is translated in a secondary language that is treated as radically separate from, but in correspondence with, the original's language. From this position, the North Korean mediators are seen confidently explaining North Korean history and answering Delisle's questions about curious sightings (see Delisle 2005: 56–63). Delisle's resistance against these North Korean efforts to translate the 'truth' of their homeland shapes and mediates his account of North Korea.

The authoritative translation offered by the mediators is in direct opposition to what the receiving culture (the West) perceives to be true. For example, in the 'baffling' activities that the North Korean mediators translate for Delisle as 'volunteers' who are working on projects of national esteem such as building bridges, the term 'to volunteer' directly opposes the outside scepticism that things like freedom and choice can exist in the North Korean society. It is a word that most 'effectively' contradicts the view that North Koreans are mobilized only by propaganda, force and fear. It is assumed in this mediation that the best translation is one that opposes – and therefore corrects – the outside 'misconception' by communicating the preferred meaning to the guest. In short, the North Korean attempts at translation and mediation take translation as a rational process: 'truth' *if presented properly* can dispel foreign scepticism. Assuming that one possesses the truth, transparent communication across cultures becomes the utmost goal in these dialogic exchanges. This transparent communication is thought possible by acquiring fluency in foreign languages to enable *accurate* oppositional interpretation in this language.

Delisle's response to these efforts of mediation illustrates that this is not quite how translation works. He reacts to these authoritative, knowing (and annoying) translations by asserting his own interpretation of North Korea that *opposes* the official version. Another layer of mediation here is how this North Korean mediation is itself a representation mediated by Delisle, the author/illustrator. How the mediators and mediation are depicted – as unreliable, inauthentic and manipulating – is part of Delisle's response to these translative acts and tells us about how translation works on him as a recipient of authoritative, knowing translations. In other words, mobilizing their own cultural resources at their disposal, Delisle and the North Korean mediators each construct positions and realities that directly oppose the 'false' North Korea the other promotes: the mediators seek to correct Delisle, and Delisle seeks to correct the mediators. Knowing translation and the detective mode are both processes of gaining control over the unknown by constraining the Other that one encounters and seeking to control how the (intercultural) encounter itself unfolds. They are efforts to replace an 'unknown' with a 'known' and a 'threat' with a 'non-threat', and are thus securitizing moves that create the state of insecurity and experiences of destabilization, as many scholars have accumulated (e.g. Campbell 1992; Dillon 1996; Ahmed 2000; Hansen 2006). Articulated in the language in this chapter, the assumption that detection contributes to (re)gaining a sense of security needs to be questioned on at least two counts, that threat is treated in an atomistic rather than relational sense; and detection relies on an ideal conception of security that treats self-preservation as necessarily in adversarial relation to the world.

In sum, while demystification assumes that by knowing the world we become not only wiser but more secure, it fails to account for how our efforts to demystify North Korea by gaining direct, intimate knowledge are always mediated by demands, techniques and subject positionings that reify the self/ Other hierarchy. Put more strongly, grasping North Korea 'better' is necessarily and primarily a creative and fictive process that is hierarchical and violent in its manner of creation. My point is that practices of detection are concerted efforts to make the fantasy of intimacy, access, mastery and security permanent in ways that privilege the self at the expense of what is rendered the Other. All the while the enactments of detective eye/I deny that seeing is an interpretative act that *necessarily* involves creation and that it is a production rather than a faithful recording.

This creative dimension of detection is more obvious in the graphic medium because it *shows* this reification process. While critics like Chute (2008) and Whitlock (2006) emphasize how the spaces between frames (the 'gutters') open up the narrative, my argument is that the boxes themselves that contain visual and textual imagery – of wind-up dolls and the sequencing exhibited in Figure 2.3 – work to magnify and punctuate the narrative by adding moments of full stop (.), exclamation (!) and perplexity (?!). My point is that rather than opening up possibilities, these forceful and explicit visual-textual panels try to stamp out other possible narrative trajectories that these intercultural encounters could enable. These visual and textual tools particular to graphic narrative are deployed to enable the narrative that Delisle has set in motion to demystify North Korea. In short, I do not think our ability to *see* (if we wanted to) these creative moments of detection make Delisle's *Pyongyang* less problematic than Church's Inspector O novels. Both function, in their different circuits, to produce North Korea self-referentially and see North Korea in a hierarchical and unidirectional mode.

Alternative modes of encountering mystery and North Korea

A series of questions about how shifts in the terms of intercultural encounter could occur emerges from the analyses of Inspector O mysteries and Delisle's graphic novel. What forms and modes of cross-cultural engagements are necessary to shift, or break away from the cycle of self-preserving subjects producing distanced Others? How do we 'know' without becoming trapped by the way our practices of detection construct our world for us? How do we evoke mystery without solving it? Can we imagine how alternative surface-level, stereotyping contacts are possible, and how they might shift the terms of the encounter to privilege the survival and transformation of *both* bodies that come in contact? I turn to Oh, Young-jin's *Pyongyang Project: Oh, Kong-shik's Wishy-washy Tale of North Korea* (2007), to begin considering how one might respond alternatively to difference, and how a non-knowing approach to translation might shift the terms of intercultural encounter.[10] I then turn to Kwon, Lee's novel *Left-handed Mr Lee* (2007) and explore how mystery and North Korea can be evoked and re-imagined to displace the prevailing modes of approaching them.[11]

Non-knowing mediation

Oh, Young-jin's *Pyongyang Project* is the author's second graphic novel based on his travel experience as a construction overseer for KEDO (the Korean Peninsula Energy Development Organization) in North Korea for 18 months.[12] Oh's earlier work, *Ordinary Citizen Oh's 548-day Stay in North Korea*, stays close to the author's experiences in the KEDO compounds and fits more comfortably in the category that Whitlock (2006) calls 'autobiographics'.[13]

Oh's second book is a travelogue with a fictionalized premise and thus has less of a problem with the term graphic *novel* because it deploys fictive circumstances and events that, while shaped by and using his travel experience, have their own trajectories and impulse. The premise of Oh's *Pyongyang Project* is an imagined artist-in-residence exchange programme between North and South Korea where his fictional alter ego, Oh, Kong-shik, travels to Pyongyang 'to increase exchange and cooperation between the North and the South' (Oh 2007: 12).

Pyongyang Project provides an illustrative example of how a traveller to North Korea can respond differently to the official North Korean mediation than Delisle's oppositional, mono-cultural reification of hierarchy. It also serves as an illustrative case for how responding alternatively to illegibility and inaccessibility can be conceived that the detective mode attempts either to efface or overcome. Admittedly, Oh's fictional travelogue can be faulted for how it problematically deploys an 'ethnographic method' to translate North Korea and make it more commensurable with the South and more readable to those unfamiliar with the North.

The term ethnography is apt because Oh studies North Korea as a cultural system of meaning by examining rituals, practices and social groupings. Oh's approach, like ethnography, privileges the internal logic of the culture in the sense that the internal relationship of the different component parts of the culture is examined. In other words, North Korea is interpreted using a cultural matrix that Oh as the 'ethnographer/translator' brings to bear in order to demystify North Korea for what it really is (i.e. not that strange or mysterious at all). Episodes in the book where Oh resorts to the idea of commonality are numerous and basic, as the episode of the children's day festival demonstrates: it is a national holiday in both the North and the South which is celebrated on different days but suggests that the parent-child relationships are alike (Oh 2007: 58–59). Oh also finds direct correspondence across cultures, for instance in the phenomenon of school bullying termed '*wang-tta*' in South Korea, and '*morajugi*' in the North (Oh 2007: 36–37). In this section, rather than offer further critical reading of these ethnographic modes of seeing, I want to focus instead on moments in Oh's *Pyongyang Project* that provide alternative ways of seeing North Korea and responding to North Korean mediation.

Like Delisle and Church, Oh is interested in revealing what everyday North Korea is like and he chooses to invent his fictional premise to aid this revelation. In the preface to his first book, which uses his travel experience in the 'non-fiction' form, Oh writes, 'A few years after the North-South Summit [4 June 2000 Summit], the North Korean society took an open approach of reform ... What exactly is happening in North Korea? How are the North Korean people coping with these radical changes of their time? I couldn't help but be curious' (Oh 2007: 7).

What is interesting about Oh's second publication is how consciously and actively it attempts to *negotiate* the meaning of his experience ('real-life events') rather than reaffirm the prevailing images and narratives of North Korea as a mysterious, sinister, unreal place – especially when his experiences allow a reaffirmation of the dominant view. The turn to a fictional premise is the most obvious way in which Oh commits to this negotiation, which the various episodes in the graphic novel richly reflect.

An illustrative episode is one that involves a tour of a 'typical' marketplace to which Oh's North Korean colleagues take him. Comrade Cho, one of his colleagues, holds the market up as evidence of North Korea's economic vibrancy (Oh 2007: 27–29). Having just woken up from a nap on the car journey to the market, Oh takes an uncharacteristically sharp line of questioning and asks, 'Wouldn't it be more accurate to say that the economic vibrancy in the market is evidence that the government's distribution system has collapsed?' (ibid.: 28). However, seeing Cho's defensive posture that his question incited, Oh quickly tries to diffuse the tension by joking around (see Figure 2.4). In response to his colleague's challenge that Oh back up his critical line of questioning (and in a sense enter into a duel), Oh breaks out in sweat and jokes:

> H-h-h-hold on Director Comrade Cho. You are truly a man of humour! How can you ask a married man to take responsibility? You're going to get me in trouble [panel 1] ... Look at the time! High noon and past the time to stuff our sausages. Ha Ha. And we still have to look around the marketplace so we can hear all your wonderful stories, eh? [panel 2].
>
> (Oh 2007: 29)

Through Oh's humorous, panicky and even nonsensical response, the host's explanation of the marketplace does not simply become evidence of an exceptionally problematic society (i.e. that North Korea is a place where people unthinkingly repeat state propaganda). While articulating the critique of the official North Korean mediation that tries to present the North Korean society in an idealized form, Oh does not reify the hierarchy between North

Figure 2.4 A tour of a North Korean market
Source: Oh 2006.

Korea and the outside by, for instance, using the incident to suggest 'Western' political and economic solutions. Rather than argue his point in a way that cancels out his colleague's position, Oh tries to continue the tour by turning into a bumbling comic. Comrade Cho looks confused and mumbles to himself that Oh's rambling does not make sense but, in the midst of the commotion, goes along with the route that Oh haphazardly proposes: to move away from a confrontational duel that seemed inevitable. Crucially, Oh has reset and transformed their itinerary and the terms of their exchange. This means that while in appearance, their roles (Cho as the guide and Oh as the ignorant visitor), what they do and where they go on their tour stay the same, the context of how they fulfil their roles and continue in these activities has changed. All these non-textual movements, which usher in a shift in the storyline, are efficiently presented through three simple panels, as seen in Figure 2.4. The tour (re)starts, but given the episodic narrative structure adopted, the potentially alternative graphic translations of the North Korean market are left undrawn and the episode ends abruptly.

Theresa Tensuan (2006: 950–51) argues that this episodic, in contrast to epic, narrative is part of the genre's various techniques (of digression, interruption, deferral) which can allow marginalized, long-ignored knowledges and epistemologies to emerge. The episodic narrative structure counteracts the ethnographic translative gaze on which Oh frequently falls back in much of the book by cutting those moments short and allowing a fresh start and theme to be taken up in the next episode. However, as the marketplace episode also demonstrates, even in those moments when alternative or marginalized narratives and images are 'primed' to emerge, the episodic structure stops short of actually representing these alternative narratives and trajectories. This openness, i.e. the falling short of actual representation of 'marginalized' knowledges and realities, is especially important if we are to avoid reifying the rhetoric of authenticity and intimate access to cordoned-off spaces.

This disruption of the easy oppositional response to 'North Korean propaganda' is not merely an issue of being as good-humoured as Oh, and there are many episodes where Oh refuses to take on his bumbling idiot persona and fights. For instance, in an episode involving the Arirang Games – a synchronized performance by the masses – Oh and Comrade Cho argue over the value of these games which mobilize thousands to perform the North Korean national narrative (Oh 2007: 99–102; see Figure 2.5).[14] This time Oh refuses to go along and play the role of a curious outsider by rejecting Comrade Cho's suggestion that he attend and write about the Games. Panel after panel, the exchange gets increasingly confrontational and the two men turn bright red in anger. Oh walks out after letting Cho know his view on the Games: 'How can you defend this gimmicky show that exploits the population to extract measly foreign currency from the tourists?' (ibid.: 101).

What is interesting is how this episode ends. Parallel columns follow the two men after their fallout; we see both Oh and his colleague Cho, from one panel to the next, turn increasingly sombre and thoughtful. Just like the market

Figure 2.5 Arirang Games
Source: Oh 2007.

scene where there is no attempt to sum up the 'real' North Korea, this episode also stays on the surface. We do not know where the men's thoughts have turned, but the panels in parallel columns register the ambiguous effect and implication of their incommensurable worldviews. They cannot stay where they were – angry, self-righteous and determined – but each, in their own space and time, shifts position. In subsequent panels, the red anger that coloured their faces in the heat of the argument colours the sky above Oh as he walks past a group of students returning from their rehearsals for the Games. Comrade Cho makes a phone call to complain about Oh but falls short; with only his back in the frame, Cho's word balloon, which has been spiky and full of unflattering and angry words, becomes rounded again, filled only with ' … '.

My point is that this shift, while ambivalent, has taken place without demolishing the Other, and it has occurred because Oh, the author, privileges the body that stands in front of his alter ego and the superficial exchanges that result. Oh's caricatures exaggerate these moments and the emotion and bodily gestures and features that stay on the surface, making significance out of these fleeting, superficial moments. Translation here is a bodily act in the sense that it privileges the bodies in the encounter, rather than a higher ideal that stands apart or above (earthly) encounters. This is not to say that survival dissipates as a concern. This concern that we saw Delisle turn into an issue of self-preservation (by creating uncomplicated, mechanical, inauthentic non-agents) does not lead to a similar turn in Oh. By valuing the bodies in relation and the present moment (rather than a later moment which will amend the situation by, for instance, writing about the encounter to reaffirm one's position *over* the Other), Oh does not see conflicting realities as occasions to assert against, attack or suppress the views that contradict his own. In short, it is not another opportunity in the long and tenuous road to convert the Other. In this sense, Oh goes some way to avoid reifying the hierarchical relationship between the detective eye/I and North Korea.

This ambiguous side-stepping of conflicting views also illustrates how translation is a bodily act in a different sense as well. The translation that ushered in the shift relied not on textual coherence or quality, but on the distraction that the verbal assuage brings about, which in turn ushers in a physical and bodily move to elsewhere. One way into this argument is to point out that Oh's humour exhibited on the tour of the marketplace is a banal play on words that even in Korean does not immediately or entirely make sense. Is Oh playing with the idea that 'taking responsibility' insinuates a situation where one is told to take responsibility for an illegitimate child? Was the phrase 'stuff our sausages' meant to be 'stuff our bellies with sausages' that has been hastily uttered? The point is that, perhaps, it does not *need* to make sense. In speaking of the agency of language, Butler, for example, conceptualizes speaking (and by extension cultural and political acts) as a bodily act. By 'agency of language' (rather than the subject), Butler points to a lack of control and mastery in interaction, and the body here becomes 'a sign of unknowingness' because the body from which speech is uttered is never fully consciously directing its action (Butler 1997: 10). To paraphrase Butler, an act always says more than it means to say, or says it differently. Drawing on Butler's insights, translation in *Pyongyang Project* is a bodily act in the sense that it involves body language (gesturing, facial expressions, words for their form not content) and bodily reaction (sweating), wherein words and verbal coherence take on a secondary function.

What is said, known and communicated must be understood in relation to both verbal and body languages as well as the survival of the specific bodies in the encounter. Put differently, *bodily* mediation is a *non-knowing* ('non-sensical' if we retain the idea of textual coherence) approach to practising translation in a way that foregrounds the ambivalence, superficiality and creativity that are inherent in any relation.

Puzzling North Korea

Kwon, Lee's novel, *Left-handed Mr Lee*, brings 'North Korea' to a surrealist Seoul of an 'ordinary' South Korean family, a loose network of North Korean defectors and the online game world where the two protagonists – Mr Lee and Miro – live most of their time. The story begins when Mr Lee, a 'reset-tled'[15] North Korean defector, takes lodging in the motel that Miro's family runs and lives in. Until chapter 13, the story does not have an easily dis-cernible direction and circles around the inhabitants of the motel. The chap-ters that follow (Chapters 14 to 39) weave in and out of different realms (e.g. cyber and material realities, adult and child worlds, dream and waking lives) and different stories (e.g. cantankerous domestic scenes, North Korean defec-tor experiences, a murder investigation, growing pains involving Miro, fan-tastical stories of the online games, etc.). Characters weave in and out of these realms and stories in ways that do not entirely make sense. For instance, Mr Lee and Miro interact seamlessly as players of an internet game, as characters within the internet game itself and as strangers in the motel, but how they move between realms is never made clear or logically possible (see Kwon 2007: 61–62, 132–39, 198–99). In both worlds, however, Mr Lee and Miro have much affection for each other.

Left-handed Mr Lee plays with the distinction between 'reality' and 'fan-tasy', blurring the boundary between the two. To be more precise, the book illustrates the multiplicity of realities and fantasies and draws a complex pic-ture of the world(s) that the characters inhabit. Kwon's novel can be char-acterized as a 'metaphysical' mystery novel. 'Metaphysical detective fiction' is a term that literary critics use to refer to fiction that 'parodies or subverts traditional detective-story conventions', which in effect questions the possibi-lity of demystification through techniques of detection, decoding, ratiocina-tion (Merivale and Sweeney, in Chambers 2009: 39). It plays with binaries of mystery/detective fiction (explicability/inexplicability, real/fantasy, rational/irrational, etc.) in a way that lays out the ambiguous spaces in between the two, not only in the structure of the novel but in its plotlines and use of metaphors of mazes, codes and puzzles. *Left-handed Mr Lee* exhibits many of these characteristics. For instance, the novel is composed of short chapters that do not neatly link up in an orderly or entirely coherent fashion. It moves from one context to the next, one group of characters and activities to another, and one world ('real world') to others (the cyber world and the dream world). This disrupts the decoding and mystery-solving activities of the characters (and there are multiple characters engaged in these activities, not just a single, lone detective), as well as the reader's effort to decode and make sense of the events that unfold in the pages. However, for the purposes of this chapter, what is interesting is how the novel couches the 'North Korea problem', and more specifically the 'resettler or defector problem', in a confusing mix of seemingly unrelated contexts, events and characters. It plays host not only to mystery and detective-related symbols and activities (e.g. labyrinths, codes, detection, murder, puzzle solving), but also the domestic scenes of a dysfunctional family, alien/UFO theories and the cyberspace of gaming. The question here is what critical insights can be gained about the 'North Korea problem' when we transpose it into a world that questions the convention of telling knowledgeable and insightful tales about pressing political and social issues of the time. What Kwon's novel compels us to think about is the larger question of fiction's role in politics.

Rather than use knowledge and knowingness either to make progress in the plotline or find a way to solve a puzzle or mystery, Kwon's novel privileges getting lost and foregrounds the complexity of trying to know what is going on. In the middle section of the novel, a reporter from *Sexy Daily* (a serious newspaper) goes to China looking for Mr Lee who, it seems, has disappeared from Seoul. Meanwhile, Mr Lee is actually hiding in one of Seoul's darkened internet cafés, escaping from his despair by living in the game world. Miro, who also has a talent for getting lost, is recruited by a mysterious woman to help scramble up the world: 'It is a sort of a job like a guide. Gather as many players as you can for this adventure. This is what I want to request of you, Player Miro' (Kwon 2007: 173).

At about the same time (but in a different chapter), Mr Lee, whose growing debt, isolation and curtailed hope push him even deeper into despair, is also told by a different mysterious woman (in the form of a toy) that he should first get lost in order to find his way. The two moments that propagate getting lost send Miro's family into his dream world where their mission is to find Mr Lee, and Mr Lee enters the dream and partakes in a role-playing game with the family. The roles the different members have to play are blindly picked, and an interesting series of re-enactments and dialogic exchanges ensues – feelings get hurt, accusations fly and the entire party becomes embroiled in a heated argument (see ibid.: 268–69, 281–95). They experience becoming another person, but what is interesting here is not that this experience then leads to a better understanding of the other person's position, but that it leads to chaos, an exchange of accusations, snide comments, outrage and denial. At its height, this chaos does not explode (i.e. become a crisis), but rather dis-solves into another completely unrelated unfolding of events in the dream. Also illustrative of this chaos is the larger series of events involving Miro's family inside Miro's dream. In appearance, the task at hand seems to involve figuring out what the dream is about and escaping it, which the characters do by reading Miro's dream journal to decipher Miro's world. However, as the characters try to solve the puzzle, their assumptions of what this game entails are constantly questioned from the lack of 'progress' their efforts yield (e.g. Kwon 2007: 180–81, 252–54). In short, puzzles, mazes and codes are there to get lost in rather than solve. To decode and find one's way out of them is to get lost in them and stay lost.

This approach to mystery, which is not to demystify (i.e. to turn an 'unknown' into a 'known'), but to let mystery unfold in its full complexity, frames the novel's various explorations of the 'North Korean problem'. I say various because while the explorations occur as part of the plotline involving the murder of a North Korean defector (which Mr Lee is suspected of com-mitting) and the stories of the various defector characters (of which there are many interwoven into each other), the explorations also occur obliquely in dialogic exchanges in cyberspace, between Miro's friends, or through Mia, the prescient and odd-ball younger sister. For instance, the privileging of right-handedness over left-handedness is used as a theme throughout the novel, which is also enacted in the fantasy world where Miro's friends get trapped. Here, the privileging of the right-handed population is reversed and taken to the extreme where the population is segregated and the right-handed minority are sent to 're-education' programmes and these 'ordinary' Seoulite teenagers become 'illegals' (Kwon 2007: 161–68, 188–94; for another example, see also 113–16). This theme can be read as an oblique exploration of the 'North Korean problem' through the surrounding plotline (i.e. the gang's latest member turns out to be a North Korean resettler).

My larger point is that the variety of discussions and narratives about North Koreans in this complex world – wherein South Korean society's paranoia, idiosyncrasies and fantasies are themselves simultaneously interrogated – are couched in decoding, codes and mazes that enable getting lost. Such embed-ding creates a 'chaotic' picture of the social and political problem that North Korean narratives and discussions by and about North Korea(ns) pose.

However, at the heart of Kwon's novel is the case of the depressed Mr Lee. What Mr Lee wants is a reality where he is not a hostage in someone else's fantasy. He wants a reality that does not rely on fantasies of redemption and God that those in more powerful positions impose on people like him (pow-erful people like Reverend Shin and the missionary David Young are mostly villains in the story; they exploit and manipulate the North Korean defectors for profit and religion). However, the reality that Mr Lee lives out is a world ordered by those who have no space for 'aliens' to enter. Mr Lee tells himself, 'In this world, order that disguises chaos is in circulation. Order is a capitalist order, an order according to those who have, a cookie-cutter order and order that privileges order before value' (Kwon 2007: 116). Mr Lee wants to escape this rigidly ordered world that is stopping him from travelling to China to find his mother (his national residency number identifies him as a defector and thus restricts his travel), denying him his former career as a surgeon in North Korea (he does not have the right documents) and making the new name Lee, Woori, which means 'we' in Korean, which he adopted in South Korea, meaningless. As the narrative asserts, there is no 'we' in South Korea, only a collection of 'I's' (ibid.: 116). Against all these restrictions, Mr Lee explodes in frustration:

> Why do we need things like fantasy? Why can't we just experience reality itself? Why can we have fantasies only in nightmares? What, because violence created fantasy? Why does my fantasy produce nothing but self-harm? Is violence from the nation and society being internalized and passed on? Why is it that we create fantasies only through violence? If this is really the case, does this mean I have to use violence to again return to reality? Could it be that if I break the fantasy, rather than to return to reality, I will live forever in the nightmare? Please, I just want to leave the room without guilt.
>
> (Kwon 2007: 186)

The problem of Mr Lee that Kwon presents is a complicated case of contradictory desires, impossible solutions and no escape.

While the murder case is solved (the *Sexy Daily* reporter, through his journalistic/detective skills, identifies Reverend Shin as the killer), the case of Mr Lee remains at the end of the novel. By keeping Mr Lee's as well as Miro's stories open, a relegation of mystery solving results. Codes can be broken and crime cases solved, but the central mystery of life cannot be solved by detection, conjuring up answers or finding resolutions. Despite the centrality of the theme (mystery, detection, puzzles), mystery does not turn into a problem-solving exercise in *Left-handed Mr Lee*. The 'incoherent' movement between worlds and the overlapping existence allow the characters multiple dimensions that are themselves fractured and not entirely whole.

As a result, deciding between North and South Korea and other binary distinctions such as real/dream, cyber/material, child/adult becomes *not* a particularly interesting project. This stands starkly in contrast not only to the popular South Korean films about national reunification and reconciliation examined in Chapter 4, but another novel that has received much attention about a 'converted' North Korean spy in Seoul, Kim, Young-ha's *Empire of Lights* (2006). Detection (deciphering, decoding, cracking the case) too becomes *not* a very central or consequential activity. Because of the way decoding and deciphering puzzles enter the story, they become activities that lead to surreal, complicating and (physically) transformative encounters, rather than activities that help pass judgement or reach a resolution. While working with mystery (e.g. puzzles, riddles, codes) and the efforts and desires to solve it, the storyline works by repetitively weaving in yet another fragmented string which alters the terrain of the mystery in terms of *what* matters and *how* it matters. Multiple fragmented and fluid individual stories are not subsumed under one overarching puzzle; instead, they occur to fragment the novel.

In a way, Kwon's approach shows us what is created in our mystery-solving and world-navigating activities: an interweaving of individual stories in fragments. The problem, of course, is that these entanglements get structured out when one overarching puzzle or narrative organizes them, which Kwon cleverly tries to elide. The translation and mediation that are needed in our encounters of North Korea(ns) are greater surface-level interminglings that can produce complexity which mediates intercultural meetings and understanding to bring about shifts in the prevailing terms of intercultural relations.

Conclusion

The mysterious North Korea(ns) is produced by the techniques, positionings and assumptions of the travelling detective eye/I. Mystery solving and solving the 'North Korean problem' assume that our encounters with North Korea(ns) help us to know it/them better. The travelling detective eye/I operates under the dictum, decode and expose. This involves 'discovering' the 'essence' of North Korea (ancient, authentic, anti-communist), or showing how inauthentic, mechanical and unfree the North Koreans are whom one encounters. In short, the self/Other hierarchy in encounters between the detective eye/I and North Korea sanctions the idea that something disorderly, dangerous and even mythical about North Korea *invites* our domination, containment and deciphering. My argument is that intercultural relations are issues of mediation and, more specifically, of translation that are never as simple as decoding and exposing a truth that pre-exists the discovery. Encountering North Korea is always mediated and creative. Such encounters are not only themselves acts of translation but also necessitate translations attuned to issues of power, relationality and difference. Translation must avoid falling into the pitfalls of translation from positions of knowledge, authority and authenticity, as exhibited by the official North Korean mediators in Delisle's *Pyongyang*. Rey Chow's critical formulation of decentring and brushes-against-surfaces helps to articulate how the question that needs 'answers' is how we can disrupt the subject/object hierarchy that constrains and produces the intercultural relations between North Korea and the international community. The final analysis is that non-knowing bodily mediations and an interrogation of the full complexity of mystery and North Koreans are translations/mediations that disrupt, suspend and shift – ever so slightly – the terms of intercultural relations.

I attempted to do two things in this chapter. First, I aimed to build a case for the necessity of shifting away from the need to know 'the Other'. The stress was on the fictive nature of practices of 'knowing-about', i.e. mystery/problem-solving, and the hierarchy in these practices. Second, I tried to illustrate how we might go about displacing our need to know. Rather than suppress, deny or become resigned to our desires, what we need is to reconfigure our knowledge practices as matters of relationality and intercultural encounters.

This chapter has attended to translation and mediation as one way to begin reconfiguring the significance of knowing. Importantly, examining detective fiction together with graphic travelogues has brought to the fore how knowing the Other as well as translation and mediation are all practices where seeing and visuality importantly compose them. Not only is detection centrally a visual practice, but seeing is never unmediated and unmediating. It is always creating stereotypes, superficial differences and caricatures. The argument has been that rather than prescribe how to see better and overcome superficiality or stereotyping, what needs further interrogation is what the inescapability of visuality and stereotypes in intercultural relations means for critical interventions.

Notes

1 Euna Lee, the other journalist, has also published a book about her experience, *The World is Bigger Now: An American Journalist's Release from Captivity in North Korea … A Remarkable Story of Faith, Family and Forgiveness* (2010).
2 The dichotomy mental/material is a product of the way detection has been discussed in the literary genre that further distinguishes it from ratiocination, which is a 'purely' intellectual puzzle that does not require roaming around the world to gather evidence. For instance, Holquist (1979: 139) makes the distinction between 'pure puzzle and pure ratiocination', and what I point to as detective work. The latter involves combing through dirt for a piece of evidence which is then used to string together a theory to crack the puzzle, while the former is 'purely' deductive (also see Rzepka 2005). My point is that regardless of the particular style of reasoning, this idea of reasoning itself is a way of approaching 'reality' that subsumes materiality under the human mind.
3 For those unfamiliar with Hergé's Tintin adventure comics, the two main giveaways of this Delisle-Tintin/Hergé transposition are the dog, Snowy, and Delisle's attire (shorts, boots and braces/suspenders).
4 Hillary Chute and Marianne DeKoven (2006) argue that the term 'graphic narrative' is more descriptively accurate since not all 'comics' are comic and not all of them are 'novels' and exist in many genres like superhero fantasies, autobiography, etc. I use the term graphic novel, graphic travelogue and graphic narrative interchangeably in this chapter.
5 His fourth volume, *The Man with the Baltic Stare*, was not available at the time this chapter was researched.
6 This construction of the grandfather figure mainly occurs through Inspector O's recollections which are prompted by people who cross O's path. All unanimously recall General O as a wise man of integrity (e.g. Church 2006: 128–29, 148, 2008: 172, 280–81).
7 Hagberg apologizes for this lack of concern for 'realism' in his title pages: 'This is a work of fiction, so I've moved some locations, mostly within the city of Pyongyang, to suit my story. My apologies to students of geography and to Kim Jong Il' (Hagberg 2009: n.p.).
8 This internet project is headed by Joel Witt, the co-author of *North Korean Reform: Politics, Economics and Security*, which argues that a more complex rationalized understanding of North Korean domestic politics could explain its foreign policies. Witt's position is that North Korea is explainable.

9 For how this issue is explored in relation to Orwell's novel, we can turn to a collection of essays edited by Gleason, Goldsmith and Nussbaum (2005), especially the essay by Edward Herman. Donna Haraway (1991) also offers interesting counterpoints on automatons and mechanization in a slightly different context in *Simians, Cyborgs and Women: The Reinvention of Nature.*

10 All translations of both Oh's *Pyongyang Project* and Kwon's *Left-handed Mr Lee,* including their titles, are my own. Oh's book title in Korean reads *Pyongyang Project: Olung-Ttung – ttang Oh Kong-shik-eui Manhwa Bukhan-gi-haeng.*

11 The Korean transliteration of the book's title is, *Wenson-jabi Mister Lee.*

12 KEDO is an intergovernmental organization that was set up as part of the 1995 Agreed Framework 'under which North Korea agreed to freeze and ultimately dismantle its nuclear program' on the condition that alternative sources of energy would be provided, including the building of two light-water reactors (www.kedo. org). KEDO's operations to meet these energy requirements ceased as of 2006.

13 Whitlock (2006: 966) coins this term in her argument that there is a need to read graphic narratives for how their generic characteristics relate to, and mediate, life narratives.

14 The Arirang Games (also commonly referred to in English as Mass Games), according to promotional material from a tour agency operating in North Korea, 'can basically be described as a synchronized socialist-realist spectacular, featuring over *100,000 participants* in a *90 minute display of gymnastics, dance, acrobatics, and dramatic performance, accompanied by music and other effects,* all wrapped in a highly politicized package. Literally no other place on Earth has anything comparable and it has to be seen with your own two eyes to truly appreciate the scale on display' (Koryo Tours 2010: emphasis in original).

15 The term refers to North Koreans who have entered South Korea through the South Korean government's 'resettlement' programme, which mainly includes a period of 're-education' in Hanawon and a 'resettlement fund' to help the 'new' citizens integrate into the larger society.

Bibliography

Websites

38North, www.38north.org/about, U.S.-Korea Institute at the Paul H. Nitze School of Advanced International Studies (SAIS), Johns Hopkins University (accessed April 2012).

Drawn and Quarterly, 'News Briefs Featuring Guy Delisle', www.drawnandquarterly. com/newsList.php?st=art&art=a41e32dcb62910 (accessed April 2014).

KEDO: Promoting Peace and Stability in the Korea Peninsula and Beyond, www.kedo. org, The Korean Peninsula Energy Development Organization (accessed September 2010).

Books and articles

Adams, Kathleen (2003) 'Global Cities, Terror and Tourism: The Ambivalent Allure of the Urban Jungle', in Ryan Bishop, John Phillips and Wei-Wei Yeo (eds) *Postcolonial Urbanism: Southeast Asian Cities and Global Processes*, London: Routledge.

Ahmed, Sara (2000) *Strange Encounter: Embodied Others in Post-coloniality*, London: Routledge.

Allen, Dick and Chacko, David (1974) *Detective Fiction: Crime and Compromise*, New York: Harcourt Brace Jovanovich.

American Morning (2009) Transcript, CNN, 24 April, 8.00 am EST.

Anand, Dibyesh (2007) 'Western Colonial Representations of the Other: The Case of Exotica Tibet', *New Political Science* 29 (1): 23–42.

Anderson Cooper (2009) Transcript, CNN, 9 June, 11.00 pm EST.

Apter, Emily (2006) *The Translation Zone: A New Comparative Literature*, Princeton, NJ and Oxford: Princeton University Press.

Baetens, Jan (ed.) (2001) *The Graphic Novel*, Lovain, Belgium: Leuven University Press.

——(2008) 'Of Graphic Novels and Minor Cultures: The Freon Collective', *Yale French Studies* 114: 95–115.

Breu, Christopher (2005) *Hard-boiled Masculinities*, Minneapolis: University of Minnesota Press.

Butler, Judith (1997) *Excitable Speech: A Politics of the Performative*, London: Routledge

Campbell, David (1992) *Writing Security: United States Foreign Policy and the Politics of Identity*, Minneapolis: University of Minnesota Press.

Cawelti, John G. (1976) *Adventure, Mystery and Romance: Formula Stories as Art and Popular Culture*, Chicago, IL: University of Chicago Press.

——(2004) *Mystery, Violence, and Popular Culture*, Madison and London: University of Wisconsin.

Chambers, Claire (2009) 'Postcolonial Noir: Vikram Chandra's "Kama"', in Nels Pearson and Marc Singer (eds) *Detective Fiction in a Postcolonial and Transnational World*, Surrey: Ashgate.

Choe, Sang-hun (2009) '2 Views of Journalists by North Korea: In West, they're Victims; In South Korea, they are Seen as Irresponsible', *International Herald Tribune*, 22 August: 3.

Chow, Rey (2002a) *The Protestant Ethnic and the Spirit of Capitalism*, New York: Columbia University Press.

——(2002b) 'The Interruption of Referentiality: Poststructuralism and the Conundrum of Critical Multiculturalism', *The South Atlantic Quarterly* 10 (1): 171–86.

——(2006) *The Age of the World Target: Self-Referentiality in War, Theory, and Comparative Work*, London: Duke University Press.

Church, James (2006) *A Corpse in the Koryo*, New York: Thomas Dunne Books, St Martin's Minotaur.

——(2007) *Hidden Moon*, New York: Thomas Dunne Books, St Martin's Minotaur.

——(2008) *Bamboo and Blood*, New York: Thomas Dunne Books, St Martin's Minotaur.

——(2010) 'Inspector O and You Know Who', *38North*, 26 October, 38north.org/2010/10/inspector-o-and-you-know-who/ (accessed February 2011).

——(2012) 'Off to the Races', *38North*, 3 January, 38north.org/2012/01/jchurch010312/ (accessed April 2012).

Chute, Hillary (2008) '*Ragtime, Kavalier & Clay*, and the Framing of Comics', *MFS Modern Fiction Studies* 54 (2): 268–301.

Chute, Hillary and DeKoven, Marianne (2006) 'Introduction: Graphic Narratives', *MFS Modern Fiction Studies* 52 (4): 767–82.

Delisle, Guy (2004) *Pyongyang: A French Cartoonist's Crash-bang Journey in North Korea* (*Pyongyang: Peu-rang-sue Manhwa-ga-eui Jwa-chung-woo-dol Pyongyang iyagi*), Seung-jae Lee (trans.), Seoul: Munhak-saegae-sa.

——(2005) *Pyongyang: Journey in North Korea*, Helge Dascher (trans.), London: Jonathan Cape.

——(2006) *Shenzhen: A Travelogue from China*, Helge Dascher (trans.) and Dirk Rehm (hand-lettered), Quebec: Drawn and Quarterly.

Denis, Benoit (2007) 'Herge-Simenon, Thirties', in Nathalie Aubert, Pierre-Philippe Fraiture, Patrick McGuinness (eds) *From Art Nouveau to Surrealism: Belgian Modernity in the Making*, Oxford: Legenda.

Dentith, Simon (1990) '"This Shitty Urban Machine Humanised": The Urban Crime Novel and the Novels of William McIlvanney', in Ian Bell and Graham Daldry (eds) *Watching the Detectives: Essays on Crime Fiction*, New York: St Martin's Press.

Dillon, Michael (1996) *Politics of Security: Towards a Political Philosophy of Continental Thought*, London: Routledge.

Dodds, Klaus (2007) 'Steve Bell's Eye: Cartoons, Geopolitics and the Visualization of the "War on Terror"', *Security Dialogue* 38: 157–77.

Drawn and Quarterly (n.d.) 'News Briefs Featuring Guy Delisle', www.drawnandquarterly.com/newsList.php?st=art&art=a41e32dcb62910 (accessed April 2014).

Fresh Air (2010) 'Ling Sisters Recount Laura's Capture in North Korea', National Public Radio, 19 May, www.npr.org/templates/transcript/transcript.pho?storyId=126613763 (accessed July 2010).

Gleason, Abbott, Goldsmith, Jack and Nussbaum, Martha C. (eds) (2005) *On Nineteen Eighty-four: Orwell and Our Future*, Princeton, NJ: Princeton University Press.

Hagberg, David (2009) *The Expediter*, New York: Forge Book, Tom Doherty Associate.

Hansen, Lene (2006) *Security as Practice: Discourse Analysis and the Bosnian War*, New York: Routledge.

Haraway, Donna (1991) *Simians, Cyborgs and Women: The Reinvention of Nature*, New York: Routledge.

Hart, Otis (2005) 'Graphic Novel "Pyongyang" Follows One Westerner's Stay in North Korea', *Associated Press*, www.drawnandquarterly.com/newsList.php?st=art&art=a41e32dcb62910 (accessed April 2014).

Hayes, Peter (2006) 'Inspector O and the Case of the Missing Tea Thermos', *Policy Forum Online* 06–105A, www.nautilus.org (accessed December 2010).

Holland, Patrick and Huggan, Graham (2000) *Tourists with Typewriters: Critical Reflections on Contemporary Travel Writing*, Ann Arbor: University of Michigan Press.

Holquist, Michael (1979) 'Whodunit and Other Questions: Metaphysical Detective Stories in Post-war Fiction', *New Literary History* 3, 1: 135–56.

Huggan, Graham (2009) *Extreme Pursuits: Travel/Writing in an Age of Globalization*, Ann Arbor: University of Michigan.

Kay, Peter (2009) 'Guy Delisle Interview', *Time Out Hong Kong*, www.timeout.com.hk/books/features/21133/guy-delisle-interview.html (accessed April 2012).

Kim, Young-ha (2006) *Empire of Lights* (*Bitche Jae-guk*), Paju: Munhak-dongnae.

Knight, Stephen (1990) 'Radical Thrillers' McIlvanney', in Ian Bell and Graham Daldry (eds) *Watching the Detectives: Essays on Crime Fiction*, New York: St Martin's Press.

——(2004) *Crime Fiction, 1800–2000: Detection, Death, Diversity*, Basingstoke: Palgrave Macmillan.

Koryo Tours (Hannah@koryotours.ccsend.com) (2010) 'Mass Games 2010 Dates Confirmed', mailing list email to Shinhyung Choi (schoi05@qub.ac.uk), 17 May.

Kwon, Lee (2007) *Left-handed Mr Lee* (*Wenson-jabi Mister Lee*), Paju: Moonhak.

Lee, Euna (2010) *The World is Bigger Now: An American Journalist's Release from Captivity in North Korea … A Remarkable Story of Faith, Family and Forgiveness*, with Lisa Dickey, Guildhall: Broadway Books.

Lewis, Jennifer (2009) '"Sympathetic Traveling": Horizontal Ethics and Aesthetics in Paco Ignacio Taibo's Belascoaran Shayne novels', in Nels Pearson and Marc Singer (eds) *Detective Fiction in a Postcolonial and Transnational World*, Surrey: Ashgate.

Ling, Laura and Ling, Lisa (2010) *Somewhere Inside: One Sister's Captivity in North Korea and the Other's Fight to Bring her Home*, New York: HarperCollins.

Lisle, Debbie (2006) *Global Politics of Contemporary Travel Writing*, New York: Cambridge University Press.

Malmgren, Carl D. (2001) *Anatomy of Murder: Mystery, Detective, and Crime Fiction*, Bowling Green, OH: Bowling Green State University Popular Press.

McCloud, Scott (1993) *Understanding Comics: the Invisible Art*, New York: Harper Perennial.

Miller, D.A. (1988) *The Novel and the Police*, Berkeley, CA: University of California Press.

Mills, Sara (1991) *Discourse of Difference: An Analysis of Women's Travel Writings and Colonialism*, London: Routledge.

Mullen, Jethro (2014) 'Kenneth Bae Worried about his Health in North Korean Camp', *CNN*, 10 February, edition.cnn.com/2014/02/10/world/asia/north-korea-kenneth-bae/ (accessed April 2014).

Naghibi, Nima and O'Malley, Andrew (2005) 'Estranging the Familiar: "East" and "West" in Satrapi's *Persepolis*', *English Studies in Canada* June/September: 1–27.

The New York Times (2009) Section Reviews Fiction, 14 December: 35.

Oh, Young-jin (2004) *Ordinary Citizen Mr Oh's 548-day Stay in North Korea* (*Botong Simin Oh-ssi-eui 548-il Bukhang-cherugi*), 1 and 2, Seoul: Gil-chatgi.

——(2007) *Pyongyang Project: Oh, Kong-shik's Wishy-washy Tale of North Korea* (*Pyongyang Project: Olung-Ttung – ttang Oh Kong-shik-eui Manhwa Bukhan-gi-haeng*), Paju: Changbi.

Pearson, Nels and Singer, Marc (eds) (2009) *Detective Fiction in a Postcolonial and Transnational World*, Surrey: Ashgate.

Pepper, Andrew (2000) *The Contemporary American Crime Novel: Race, Ethnicity, Gender, Class*, Edinburgh: Edinburgh University Press.

Picker, Leonard (2008) 'Intrigue in Pyongyang: A Popular Mystery Set in, of all Places, North Korea', *Korea Herald*, 9 August: 32.

Porter, Dennis (1981) *The Pursuit of Crime: Art and Ideology in Detective Fiction*, New Haven, CT: Yale University Press.

Pratt, Mary Louise (1992) *Imperial Eyes: Travel Writing and Transculturation*, London: Routledge.

Rzepka, Charles J. (2005) *Detective Fiction*, Cambridge: Polity.

Sacco, Joe (2008) 'Burmese Days', *The National*, www.thenational.ae/article/20081107/review/153320036/-1/sport (accessed May 2010).

Slavin, Barbara (2008) 'Mystery, Diplomacy in North Korea', *The Washington Times*, 14 December, Books Section: M28.

Tensuan, Theresa M. (2006) 'Comic Visions and Revisions in the Work of Lynda Barry and Marjane Satrapi', *MFS Modern Fiction Studies* 52 (4): 947–64.

Whitlock, Gillian (2006) 'Autobiographics: The Seeing "I" of the Comics', *MFS Modern Fiction Studies* 52 (4): 965–79.

Wittig, Louis (2007) 'CSI: Pyongyang: The First American Detective Novel Set in North Korea Exposes more than Just Whodunit', *KoreAm Journal* 18 (7): 27, www.iamkoream.com (accessed January 2010).

3 What 'seeing' suffering demands of us

Photographic engagements with North Korea(ns)

Now, we know of his [Kim Jong-il's] land that is land where freedom is in shambles, human dignity ridiculed and hope repressed. So what then must we do? All we can do is pull the alarm, thus free citizens of the world. So, if we are here [at this United Nations special session] on North Korea it is because we believe North Korea needs our help, needs the help of the United Nations, needs at least the very idea that they are not alone. That we are here to hear their cry and we will help them. Yes, I have spoken before to the Security Council. Before I spoke here in the United Nations on anti-Semitism, I spoke at the first ceremony on, the Holocaust ceremony here, a remembrance ceremony in the United Nations. This is part of the same concern. Part of the same obsession that the victims should never feel abandoned. The victims in North Korea should know that there are people in the world who feel, who try to feel their pain, their anguish and their despair. We are their hope. Let's not deceive them. Thank you.

(Elie Wiesel at UN ECOSOC (Economic and Social Council) special session on 'Failure to Protect: A Call to the UN Security Council to Act in North Korea', 2006)

Introduction

In 2006, Vaclav Havel, Kjell Magne Bondevik and Elie Wiesel commissioned a report to make a case for a United Nations (UN) Security Council action against North Korea under the 'responsibility to protect' doctrine. A special meeting was held in 2006 hosted by the then UN representative of the Czech Republic, attended by these three dignitaries. A second follow-up report was commissioned in 2008 (see United Nations 2006; DLA Piper LLP and US Committee for Human Rights in North Korea 2006; DLA Piper LLP, US Committee for Human Rights in North Korea and Oslo Center for Peace and Human Rights 2008). Just as I am putting the finishing touches to this chapter, another round of UN calls for action in the name of humanity is unfolding, this time through a report commissioned by the UN Human Rights Council. This 2014 report, 'Human Rights Council Resolution 22/13', was mandated by the Commission of Inquiry on Human Rights in the Democratic People's

Republic of Korea (DPRK), 'to investigate the systematic, widespread and grave violations of human rights in the DPRK, with a view to ensuring full accountability, in particular, for violations that may amount to crimes against humanity' (UN Human Rights Council 2014: 5). This chapter questions the underlying logic that structures these recurrent expressions to *do something* (anything!) about North Korea.

The previous chapter discussed how our desire and sense of entitlement to know and make truth claims from positions of authority over-determine our encounters with North Korea. This chapter focuses on one aspect of this knowledge hierarchy – that between what Luc Boltanski (1999) calls the fortunate (self) and the unfortunate (Other) – wherein the world is divided by singling out the Other for its misery and suffering. When suffering is seen as a problem in the sense that something is wrong with *them over there* that *we over here* must do something about, we enter the realm of obligation and responsibility. The worldview that assumes that we are more fortunate, better off and 'are their hope', as Elie Wiesel put it in the epigraph, undergirds this sense of obligation. This sense, in part, is a product of feeling that we can do something about the suffering of Others because of our outsider position in relation to this misery. It is also an all-around good feeling that is produced through feeling sad and outraged – we feel good about ourselves because we are capable, empowered and in the right. We feel good because we feel that we can and must do something about the world's problems. This self-image is possible because we assume that we stand outside, i.e. that there is a distance between us and the most miserable, unfortunate, abject human condition.

Contrary to Boltanski who frames acting on the suffering of Others through the limited realm of pity, I want to begin interrogating the hierarchy of fortunate/unfortunate more broadly. I want to question the sense of obligation and responsibility to act which stem not only from pity but a number of other similar emotions (e.g. compassion, guilt, anger, empathy) that produce a hierarchical gazing down at suffering from a position of superiority and distance. This is to understand these emotions as sharing, in varying degrees, the hierarchical structure found in pity that views suffering as a 'lack' and as an unambiguous object of our (knowledgeable) action. Elie Wiesel's status as a holocaust survivor (i.e. from a position of having 'been there') is an especially interesting enactment of this hierarchical relationship between fortunate international subjects and unfortunate North Korea. It illustrates the complex composition of the active 'us' as well as the indispensable role of 'insider' interlocutors, which I discuss in Chapter 5. While an outsider in relation to North Korea, Elie Wiesel speaks with authority from having been in a similar position of suffering. His status as a holocaust survivor provides him a special position of proximity that makes him an asset in an international moral case for action on the North Korea.

This chapter focuses on the prevailing assumptions undergirding the distance between 'us' and 'them' more broadly which hierarchically constructs the world. Framing the 'North Korea problem' as a special case of dictatorship (or in the international legal language, a case of 'failure to pro-tect') is to understand suffering like poverty and political oppression as situations particular to 'Third World' countries like North Korea where dic-tators can reign. Here, North Korea is produced as an object of intervention by international humanitarian organizations, international bodies like the UN Security Council and the international human rights framework.

I examine how this dominant imagining of North Korea as an object of international help and concern is visually constructed, i.e. how images and stories that are captured and told through cameras try to turn North Korea into a target and object of outside help.

At the heart of the present examination of images of suffering in need of intervention is a deep scepticism of the prevailing notion that suffering is a condition that sufferers *have*. That is, suffering and pain reside inside and belong to the sufferers which renders suffering an inert and objectifiable experience with some stable base that is graspable. By placing and enclosing suffering inside the sufferer, the *inaccessible* nature of experiences of poverty, oppres-sion, violence and misery becomes a problem. In this formulation of suffering, the gap between suffering and representations of suffering, as well as the distance between sufferer and spectator, become spaces that need to be reduced and closed. They become obstacles that need dodging or facing up to in efforts to respond and act responsibly to the suffering Other. The static and objectified understanding of suffering at the same time leads to the reception and treat-ment of testimonies of suffering as requiring scrutiny and 'healthy' scepticism in an effort to differentiate authentic pain from inauthentic or falsified claims.

By interrogating suffering in need of intervention, the first part of this chapter foregrounds the relational nature of suffering through related ideas of contingency, touch and ungraspability. The discussion more specifically turns to the way photographs – the capturing of suffering through the use of a camera – operate as privileged evidence of North Korea's poverty and oppression. I explore the problems as well as the politically productive effects of privileging camera images in picturing and responding to suffering. I argue that the assumed intimate relationship of camera images with witnessing can help to foreground the contingent nature of suffering and problematize the pre-valent ways in which distance between spectator and suffering is acted upon.

The second section of this chapter examines images produced by photo-graphers in the 2000s who have focused on documenting poverty and oppression in North Korea. The analysis is mainly of three photo books: Choi, Soon-ho's *Defectors: Their Story* (2008), Ri, Man-geun's *Landscape of the Everyday North* (2005) and Philippe Chancel's *North Korea* (2006). Each of these photo books pictures different dimensions of suffering in North Korea, but collectively, they affect a singular positioning of North Korea as an object of outside intervention. I illustrate how the production of this sin-gularity occurs through the use of established photographic aesthetics, mainly the sequencing of photographic images in book form, and the use of texts and captions.

The last section turns to an image of North Korea choreographed by Area Park to re-imagine what is involved in responding to the pain of Others. I argue that rethinking suffering in North Korea is not about the production of new images but about a different way of seeing suffering and positioning the self and the Other. Responding to suffering is reconceived as an issue that lies far beyond the idea of merely 'helping', a power relationship of an active and benevolent 'we' taking action upon, or on behalf of, the deviant, unfortunate, needy Other. Responding and responsibility to suffering are broader issues wherein material aid is but one small aspect of what they mean, one that is undoubtedly important but also in dire need of more creative and heterogeneous approaches that acknowledge its smallness, ambiguity and contradictions.

Encounters with suffering

Suffering has long been described as an experience that is surrounded by silence. Reasons vary – from the physicality of pain as an experience that means it escapes language, to the plurality of experiences we categorize as suffering, to how all experiences gain their status through existing languages and images, which leaves much 'unspoken' and 'unrepresented' (see Kleinman *et al.* 1997a; Sontag 2003; Reinhardt *et al.* 2007; Dauphinee 2007).[1] What I am pointing to here is the discordance in experiences of suffering that can never be perfectly aligned. The narrow range of accounts of this diverse and inherently unstable condition with emotional, physical, social, cultural and political dimensions directs us to the work of power. The static understanding of suffering points to how culture is mobilized to produce this singularity. It also draws attention to the socio-political function that these privileged images, narratives and conceptions of suffering perform. Put differently, dominant social, cultural and political forces are too centrally constitutive of suffering for it to be heard, seen and experienced in all its multiplicity and complexity.

Thus, in highlighting the silence and incommunicability of suffering, it is important simultaneously to acknowledge that silence and incommunicability are also products of power. Mustapha Pasha, for one, places greater emphasis on how silence itself is something that is constructed in conceptualizing poverty in global politics, and defines the poor as 'those that lack not only the material capacity to satisfy culturally informed needs but the ability to live meaningful lives' (Pasha 2009: 335). What we define as 'poverty' and who we define as 'poor' are determined, not by the lack of an essential set of material resources or material capacity, but by the lack of means to represent and live their lives (i.e. to communicate meaningfully about their lives and to inhabit 'their lives'). In other words, silence and incommunicability are also products of political, cultural and social forces; they are works of power. As Bhambra and Shilliam (2009) stress, silence cannot simply be understood as absence but rather approached as a concept that can inform issues of voice, representation and responsibility. Silences are productive, heterogeneous and even communicative, which is to say interrogating and responding to how the poor and other groups of sufferers are silenced and deprived of expression is a complicated endeavour that necessitates following 'silences' to listen to what they do tell and communicate. This formulation of silence as a political-cultural-social construct that is productive and communicative helps to dispute the idea that those excluded (the Others who are marginalized, silenced, forgotten) are suffering in a way that our action to alleviate can help in any direct sense of the word. It also challenges the idea that we encounter suffering unambiguously as a bystander, a benefactor, a donor, a protector or a saviour – we are also an accomplice, an agent and a facilitator of the silence of suffering. In short, prevailing understandings of suffering are problematic because they disempower Others by casting them through 'lack', position suffering as a comprehensible experience and reduce suffering to a solvable and measurable problem of pain reduction.

Contingency of suffering

Spectatorship of suffering is an encounter, i.e. a coming into relation with an Other. Because suffering is often assumed to be an objective bodily condition, the distance or separation between the spectator and the sufferer is foregrounded as the encounter's main conundrum. The key set of questions in this framework is about how we can overcome the problem that distance and separation pose to our efforts to understand, alleviate and/or contain the condition of sufferers. This problem is taken up in Lilie Chouliaraki's *Spectatorship of Suffering* (2006: especially 201–17) as an issue of expanding the circle of moral/political community to reduce the distance, or at least constantly work towards this goal. Building on Luc Boltanski's (1999) idea that political action based on pity is possible in cases of suffering (thus maintaining the structure of 'the fortunate spectator' and 'the unfortunate spectated'), Chouliaraki and others explore how more rigorous forms of pity, such as compassion, empathy or fellow feeling could be nurtured (see Moeller 1999; Silverstone 2006; Morris 1997; Andrews 2007). Interestingly, love is not examined as an alternative, which is the focus of my next chapter. Most notably, Chouliaraki (2006) argues that a politics of pity (which she believes plays an important expansionary role), must be coupled with justice and de-coupled from an 'ethics of proximity' (i.e. a sense of responsibility tied to an 'us-ness'). Silverstone (2006: especially 118–35) argues that distance is not just about physical proximity but is virtual and mediated. This requires that we understand better the role that 'the media' plays in reducing distance and strengthening connectedness. I question these efforts to *overcome* the distance created by suffering. My question is: what if the spectatorship of suffering is not an issue of distance, hindered fellow feeling or even misfortune? What if suffering is not a problem that can be solved *by us* with *our* models of cosmopolitanism and global citizenship, as variously argued by these writers?

   Sara Ahmed's (2002) discussion of spectatorship of suffering through the idea of contingency is useful here. Spectatorship, for Ahmed, involves being touched by what one encounters, and thus becomes part of the latter, through the act of witnessing in all its ambiguity. We feel pain when we touch or are touched by another object that is in pain or that causes pain. While still spatially conceived, the encounter is conceptualized in terms of proximity, touching, coming into relation rather than that of distance, lack of or deficiency in proximity or clarity. This is because proximity to pain is conceived as a proximity to an unknown – there is no such thing as pain. Treating pain as an 'it', an object that one can know, describe or locate, is to simplify pain and what the spectatorship of it involves. Ahmed writes:

> the feelings and sensations that we come to identify as pain are 'read' in that moment of identification; they are interpreted as pain, as something against me, as something to be pushed out, moved away from. This does not mean that these experiences are not real. The intensity of pain and pleasure can burn through us. But it means that my pain cannot be simply grasped in its 'thereness'. Pain is more than there even when it is so there that it feels that it is all that there is.
>
> (Ahmed 2002: 24)

Her point is that the pain, whether one's own or that of Others, is ungraspable, relational and interpretive. Pain is in the touch; it is a *relational* experience. Touch, contact and the encounters between spectators and suffering render the experience of suffering *contingent*. Suffering is reliant on the contact of two (or more) differently positioned bodies, but this touch, this contact, does not reliably happen. It is an uncertain occurrence liable to happen or not, and unfolds in ways that are unruly, excessive and uncontainable. This means the authenticity and veracity of claims of injustice, deprivation or oppression are always subject to questioning and contestation.

In short, the ungraspability of the pain of Others is what defines the experience of the spectator who is touched by suffering. Touching, or being touched by, another's suffering is not to *share* another's pain; that is, my witnessing of suffering has, at best, a tenuous relationship with those more directly, materially and corporeally entangled in the experience of suffering. A spectator's encounter with suffering 'involves being open to being affected by that which one cannot know or feel' (Ahmed 2002: 24). As formulated by Ahmed, contingency denotes touch, contact, being moved and stirred as well as moving, stirring *with* affect that is ungraspable because it exceeds speech, understanding and meaning. Thus, conceptualizing suffering as contingent (i.e. seeing suffering as a kind of touching or being touched by pain) avoids understanding the distinction between spectator and sufferer as that of distance. Rather, suffering is a site of social relation that, while predominantly enabling hierarchic enactments of social relations along seer/seen, fortunate/unfortunate, empowered/helpless and so on, it is also a site that can bear alternative social relations because of the particular kind of contact that is specifically possible in this site.[2]

Imaging suffering

Variously referred to as iconic, indexical, referential, literal or authentic, photographs occupy a position in visual culture as images that stand in close proximity to the referent (Hirsch 2001: 13–16; Scott 1999: 17–45; Barthes 1993; Friday 2002; Price and Wells 2004: 31–34; Horstkotte and Pedri 2008: 12–17). As Horstkotte and Pedri (2008: 13, n.16) point out, the contentious nature of this privilege only comes to the fore when conceptual clarity is pursued, and even sceptics admit that in everyday and public uses of photographic images, this privileging of the real is hardly ever contested. For me, this points to how part of photography's privileged relation to immediacy is the invisibility of this privilege. A photograph, as Barthes put it, contains '*the thing that has been there*', which differentiates it from a sketch, painting or installation (Barthes 1993: 76, emphasis in original). It is an image that is a product not only of being close enough to touch (if not literally, at least metaphorically) but also of light's penetration of the referent to produce a virtual version – an 'emanation' – of the referent (ibid.: 80).

Sontag (1979: 154–56) writes about photography as a form of *acquisition* of 'a trace, something directly stenciled off the real, like a footprint or a death mask'. The photographic image is taken here as a depository, and the possession of the photograph is seen as a surrogate acquisition of the thing, person, event, experience or information. This depository nature of the photographic encounter, its supposed literal proximity to the authentic, keeps open the grounds for seeing photographic images of suffering as potentially revelatory.

What the photograph's privileged relation to the real and immediacy keeps alive is the belief that we can speak to power directly to alleviate suffering and galvanize support, resources and information. In other words, at work here is the idea of 'if only' – if only we could speak to power directly and uninhibitedly … We assume that change is possible only through the *powerful* (i.e. agency resides with the powerful) and that suffering is the target object that must be eradicated, contained or managed. This is to place *spectatorship* in a position of power, masking over the contingency of suffering as well as the particularity of a given encounter with 'suffering'.

In the Western tradition of socially conscious photography, John Tagg points out how those that photographers speak *for* are positioned as lacking, and are produced as a '"feminised" Other, as passive but pathetic objects, capable only of offering themselves up to a benevolent, transcendent gaze – the gaze of the camera and the gaze of the paternal state' (Tagg 1988: 12). At work here is the idea that those with relative power are able to speak *about or for* those positioned as suffering by producing various imageries of lack. Scenes of suffering in this mode become pictures that identify victims, the weak and the unfortunate within the frame to make them visible and speak to us. 'Suffering', then, is a code for 'lack' (whether bodily, economically or politically) that *should not be*, but which *can be redeemed* by our institutional practices, processes and manpower – an assumption that produces a particular visualization of helplessness (Malkki 1996; Prosser 2005: 89–121; Campbell 2003, 2007; Manzo 2008; Campbell *et al.* 2005; *Imaging Famine* n.d.; Sliwinski 2006; Bleiker and Kay 2007; Hutnyk 2004; Nyers 2006; Shim 2010: 16–23). These photographs of suffering can be images of abjection, extreme deprivation or infliction of violence, such as starving, unclean children, wounded bodies and anonymous mass or individual portraits of misery. They picture victims as passive and pathetic figures who compel a response from the viewers. They can also be positive images of innocent children, wholesome women or hardworking, honest natives. Both the negative and positive images turn the subjects in the photograph into objects *deserving* of *our* help. As Jay Prosser (2005: 91) put it, 'Documentary photography had to convince us that the sufferings were worthy of redemption, that there was nobility even in abjection'. This points to the role that aesthetics plays in speaking to those with relative power about who is deserving of their supposedly scarce, but life-changing attention, i.e. their benevolence and problem-solving powers. We can help only to the extent that we can admire (i.e. accept as noble or beautiful) and can grasp and make sense of (i.e. comprehend through existing narratives, images and conventions of knowledge and representation). This means turning what stands in front of the camera into recognizable forms that will make the image worth looking at, printing and circulating within established conventions of photography.

While problematizing the hierarchic nature of prevailing documentary practices, scholars like David Campbell (2003, 2007), Ariella Azoulay (2008), Sharon Sliwinski (2004, 2006) and others also recognize the political potency of the affective, sensational dimension of the various moments of photographic *contact*. Campbell, for instance, writes that 'we need to depart from an understanding of photographs as illustrations and carriers of information (which a focus on their content would suggest) to an appreciation of pictures as ciphers that prompt affective responses' (Campbell 2007: 379). What the camera gives the viewer might not be as clear as realist or moralist documentarians want, but the picture has a particular effect on us partly because it is a photograph ('*the thing that has been there*'). This sense of 'immediacy' – of having touched, penetrated or accessed the referent – attributed to images captured by the camera is part of why photographic images of suffering 'haunt us' (Sontag 2003: 115). However, being haunted by these photographs is not a monolithic or singular experience and it is difficult to know what the right way of being haunted is. Linfield helps us to admit, 'it is hard to get our feelings "right"', and in fact photographs are better understood as a way to 'discover what our intuitive reactions to such otherness – and to such others – might be' (Linfield 2010: 25, 22). In short, while photographs (especially single-frame images) tell us very little about what it is we are seeing – and as demonstrated later, captions and other narrative tools often do the work of telling us what to see, or even what to feel – it moves us, whether this be to stillness, shock, despair, sympathy, condescension and a sense that someone needs to do something about it. Even indifference and lack of feeling can be ways of being moved by photographs, since the feeling that one should feel otherwise, or is expected to feel otherwise, accompanies such indifference (Lisle 2009). Ariella Azoulay's explanation of the photographic contact – the tactility and touch of photographic images – is especially useful here (also see Hirsch 2001: 16, 24). Photographic images and their supposed proximity to the imaged subject help us to see, feel, be affected by relationality in the visual form. The relationality here is not a triangular one between the photographed figure that is the subject of the photograph, the eyes behind the camera and the consumer of this image, but rather, it is about the broader social relations that have made the photograph possible:

> A photograph does in fact attest to what 'was there', although its evidence is partial, and only in this sense is it false. What was there is *never* only what is visible in the photograph, but is also contained in the very photographic situation, in which the photographer and photographed interact around a camera. That is, a photograph is evidence of the social relations which made it possible.
>
> (Azoulay 2008: 127, emphasis in original)

Photographic contact with what 'was there' does not mean the photograph itself can be taken as factual evidence of the subject that is photographed. It serves as evidence of *the contact* and only *part* of what 'was there' that 'sometimes is only a *point* of departure to arrive at what "was there"' (Azoulay 2008: 312, emphasis added). Azoulay writes that the spectator has a responsibility towards photography itself, i.e. the photographic situation, which always exceeds what simply 'was' as well as what is visible. It is something that must always be 'reconstructed' through the photograph that is in effect evidence of the limits of photography, viewing and witnessing (ibid.: 312).[3] Azoulay is pointing out how instead of staying with what we see (i.e. the visual, the content of an image), what is valuable in visuality and photographic encounter is how they enable us to imagine more rigorously what lies outside the line of vision. It makes political imagination more mobile in that thinking travels to multiple spaces, positions and perspectives rather than just staying put in one or two positions and perspectives (one's own or the Other's). This mobility enables a political imagination that privileges the specificity of the context, the relationality that produced the context and the positionality of the viewing culture (the viewer, the photographer, and the circulation and production system).

   These critical treatments attending to the affective and relational dimension of photographic contact are important but these formulations, including Azoulay's, retain a dimension of the socially conscious documentary tradition that they critique. I have argued that the problem with the prevailing Western tradition of socially conscious photography is the assumption that the suffering imaged in the photographs can be alleviated by presenting images of suffering directly and appropriately to those in power. It channels images to induce a particular kind of action *from us* that intervenes and treats suffering as a lack and negation. The critical arguments of Azoulay and others also retain another important assumption that privileges the rationality of our interpretations and our action in the face of suffering; that is, they assume that photography should move spectators toward contemplation, critical reflection and digging. For example, Linfield (2010: 29) writes that feeling something (albeit never quite right) when one views a photograph of suffering makes us 'dig, and even think, a little deeper'. Here, she returns the work of affect to a thinking self, which is also what Sontag does when she argues for the importance of examining and looking at photographs of lynching, atrocities of war, violence and 'barbarism', because our ability to engage with them is 'a benchmark of civic virtue' (Sontag 2003: 84). Campbell in a blog also posts, 'But photographs do force us to think hard about what is happening and why. And as Barthes observed in *Camera Lucida* "ultimately, Photography [sic] is subversive, not when it frightens, repels, or even stigmatizes, but when it is pensive, when it thinks"' (Campbell 2011).

My main contention is that, for these scholars, the point seems to be that photographs should move us to *think*, and that a thinking photograph helps us to do this better. Thinking, more pointedly a 'thinking us', is the only recognized channel for change articulated by these critical approaches. Put differently, they variously operate with a narrow idea of 'if only' that centres *us and our thinking action*, i.e. if only *we* thought more deeply, asked harder questions, knew our complicity more acutely, then maybe *we* could create change. I have no problems with the possibilities that this line of thinking creates, but I take issue with how even their digressions to the affective register continue to reinstate a *rational, thinking self*. As I show below, there are other ways, more relational understanding of responsibility that spans far beyond the remit of our rationality and action. Also, the ways in which the accent stays squarely on the self (its agency, action, improvement) in the self-Other relationship are devastatingly left uncommented. The 'self' for these critical thinkers is a relational, performative, self-questioning one, but I am wondering whether there is a need to displace more foundationally how the self remains the *main* site of activities, theorizing and change. I ask, what is the basis of our optimism about ourselves?

Trinh questions our impulses as inhabitants of a rational(izing) world by placing critical emphasis on reflecting on how we go about analysing, dissecting and exposing dominant framings and logics. For Trinh, feeling can be a way of thinking, and thinking might have different feelings where we can 'see what the eye hears, and hear what the ear sees' (Trinh 2011: 2). In other words, thinking must be done differently, in a way that makes strange our routinized processes of thinking and feeling. Thinking must, *in its very expression and enactment*, draw attention to the importance of heterogeneity and openness in sites that particularly come to be associated with suffering. If the task at hand is to keep sites of suffering open to multiply positioned interpretations and contacts with pain, and if the goal is to enhance the capacities of sufferers and suffering to make meanings, then the way these sites are kept contestable, unstable and critical must itself express this heterogeneity and multiplicity of worlds, positions, relations and modes.

It is in this context that I argue that our response (i.e. the self's political action in the face of power and violence) has to problematize more intimately the self's agency in alleviating, acting and responding to suffering. This is not to say that no action is a good action, but that the privileging of the self and its agency – this includes the privileging of the self's potential to produce a more ethical, reflexive, questioning self – are a continuation of the production of the world as a target for *our action* and as a place composed of objects for us to act upon. The way Trinh goes about theorizing politics, responsibility and action is useful because she focuses her critical energies in its *expressive* articulation in order to heterogenize critical spaces, modes and practices. By insisting that we feel, think and see differently, Trinh shares with other critical engagements the view that we must explore what a shift away from this preoccupation with images of sufferers and victims (as subjects who lack power, agency and will) opens up and brings about (e.g. Bernstein 2004; Dauphinee 2007; Lisle 2011). However, the questions we can ask through Trinh's expressive, heterogenizing approach are more creatively oriented. What happens if we privilege the contingency of the encounter with suffering (as something other than pain, lack or victimhood) *in 'all' its complexity*? What does it mean to say we must allow complexity of the contingency of the encounter with suffering to (dis)order response, responsibility and intervention? What comes after (in what mode, where, for whom, at whose cost) complexity and contingency? I dwell on these questions as a starting point to open up a discussion about photographic representations of North Korea.

Suffering North Korea

The poverty and oppression in North Korean society are pictured in varying gradations of abjection, but all these photographic contacts converge to insist that North Koreans inside and outside North Korea are suffering in a way that *we* can significantly help with *our* direct action.

Documenting suffering and distance

Choi, Soon-ho's photo book, *Defectors: Their Story* (2008), takes the position that abject misery is just waiting inside North Korea to be pictured, and that all it needs is the cameras and photographers to 'document' it.[4] Inhibited by his status as an outsider (Choi is South Korean), the photographer circumvents the North Korean government's censorship by photographing 'North Korea' from outside the territorial bounds under DPRK. Choi photographs the North Korean landscape from the Chinese side of the North Korea–China border and extends out to take pictures of North Koreans who have left North Korea and reside in China, South Korea and the USA. *Defectors* strikes me as a photo book that is preoccupied with achieving spatial and moral proximity with the suffering North Korea. The message of the four sections (or 'Stories', as Choi calls them) of the book seems to be that life inside, and in close proximity to, North Korea is hard, bare and miserable. Photographic arrangement begins with images of dejection and the hard, bare life defined by material lack: bare landscapes, sparsely populated snow-covered villages, borders, desperate border crossers and homelessness. It progresses then to photographs of defectors who are now resettled in South Korea and the USA. Interesting is how narrative progression of the book that journeys from North Korea→China→South Korea→USA is not strictly linear – i.e. the USA is not on the topmost tier in the journey to, as the book put it, 'heaven'; instead, South Korea occupies the brightest spot in the sense that this section contains the highest number of dignified photographs of North Koreans (e.g. personality profile portraits of a pianist, boxer, college student, etc.). The main ways Choi constructs this narrative of 'North Korea' as a place and social group of heart-wrenching misery are through the use of text that together with the image exploits the idea of referentiality, and the careful composition of the image. The insertions of defector texts that are autobiographic, biographic or explanatory are together an integral part of the photo book. Following a series of photographs of wires, fences and borders, next to a nondescript photograph of an unpaved country road, presumably in a North Korean border village, is an excerpt from a defector memoir which appears in blaring white text against the black page:

It didn't matter whether you were standing in line or walking on the street. If you spotted a kernel of corn or pea, you ate it even if it meant getting beaten up. Once I was so hungry that I walked with my eyes glued to the ground and spotted three kernels of dried corn mixed in with cow dung. The cow must have had a hard time digesting the corn seedlings it had swallowed. I ate those three measly kernels barely wiping the crap off with my sleeve. I was slowly turning into an animal.

(Shin, in Choi 2008: n.p.)

This text functions to fix the meaning, not only of the image next to it, but also retrospectively of the preceding photographs of the North Korean/border landscape. The insertion of the text here implies that even at this great distance from the Chinese side of the border, these landscapes should be interpreted as 'empty' and 'bare' and thus defined by scarcity and dehumanizing hardship. Here, the referential character of first-hand accounts and photography are used to their full potential to draw a singular picture of North Korea; it is abject, helpless and deserving objects of help. One other type of textual narrative deployed in the book is that of an expert, which occurs only once to explain the human rights condition of North Korean defectors in South Korea. It is a two-page description given by Yoon, Yeo-sang, an associate director of the North Korean Human Rights Information Centre, based in South Korea, and echoes the larger message of the book.

Choi's *Defectors* mobilizes the widespread opinion that first-hand accounts and photographic images refer to a reality and truth that exists out there without mediation. This is achieved by carefully using layouts and editing options available to the book form. To return to the page where the first text appears in *Defectors* – Shin's account of his escape from prison – the picture next to this text, and the pictures that precede and follow it are not labelled. We nonetheless assume that they are pictures of the North Korean landscape and the border area captured from the Chinese side. The accompanying text about an experience in a labour camp helps us to arrive at or retain this assumption even though the images are nondescript. The 'authenticity' of the text works to make the images speak and perform their referential function of 'showing' and 'pointing at' the reality of North Korean poverty out there. Important here is that this referential use of photographic images and first-hand accounts is aided by Choi's discarding of *other* referential layout and captioning methods, for example, withholding the dates and locations of the photographs, or using texts that are not 'referentially' linked to photos. The absence of direct captions for the photographs allows the almost immediate association of the occasional text pages and the images surrounding them. The pages of the book are not numbered either, and the only way the book is 'paginated' is through the four dividing pages that give the number and the title of the 'Story' that also functions as a guide for interpreting the images that follow. Moreover, the images and texts are inlaid in black (the texts appear in white to contrast with the black background of the pages) accentuating the (black) *vacuum* in which the images and text are supposedly freely, uninhibitedly floating. Thus, one gets the impression that within a 'Story', the relationships between the images, and between the images and the accompanying texts, are interchangeable. Once the text-image pair and their shared 'reference' are registered (e.g. hunger), all the photographs in surrounding pages feel as if they 'refer' to this same anchor.

The point here is not that with the proper markers, indicators and deployment of text, the referential 'failure' of Choi's book can or needs to be remedied. Failure to refer to reality itself and close the distance between the spectator and suffering is an inescapable part of representational practice. Choi assumes otherwise and tries to overcome the problem of distance by an idiosyncratic deployment of referentiality, taking full advantage of the prevailing acceptance of memoir and photography's claim to proximity to the authentic experience. I believe this gesture, however well intentioned, produces another layer of violence to the reality that he supposedly holds sacred and acts on behalf of. At the same time, the problem of distance remains in Choi's *Defectors*, since his images of North Korea and North Koreans are still from afar. Choi's photographs of the landscape are views from a great distance. The photographs of the North Korean defectors perhaps say something about their condition in general or superficial way (or about the photographic encounter) but they cannot in their visual representation *show* the poverty *inside* North Korea. Moreover, the use of defector accounts highlights the temporal distance that also poses a problem in Choi's effort to overcome the distance that exists between spectators and actual sites of misery. As productions of memory, these accounts of misery are acts all too aware of, shaped by and the product of the distance between 'the here and now' and North Korea of their past of which the defectors claim ownership. In other words, in using defector accounts of their past to overcome the problem of distance between us and North Korea, *Defectors* simply and unfortunately creates a different kind of distance.

This distance is also achieved through the use of stylized composition to produce abjection. This is especially poignant in one of the most wretched images in the book, that of an amputee whose stumps are foregrounded while her head is cut from the frame but shown as a reflection in a strategically placed mirror. Accompanied by an account of an anonymous amputee's escape from North Korea, Choi deploys a visual fragmentation of the body to symbolize the amputee's brokenness as a result of state violence against her body, agency and humanity. We assume this text is the story of the woman in the picture, but not only does the image lack a caption, but the text, too, includes no citation, date or even an indication as to whether it might be a product of an interview, a public testimony, a report or some other form of communication. Not only has her body been mutilated by the state, but her entire being has been dismembered. The photographer wants to read this dismemberment as simply a product of North Korean state violence. I want us to read how this image is contributing to the dismemberment in the way the photographer has visually and aesthetically arranged the shot which makes it a visual rehearsal of the prevailing idea that victims are immobile, docile and abject bodies.

While Choi claims to have succeeded in witnessing the misery in North Korea as up close as possible (keeping in mind that government censorship from both Koreas prevented him from getting 'inside' North Korea), what he actually produces is a more profound geographic and temporal distance along a fortunate/unfortunate hierarchy. This image of immediacy operates on the assumption that the more abject, visibly destroyed the North Korean body (and the human body occupies a privileged position in our conceptions of suffering and violence), the more effective the image in mobilizing action for justice, retribution and action. One of the main implications of this photograph is the question of how this image of dismembered North Korean defector that symbolically stands in for North Korea feeds into, and is produced by, South Korea's national unification machinery. I turn to this point in the next chapter.

While Ri, Man-geun's (a pseudonym) *Landscape of the Everyday North* (2005) challenges the dominant logic at work in Choi's *Defectors* – that the more extreme the suffering in the photograph, the better – Ri shares the concern for North Korean poverty that produces unnecessary suffering.[5] Ri, however, unlike Choi, was able to take photographs from inside the North

Korean territory which produces a network of concerns, attachments and distancing different from what we see in *Defectors*. Ri's photography project exhibits its own politics and hierarchy, which I want to examine.

Landscape of the Everyday North is a collection of photographs that Ri secretly took over a span of seven years (mostly of North Hamgyong province) during his assignment in North Korea as an official photographer for KEDO.[6] As the introductory essay in Ri's *Landscape* by Ahn, Hae-ryong, a well-regarded 'leftist' documentary filmmaker, insists, 'This photographic record pains us because it contains the suffering and strife of the North Korean people. Their suffering and strife are the reality and truth that we must register rather than hide or avoid. Because they are real, they hurt even more' (Ahn 2005: 17). In other words, these photographs of North Korea move us because they are reflections of the reality in and truth about North Korea that it is poor and suffering.

Because Ri takes the idea of a 'photographic record' literally – as 'non-interpretative reproduction' and 'a detailed observation, meticulously researched and verified' – the photographs are arranged according to what the images tell us about – how they correspond to – North Korea (Ri 2005: 9; Ahn 2005: 17). Beginning with the section entitled 'Our way of life' – 'our' here in reference to North Korea that takes on speaking position *as and behalf of* ordinary North Koreans – the photo book is composed of seven sections meant to provide a visual ethnography of rural North Korea. Much like Oh, Young-jin's graphic novel *Pyongyang Project* examined in Chapter 2, this ethnographic view allows a conveyance of a knowledge-based understanding of a different culture by studying their rituals, architecture and everyday practices.

The idea of documentation is also reflected in its photographic style that is 'natural' and 'unstylized', sharply contrasting with the images in Choi's *Defectors*. Many of the images lack the thematic and technical sharpness, colour contrast and tight framing common in 'Western' photography and photojournalism (see Clark 2008: 114–18; Edwards 2007: 79–83; Lutz and Collins 1993: 261–64; Price 2004: 108–9). Ri claims that these 'flaws' were unavoidable, given the context in which the photographs were taken, as he had to take them quickly and undetected. We do not have to accept Ri's explanation, especially given that well-framed and more composed photographs have been taken of North Korea in tense moments or surreptitiously. For instance Gary King of VII Photo has produced some images of scenes on trains and from train tracks that best contradict Ri's claim (while these particular pictures are no longer on *Life* magazine's website, see King's other photographs at www.garyknightphotography.com). My point is that the natural and unstylized style actually works in favour of Ri's idea of a 'photographic record', since the sense of spontaneous composition in a select number of images gives the collection as a whole an aura of authenticity and immediacy. The collection feels 'raw', as if just zooming in on reality and recording it as it was without the photographer's interpretation. This facticity effect is enhanced through a text that accompanies each photograph, providing detailed information 'related' to the image. I put 'related' in quotes because the texts involve a wide range of descriptions of the North Korean system and society more broadly, which frequently refers, but not always, to what is specifically in the photograph.

The texts and the photographic 'recording' of rural life work together to produce a picture of North Korea as a place of hardship, scarcity and physically taxing labour. In a way, *Landscape* affirms Choi's point that North Korea is a painfully poor country, where people struggle just to survive. For instance, in the image-text pairing titled 'street wear', we see a group of children standing about in front of 'harmonica houses' – a common form of communal housing built after the Korean War as temporary shelter (Ri 2005: 49; see Figure 3.1). The accompanying paragraph begins by pointing out the details captured in the photograph, such as the old man's attire and cart, but the rest of the text is about the general scarcity of clothing which explains why the adults and children like to wear one outfit for the outdoors. The photograph affirms this point: the boys are wearing exactly the same clothes which could be their school uniform, the girl in the centre is wearing a tracksuit (which we know from the text doubles as a school uniform), and the man's trousers are badly soiled and creased while his jacket looks heavily worn. The message here is clear: the severe poverty in North Korea has a

Figure 3.1 A view of a street in the southern province of Hamgyong
Source: Ri, Man-geun 2005.

dehumanizing and depersonalizing effect expressed, for example, in the limited clothing available.

What is interesting about Ri's photographs – and what distinguishes them from Choi's collection – is their busyness: people are going places, moving things and animals, working, marching, playing. People are often in groups and engaged in communal work, play and loitering. In short, these are images of activities and people in motion. The accompanying texts point out the ingenious ways in which people have coped with deprivation in their farming, ways of getting around and making do, despite the scarcity of fuel, clothing and food. These are not docile suffering bodies; they are active, working, moving bodies that are coping admirably with strife. Moreover, because Ri is interested in providing an ethnographic view, many of the images are not only full-body shots but pull back to include much of the background scene, catching many people 'in action'. This interest in producing active, full frames with little room for blank space contributes to the sense of busyness in Ri's images. We see this when we return to Figure 3.1 and notice that it includes in its frame the man pushing the cart, groups of children scattered on the street and the harmonica house partly in view. The frame is fully occupied by subjects whom Ri is interested in recording.

However, an important dimension of Ri's conception of North Korean poverty is the sentiment that 'They are still stuck in the 1960s!' (see Ri 2005: 9). Ri uses his memories of 1960s–70s South Korea to read North Korea of the 1990s and 2000s. Here, Ri casts rural North Korea of his record-creating project as an historical past of his own culture – North Korea is *pre*-modern, traditional, backward (i.e. inferior), just as we were in the 1960s *and thus* is in need of change to become more like us today (see Lisle 2006: 212–14; Inayatullah and Blaney 2004: 50–123).

Ri's unreflective use of his own reference point to interpret the image has a way of writing over the busy and full image that can potentially travel in multiple directions. Nostalgia is an important ingredient here, which comes through most strongly in the picturesque image of an old man walking with a goat in tow used as the book cover (it also appears on page 209). Ri finds the rural life that he sees in North Korea sad (their poverty pains him) but he is also nostalgic for this pre-modern state. The way nostalgia entangles ideas of beauty and nobility in suffering is an important dimension of Ri's book. This sentimental attachment to *his own* past (which romanticizes rural life in general and the South Korean past) not only sees contemporary, rural North Korea through the modern/pre-modern binary, but also projects this reading towards a utopian future where North Korea can be redeemed.

Ri's photographs are also 'busy' in a different sense which unwittingly opens up another way of reading them. Because Ri takes these photographs surreptitiously (to dodge censorship but also perhaps for authenticity), obstructions, croppings and lopsided angles characterize many of his images that foreground the act of seeing. Included in these frames are reminders of photography's relation to the subjects in the photograph. For instance, in the image of a roadside, the interior of the car from which the shot was taken is included in the frame, creating a dark blurry outline on one side of the photograph (see Figure 3.2). The accompanying text explains the image as a scene of inspection of goods for the marketplace and the scene as part of the upsurge of ordinary people selling foodstuff and small household goods. While the image can be read to refer to the 'reality' of ordinary North Korean people, it can also be read for what it tells us about the photographic encounter: that the camera was inside a vehicle and that it is hard to know what is going on in the frame, not least because one of the main figures in the picture has his back towards us.

These obscured views (i.e. perspectives from behind or beside, where people and vehicles have their backs squarely or partially towards us), are common recurrences in the book (for instance, see Ri 2005: 59, 67, 121, 129, 171, 181, 193, 227). These images with turned backs, lopsided and poorly angled shots, obstructed views, collectively produce a busy, 'distracted', 'flawed' perspective, but also the sense that these images are more 'real' because they are less composed, stylized and aestheticized.

My point is that these images are visual reminders that our relationship with poverty in North Korea is obstructed, lopsided and unfocused both thematically and technically. Unlike Choi's stylized photographs that try to mask the distance and obstruction that makes imaging 'suffering North Korea' an opaque process, Ri's 'technical flaws' foreground the contingency

Figure 3.2 A view from inside a car
Source: Ri, Man-geun 2005.

of the spectatorship of suffering. By, in effect, including the photographer within the frame itself, what is pictured here more explicitly is the moment of touch, i.e. the encounter itself. In this sense, these are photographic records not so much of 'the suffering and strife of the North Korean people', but perhaps more tellingly of moments of contact between the photographer and his subjects. They compose an illustrative record of what Azoulay highlights about photographic encounters wherein the photograph is to be viewed as a point of departure from which particular social relations become 'visible', imaginable and possible through photography. They foreground an ungrasp-ability that defines our spectatorship of suffering and how the suffering Other is always mediated and often obscured by cultural resources and technologies that make the encounter possible in the first place. Rather than a knowledge exchange about North Korea in a moral community, reading photographs is a reconstructive, imaginative process that wrestles with issues of relationality, contact and touch that goes into creating a moral community.

Picturing oppression from 'where art, documentaries and journalism meet'

Philippe Chancel's *North Korea* (2006) sets out to visualize oppression that pervades in North Korean society at large. It does this not by circumventing North Korean censorship, but by subverting the 'North Korea' that officials present for outside viewing. Chancel photographs Pyongyang following the official regulations and guidance for tourists which usher them towards public marches and celebrations (big and small), museums, schools and other visitor attractions around Pyongyang. However, the photographer's point is that what he sees in them are not tourist sites and spectacles but 'the political system that controls every detail of life in that country' (Chancel n.d.). In his Artist Statement for *Moving Walls*, a documentary photography exhibition run by the Open Society Foundation, Chancel presents his insight into North Korea as something that unfolded naturally:

> What fascinates me is the near perfection of each scene. All the elements of the composition – the sets, the setting, and above all the characters – slot naturally into place as if everything has been rehearsed. The ideas and ideology that motivate the country and its people remain for me unknown and incomprehensible. But what I saw through Western eyes is the narcissism of power.
>
> (Chancel n.d.)

Here, the pictures just happened to his camera. This is a curious statement in several ways. While the photographer feigns not to understand his subject (North Korea and its people), he at the same time claims to know what he sees (political system, control, narcissism of power). This knowledge of what he sees (how a political system works to control its population and display power for itself) is assumed to derive from reality, and it is the naturalness, the spontaneity – again a claim to photography's proximity to the real, the thing that has been – which gives this knowledge its authority. At the same time, Chancel expresses this truth and reality as a perfection of a scene or composition, speaking of the formal and aesthetic components of the picture rather than of the situation or the subjects that stand in front of him and his camera. The biography page of Philippe Chancel's photography website states how his recent photography projects explore 'the complex, shifting and fertile territory where art, documentaries and journalism meet' (see www. philippechancel.com/biographie.php). In a way, this curious statement illustrates how Chancel's photography is an exploration of 'the complex, shifting and fertile territory where art, documentaries and journalism meet' that confirms what we already 'know'. Implied in the sophisticated method towards photography is the idea that an intersection of art, documentaries and journalism can open up the complex, shifting, fertile space of encounter between photography and North Korea. At best, the effects of this innovative method are ambiguous, and a harsher assessment of *North Korea* would be that the intersection of different modes of reality production picturing North Korea as a land of the oppressed adds spectacularly little to how to respond not only to suffering in Other places but unfamiliarity, censorship and state power.

Dwelling on this latter reading of *North Korea*, we see journalism and art criticism work in conjunction most obviously in the two introductory essays to Chancel's images, one by a journalist knowledgeable about East Asia (John Fenby) and the other by an art critic (Michel Poivert). Beginning with a description of North Korea as 'a giant Gulag, ruled since the defeat of the Japanese occupation in 1945 by father and son autocrats', Fenby gives an animated account of North Korea's history (Chancel 2006: 19). Poivert writes in equally dramatic terms, praising Chancel's photographs and comparing them to those of German masters like Candida Hofer, Andreas Gursky and Thomas Struth for capturing 'the [North Korean] facade of normalcy in its most spectacular form' (ibid.: 6).[7] While the use of text ends here and the book makes minimal use of captions for Chancel's images, these introductory texts play an important role in framing the images that follow. By keeping the explanatory texts separate (and written by others), the implication is that Chancel, the photographer, speaks only through his images, which as quoted earlier, are believed to construct themselves. In short, his photographs speak for themselves.

My point, however, is that texts, i.e. explanations and interpretations in Chancel's book but also in wider circulation, *make* the images speak. Most prominently, Poivert's introductory essay interprets the images closely and serves as a guide for the reader. Poivert is distrustful of the appearance of order, grandiosity and harmony in North Korean public spaces and stagings: 'For deep down, even where there are no tears or visible wounds, horror is never far away, scarcely concealed by the theatricality of the poses and props. It is a cold horror, a silent pain, and it does not need the chaos of bodies to make the spectator feel it' (Poivert 2006: 13). Poivert's 'interpretation' of Chancel's images in his introductory essay does a lot of work to frame the images and produce a preferred meaning for these images, but this interpretative text is unnecessary as these images and Poivert's interpretations of them too easily resonate with the wider circulation of texts, narratives and images about North Korea.

Chancel's images do have their own way of 'speaking', though not, as claimed by Chancel, of capturing what simply happened in front of his camera. Not only does the photographer use various techniques of image composition (such as scale, colour, clean lines), but he also uses image sequencing and pairing in the book to create a clear picture of North Korea with an established meaning. The photographs speak their own language insofar as they speak not textually but pictorially. I would like to focus on two inter-related themes articulated through the recurring image composition and sequencing in the book: state displays of power and artificiality (death) in North Korea.

In a way, Chancel echoes Delisle's graphic novel, discussed in Chapter 2, which presents the North Korean people as mechanized automatons, i.e. life-less, soulless machines for the state. Especially pronounced in Chancel's pho-tographic images of North Korea (or to be more precise, Pyongyang) is that this place inhabited by mechanized automatons is cold, silent and still.

Responsible for this cold stillness is the North Korean state. Chancel finds the North Korean state's display of power sinister in its pomp, grandeur and spectacle. This is communicated, most plainly, through the recurring large, high-resolution photographic images of the Arirang Games in full double-page spreads. Chancel reproduces the state's grandiose display of power by the sheer size of these images which, given the size of the book (12 inches by 10.9 inches), and when repeated page after page in their full glossy spreads, has a spectacular visceral effect. Figure 3.3 fails to capture the experience of the size and weight of the photo book, especially when it opens up to double-page full spreads such as the image in Figure 3.3 (due to the sheer size of the original spread, the figure is a partial reproduction).

These large-scale, high-resolution images perform the double function of showing how state power in North Korea is displayed, and of showing the human cost of such large-scale mass mobilization of people and resources in the production of spectacular power. In intermittent images, we see specks of human figures compose this mass spectacle. The smallness of each individual figure and the sheer number of these figures register their insignificance as human beings and the 'cold horror' and 'silent pain' involved in such a display of power (Poivert 2006: 13). As we see in Figure 3.3, part of the horror is the uniformity – the row after row of dancers in perfect straight lines making perfect uniform gestures, and the sea of human bodies behind each barely visible placard that, in their uniformity, create the gigantic North Korean national flag – the state symbol. We know this latter detail from the preceding page and, indeed, the photo book as a whole gives the image meaning by providing a narrative pictorially. This use of scale and reproduction of state

Figure 3.3 Flag formation in the Arirang Games (detail)
Source: Chancel 2006.

power occurs in the book not only in the images of the Arirang Games but also in images of public buildings and urban landscape. Here, the shiny, grand public buildings and vast modern roads – meant to express modernity, prosperity and power – dwarf the human figures. Particularly memorable in my reading is the play on scale in a small image: a photograph of Kim Il-sung's mausoleum which accentuates the ridiculous size of the official structure through a tiny, single soldier standing in the left-hand corner, dwarfed in comparison (Chancel 2006: 42).

Chancel also tells this narrative of oppressive state power through the arrangement of his images. Particularly significant is Chancel's use of repetition. For instance, for five consecutive pages, the two framed portraits of the father Kim and the son Kim reappear on the same part of the page, while the scenes of the photographs change (e.g. from auditorium to library, study room and public building) (Chancel 2006: 184–91). The room is empty in the first of these pictures, then becomes increasingly populated by figures who neatly and uniformly – much like the lines of dancers in the Arirang Games in Figure 3.3 – sit facing the framed pictures of the Kims and with their backs towards the camera. The final picture of this sequence is a portrait-style framing of a woman in a rouge traditional Korean dress with the Kim portraits in the background, gesturing in a formal manner towards the table which, the caption tells us, used to be Kim Jong-il's desk as a student.

The anonymity and uniformity of North Koreans is consistently contrasted with the personality cult surrounding the Kims. The photographs I found most disturbing in relation to this theme are those that picture human beings become lifeless objects. In a set of photographs that makes use of the double-page format of the book form, two images mirror each other: one of dance students rehearsing, and another of stuffed birds in a glass display case (see Figure 3.4). The two images together, again too big to allow a full double-page reproduction of the photo book here, are startling because of their similar colour schemes: the young dancers are wearing black tights, white socks, white hair bands and red hair clips, while the stuffed birds are also black and white with even a hint of red in the throat area. We feel they are versions of each other, and the juxtaposition accentuates how both are, in a sense, in glass cases; both are on display to serve the interest of those who encased them (the birds), or trained them to move (the young dance students).

Another picture that resonates with this idea-image directly follows on the next page, in the Children's Palace, a special art school for training talent, where the dance class photograph was taken. This time, we see a single picture of a singing class with one girl in the centre singing and dancing, while in the background her fellow classmates, perhaps awaiting their turn, look on (Chancel 2006: 119). With her hand raised, one of her feet slightly turned inwards, unnaturally, she looks like the ornamental birds on the wall against which her peers sit watching. This again plays with the idea of human beings in North Korea being turned into something non-human. The juxtaposition of the fake and dead with the real and alive recurs in other scenes, from hotel shops to museum displays, workplaces to family outings. In short, the power of Chancel's images is that the ideas – i.e. the artificiality, death, lifelessness in uniformity, anonymity and mechanization – are repeated through the use of different compositional techniques, scenes and themes, not only in the composition of the camera frame but also in the careful composition and sequencing of images in the book.

Chancel's book suggests that what is insufferable about the Kim regime's despotism is the dwarfing and distortion of the human into inanimate

Figure 3.4 Stuffed birds in display and dancing girls (detail)
Source: Chancel 2006.

structures and objects. What needs saving is, as Poivert writes, 'the humanity rising visibly to surface through the softness of bodies and attitudes, seemingly rejecting all these luring images of authority in its own heart of hearts' (Chancel 2006: 8). This focus on humanity that identifies 'the human', 'the grace', shimmering just below the surface is what produces the deserving objects of 'our' compassion. In other words, Chancel's *North Korea* constructs the object of our benevolence through dichotomies of human/non-human, soft/hard, warm/cold. What needs to be saved, helped and attended to is the fragile humanity, i.e. the warm, soft, human dignity and grace that shines through. We see this in the photographs that juxtapose soft bodies with the death and artificiality that surrounds them (and which they risk becoming). We also see it in the interspersed portraits of North Korean women, some as close-ups or medium close-ups, but all posed, 'dignified' photographs that punctuate the cold, glistening, grey urban landscape of Pyongyang (see Figure 3.5). These posed photographs, which use techniques of portraiture to enhance the dignity of the subjects, by supposedly giving control to the subjects over their own representation, foreground the beauty and the dignity of North Koreans.

However, Deborah Poole (1997) reminds us that even such pictures composed by the pictured follow Western bourgeois aesthetics that is racialized. Poole's argument is that this aesthetics is in wide circulation and that the subjects themselves seek to appear dignified or beautiful. Poole and others, moreover, point out that photographers and other editors of portrait images

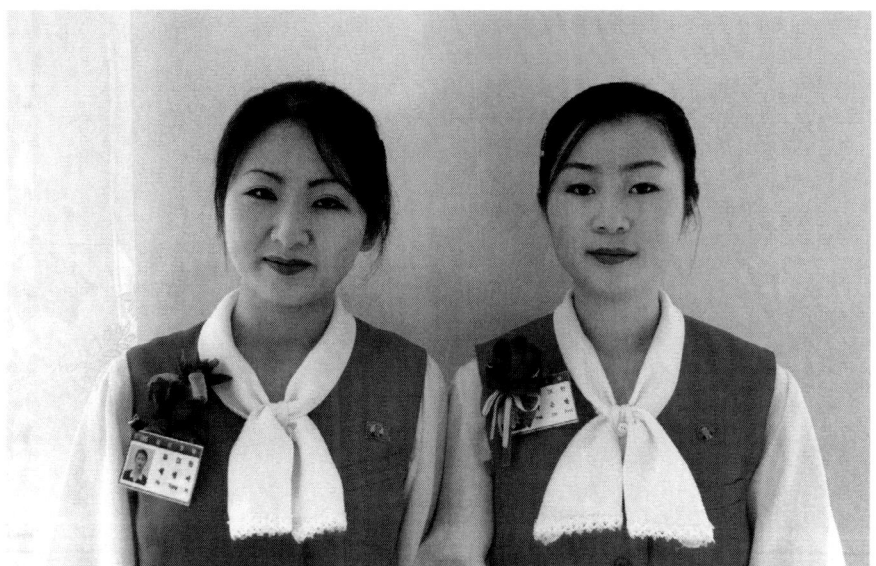

Figure 3.5 Two waitresses
Source: Chancel 2006.

can manipulate the intentions of these subjects to accentuate facial or other physical features (through lighting, for instance) according to what the producers – rather than the subject – want to make visible (Poole 1997: 121–41; Lutz and Collins 1993: especially 119–53; Clarke 1997: 101–21). Crucially, picturing humanity in a recognizable (beautiful) form in those who are 'less fortunate' or 'inferior' historically has been an important part of socially conscious photography, not least going back to colonial practices of photographing natives in official and leisurely explorations (Ramamurthy 2004; Poole 1997; Ryan 1997). Complicated efforts to photograph the 'humanity' of the Other is that they involve the deployment of widely recognized aesthetics, which in the contemporary context draws from and/or echoes the conventions of fashion and advertising photography (see Lutz and Collins 1993; Ramamurthy 2004; Edwards 2007; Clarke 1997). In short, self-composed 'dignified' photographs and photographing humanity is riddled with issues of power in its aesthetics and relations of production.

The portrait in Figure 3.5 is interesting in many respects – the brightness of the close-up, the size of the image in the book (full page), the focus solely on the faces of the two women, the subtle differences and similarities in the two faces and their makeup, hair, accessories – but, in the context of North Korea, the portrait contributes to picturing a form of North Korean humanity that appeals to established aesthetics of humanity (not to mention female beauty). This is in part because images of (beautiful) women are at the heart of seeing North Korea's humanity, not only in Chancel's photo book, but in many other photographic engagements with North Korea.

For instance, Eric Lafforgue takes a stylized ethnographic approach to photographing North Korea. His photographs (many of them youthful North Korean women) are so photogenic that they are sold on his website (www. ericlafforgue.com/prints.htm). His Flickr page (www.flickr.com/photos/ mytripsmypics/sets/72157604812751507/?page=5), gives a better overview of his work. Charlie Crane's photo book, *Welcome to Pyongyang*, is a collaborative project with the North Korean tourist board and mainly includes portraits (of women in traditional dresses and uniforms) and pictures of Pyongyang resembling those found in Chancel's book. Mark Harris's work focuses on the North and South Korean border and bordered-ness, but Christopher Morris more playfully juxtaposes the two Koreas (see Morris's Korea portfolio on his website, www.christophermorrisphotography.com).

Tomas Van Houtryve's undercover photographs of North Korea were taken while posing first in 2007 as a member of a solidarity tour and then in 2008 as a potential investor in a chocolate factory in North Korea. Van Houtryve's photographs of North Korea are in wide circulation in US-based magazines, including *Foreign Policy* and *Life*. They are also part of Van Houtryve's larger project, '21st-Century Communism', documenting Nepal, Laos, Vietnam, Kalmykia and China. While still in production, the photographs of North Korea already in circulation see its 'strangeness' coupled with 'outdatedness', 'corruption', 'suffering' in a recurring theme (see VII Photo Agency website, www.viiphoto.com/networks.php?photographer=Tomas%20van%20Houtryve and his personal blog, tomasvanhoutryve.wordpress.com). All have a focus on women.

In short, feminizing the Other who needs to be saved is a common way of accentuating the helplessness and victimhood of the object of our benevolence (e.g. Campbell 2007: 368; Malkki 1996: 388; Clark 2008: 89–91; Chow 1999/ 2000). Chow's argument is pointed, that the feminization of a culture – whether this is one's own or an Other – is a complex symbolic practice of conferring or claiming a state of weakness, demise and vulnerability (Chow 1999/2000).

Indeed, feminization of North Korea is not solely a product of the photographers' gaze. The mediating role of the North Korean state is an important part of the picture. The North Korean state has placed women in positions of 'public relations' in the cultural and leisure sectors, i.e. as hotel waitresses, museum guides and tourist shop workers, which Chancel and many others cannot seem to resist using to 'humanize' the country. Kim (2010: 205–59) explains in detail how the state has driven and orchestrated the visibility of women in North Korea's public spaces which in particular outfitted women in the Korean traditional wear while the men were not. The feminine beauty of Korean traditional wear, *hanbok*, on women is a state-driven ideology to effect a nation that is benevolent, whole and in possession of *juche* (self-reliance).

Chow's thesis could be interrogated further in the North Korean context to explore the relationship between feminization, a state of weakness and the idealist national self-imaging. That is, could it be that despite many visiting photographers' deep suspicion of, and revulsion for, all official narratives, personalities and guidance, their attraction to a feminized North Korea speaks to the important mediating role that *desire* is playing in visual narratives of North Korean suffering?

An interesting set of photographs in this cultural context of North Korea are Chris Morris's, which veer away (though not entirely) from photographing the brightly dressed North Korean women. Instead, he photographs groups of male soldiers, officials, etc. in interesting contexts (see www.viiphoto.com/ detailStory.php?news_id=443). While somewhat different, these images do not move radically away from producing a feminized North Korea; in fact, one might argue that these photographs of North Korean males who are often in groups, uniforms, and in awkward and childish positions, can be interpreted as a way of continuing to do so through a linked process of infantalization. Put more decisively, these photographs seek out and create humanity, vibrancy and dignity in North Koreans mainly through and for the satisfaction of the producer and consumer culture's desires. Important to remember here is that the Koreans who are photographed take a significant part in the production but do not participate in the consumption of these images. This search for the humanity of the Other is driven by now producer-consumer culture's assumption that there need to be likeable, desirable qualities – feminine-human-soft-shimmering – in North Koreans. If such qualities cannot be found, will we, the benevolent outsiders, not care?

To sum up, the Pyongyang that Chancel accesses, where he 'sees' suffering everywhere he turns, is a capital city, which like all capital cities is created and maintained to produce the desired image of the state. In the case of North Korea, Pyongyang is a site of privilege projecting an image of a 'socialist paradise' free of destitution, inequality, marginalization and violence. Chancel, however, is horrified by this official image; he perceives it as distasteful and an appalling display of state power because of what we know about the country's political prisons, food shortages and human rights violations. To address visually the issue of oppression and suffering in North Korea, photography has to touch suffering *more specifically*, rather than thinking (as, for example, Chancel and his supporters do) that it can be encountered and confronted by simply stepping into Pyongyang.

This is my position, and that photography, moreover, must explore how to do so without resorting to a dominant and hierarchical politics of pity. Chancel's photographic project is constrained by how it fails to engage directly with *sites of suffering* (poverty, marginalization, state brutality). While Choi's and Ri's engagements are problematic because they conceive of suffering reductively as a static condition of uncomplicated negation, Chancel's imaging is problematic because it does not engage sites of suffering despite his interest – in abstract – to do so. In effect, what Chancel's photographs mostly visualize is the hierarchic relation in the photographic encounter – a cold, evaluative, yet titillated camera gaze meeting North Korean subjects eager to show off, please or correct outside judgement. In other words, Chancel's *North Korea* is a record of intercultural encounters that visualize power asymmetry between 'the outside world' and 'North Korea'.

Alternative imaging of suffering and North Koreans

As discussed above, the dominant assumption in the images of North Korean suffering is that suffering *should not be*, and that suffering over there can and must be alleviated by us. There is a shared assumption in all these photographic engagements that denies the contingency of suffering, touch and relation, and fails to articulate how suffering always escapes textual as well as pictorial representation. In this final section of the chapter, I explore how foregrounding the touch of the encounter, that the inescapable relational dimensions of suffering, might help us to reconceptualize responses to suffering as involving a more intimate commitment to suffering and the Other than the prevailing rhetoric of international intervention would lead us to believe.

The return gaze

Images that contain a 'return gaze' are useful in rethinking what it means to respond to North Korean suffering. To revisit Ri's photograph in Figure 3.1, a girl is standing in the centre of a busy photograph looking directly at us, squinting. Perhaps it is her expression, her rosy cheeks or the way she is standing. Perhaps it is that the children, including the girl, are standing caught in the act of staring, talking in various positions, facing different directions and wearing curious expressions that as adults, as outside onlookers, we find attractive, curious. I like the way the children are looking right back at us in different ways, but only if they care to, and in a way that questions our presence. I like the girl face-on, gazing back at us. I even like how the image, in the process of digital conversion seen in Figure 3.1, adds another layer to the flawed photographic encounter with the faint, shiny vertical column (imperfect scanning) interrupting our line of gaze and appreciation of the image. Failures of reproduction for circulation, and the labour of circulating reproductions, are laid bare. Actually, perhaps the power of the image has nothing to do with the image but the context in which Ri's book was encountered. Perhaps it has more to do with Susie Linfield's cover for her book, *The Cruel Radiance: Photography and Political Violence*, which I was reading while researching this chapter. Linfield's book cover is a reproduction of another anonymous young girl, a mug shot, from the archives of the Cambodian Khmer Rouge's torture centre, Tuol Sleng, in the years 1975–79. Images disrupt specifically, contingently and inescapably through the mediation of other images, larger conversations, the subject's preoccupations.

Focusing on the return gaze in the photograph is one powerful way to foreground the touch and relationality of the photographic encounter. As already hinted, I am not alone. Many who write about photographs of atrocities time and again return to portraits of 'sufferers' (as well as the 'perpetrators') for how they destabilize the viewer and the act of viewing (see, for instance, Linfield 2010: 125–29; Azoulay 2008: 18–20, 375–76; Lisle 2009). As discussed earlier, portraits are posed moments in which subjects stand or sit still, face and look into the camera. It is part of a meeting of efforts to control what gets visualized between the photographer and the photographed subject, along with others invested in the visual product, including the viewer (Poole 1997: 3–4, 107–19). This might explain why many portraits and return gazes in posed photographs are neither destabilizing nor interesting, but actually resemble one another. At the same time, portraits and the return gaze *can* be effective in destabilizing the viewer and the act of viewing, and in its stillness it can stir movement, contemplative wondering and an explosion of questions.

Area Park's large-scale portrait of three North Korean teenage boys in South Korea is interesting for this reason. Titled 'Boys from the North [*Talbuk-sonyon*] Frozen for 3 Seconds', it was part of Park's 2006 exhibition, 'The Game: Revisiting the Landscape of Divided Korea [*bundan*]'. This installation included images from events and non-events in South Korea that Park connects to the division of the Korean peninsula. The title of the photograph is my translation of Park's original Korean (here, '*Talbuk-sonyon*' literally translates as 'defector boys'). As others have noted, 'The Game', of which the image in Figure 3.6 is a part, forms a conversation with other photographs of '*bundan*' ('the division'), most notably, photographs of US military base towns by Kang, Yong-suk, and more recently Noh, Suntag's photographs of clashes between the military and civilians and of military weaponry and technology.

I encountered this picture in a collective exhibition in Seoul, 'TransPOP: Korea Vietnam Remix', in 2008, which I went to see after reading a newspaper article about the exhibit that contained a reprint of Area Park's picture (Oh 2008; for image see Figure 3.6). Actually, the article had two art reprints, one Vietnamese ('Go to Market', by Nguyen Manh Hung) and one Korean (Area Park's photograph). While I do not remember that much from this exhibition, just a vague memory of how big Area Park's photographs were on display, it must have made some sort of impression because I packed this newspaper clipping a few months later with all my worldly belongings when I left Seoul for Belfast to start my PhD. I did not know at the time that I would be writing about North Korea, photography and aesthetics (my PhD application proposal was about something else entirely), but I quite naturally, as if I had half expected this, dug it up when I began working on this project. My thoughts on the image have undergone many turns, and the person who clipped the newspaper article and went to the exhibition would not recognize my reading of this image as it is about to go into print.

Three teenage boys are looking directly at the camera, standing still, two of them leaning against a tree – perhaps to help them stand still. The other boy is free standing, slightly apart from the other two, surrounded by a busy commercial pedestrian street. Busyness is visualized by the blurring of bodies

Figure 3.6 Newspaper article with Area Park's photograph of teenage boys in a city
Source: Oh 2008.

on the move, which includes most of the figures in the background of the photograph except a few others who happen to be still for three seconds, the length of the boys' frozen state. The boy on the left, standing slightly apart, reminds us of a commonly forgotten dimension of portrait photography: to look into the camera and be free standing (for three seconds) can be a hard and awkward request to oblige. His companions can nonchalantly lean against the tree and assume 'too cool to care' expressions, but the boy on the left stands awkwardly apart, holding his camera with both hands (to ground his standing pose?) and looks uncertain. He is not quite frozen in the sense that he seems to be watching the camera, just waiting for the go-ahead from the photographer to move again. This uncertainty in his gaze, body and posture – which requires 'reconstruction', (re)imagining, with the help of the photograph – makes the stillness of the portrait ambiguous, mobile and useful as an image of North Korean suffering. Contrary to the frozen-ness that the title of the photograph accentuates, the photograph makes visible the not-quite-frozen-ness, the ungroundedness of the portrait, the bodies and this particular scene.

When I point to these ambiguities as useful in conceptualizing alternative images of North Korean suffering, I am not referring to how familiar these North Korean defector boys look, with their ubiquitous digital cameras, trendily loose jeans and shorts, and almost identical tennis shoes. Contrary to the position that the poet Park, Hoo-gi takes which celebrates inter-Korean commonalities in his comment, 'If we were not told they were defectors, no one would have known that they were' (Park n.d.), what makes the portrait useful is not that it visualizes how much they look just like us. Rather than gesture to a commensurability between us and them to say we should care for them (or even that they do not need our help), I am pointing to how Park's picture of the boys accentuates the contingency of suffering. By a contingency of suffering, as discussed earlier, I am pointing to the touch; that is, an encounter with pain where what 'it' is and its 'it-ness' come into question, making suffering an experience *open to being affected by that which one cannot know or feel.*

Questions to begin thinking about contingency of suffering in the context of North Korea include: What can you ask three boys on their day out in the city? How does asking if they are happier now in South Korea than they were in the North, or whether they think communism has failed them, suppress the contingency of suffering or their experience? Do these questions not turn them into symbols, that is 'evidence', in arguments for or against aiding or investing in North Korea? As discussed in the Introduction, Stephen Haggard and Marcus Noland do exactly this with the 'refugee' issue (see Haggard and Noland 2006, 2011). Do these boys count as evidence against the Kim regime for crimes against humanity? Could they be part of the 'evidence' to which the international norm entrepreneurs who wish to treat North Korea as a case for the Responsibility to Protect can refer? For instance, could they be part of Vaclav Havel, Kjell Magne Bondevik and Elie Wiesel's call for UN Security Council action against North Korea under the Responsibility to Protect doctrine that uses the experiences of defectors as evidence for their case? Both the 2006 and 2008 reports commissioned by these dignitaries heavily rely on the conditions of North Korean defectors and their sheer number to make arguments for action (see DLA Piper LLP and US Committee for Human Rights in North Korea 2006; DLA Piper LLP, US Committee for Human Rights in North Korea and Oslo Center for Peace and Human Rights 2008). If not evidence, are they useless to our understanding of suffering in North Korea? What does their irrelevance in such initiatives for action say about our under-standing of, and our relationship to, North Korean defectors and suffering?

Park's image helps us to question the assumption that we understand what/ who we are seeing or that we know what to do with such 'knowledge'. What the return gaze and the mobility in stillness foreground is the ungraspability of not only suffering but the 'referent'; that is, suffering and 'North Korea' in their 'it-ness' escape. They are always something other than they seem. Area Park's photograph represents an encounter with the ambivalences inherent in the subject position and the site marked as 'suffering North Korea'. It is this ambivalence that is stirred into movement in the return gaze. So, how do we respond to an encounter with ambivalence that is marked with suffering North Korea?

Response and responsibility

I want to return to the quote by Trinh (2011: 2) introduced in the beginning of this chapter – 'to see what the eye hears, and hear what the ear sees' – as a way to argue for staying close to sites of suffering but in a way that involves not only seeing differently but also being differently more receptive to Others/ Otherness. This is to conceive of encounters with North Korean suffering as a larger issue of alternatively dwelling in the world that disrupts and displaces the hierarchical fortunate/unfortunate matrix. It is from this broader concern that any action by international bodies like the UN Security Council must be conceived and considered. Put differently, the self's position as the more for-tunate, privileged, superior, knowledgeable subject raises many questions about relations, how different bodies, things and subjects are differently posi-tioned and positioning, and intercultural dimensions of international rela-tions. Prevailing positionings of the self in encounters with suffering seek to discipline and contain ambivalence, unruly bodies, powerful emotions and inescapable relationality that are productive in such encounters. Thus, rethinking response/responsibility to sites of suffering, for me, begins with – but must go far beyond – reading images of suffering in terms that are more than just one's own. Rethinking must begin in a way that makes response/ responsibility strange to itself and thus disrupts the self and what evolves from encounters in sites of suffering. It must enable encounters in sites of suffering to affect more pervasively and disruptively an intercultural relation-ship that emerges from such sites which refuses to contain suffering whether it is one's own or that of Others.

In a lengthy but useful passage, Trinh discusses this point about response/responsibility in its complexity:

> In Asian cultures, it is commonly said that one should not receive a word by hearing it only with one's ears when one can develop the ability to receive the same word with one's mind and heart. Caught in a shifting framework of articulation, words and concepts undergo a transformative process where they continue to resonate upon each other on many planes at once, exceeding thereby the limit of that very plane where all the 'actions' are supposed to be carried out. To develop the ability to receive with more than one's eyes or ears is to expand that part of oneself which is receptive but can remain atrophied, almost closed, when its potential lies dormant. For even though everyone is endowed with such a potential, almost no one is 'naturally' tuned to this pitch of acute intensity where music, flowing both outside and within us, defines all activities of life. Wrote a thinker of the West, 'the faculty of being "receptive", "passive", is a precondition of freedom: it is the ability to see things in their own right, to experience the joy enclosed in them, the erotic energy of nature … This receptivity is itself the soil of creation: it is opposed, not to productivity, but to destructive productivity'. *Meeting and parting at crossroads, we each walk our own path.*
>
> (Trinh 2011: 56, emphasis in original)

The most immediate point here is that responsiveness to the ambivalence one encounters in the site of 'suffering North Korea' means learning to move, and be moved, in ways that one does not understand while resisting the desire to gain an understanding. Responsiveness, in this sense, is to privilege non-knowingness in the encounter. What Trinh's articulation here expresses particularly well is how this non-knowingness often jars with the accepted intellectual language we commonly use when talking about openness to ambivalence, Otherness and alterity. This extract speaks in a language of nature, Asian culture and heart, and in its juxtaposition with 'Asian culture' and a passage from 'a thinker of the West' hints to the work of translation and the intercultural dimension of this discussion. What is important about Trinh's language that jars and disrupts is not only what it says but also, and perhaps more so, its jarring, disruptive effect. While one can criticize Trinh's articulation for being essentialist, reductive and even mystical, as many have done (e.g. Gandhi 1998; Bonnett 2000), we can also receive the quote above as an expressive mode of registering the need to accept heterogeneity and Otherness, *including the heterogeneity of critical modes.*

A lot more can be and must be said in relation to Trinh's statement above, but what I wish to clarify, for now, is how action and response to Others and Otherness are conceived in the passage above as issues of reception, being receptive 'with one's mind and heart' rather than giving aid or helping in ways that reinforce dominant asymmetries. This is not to say active forms of response through individual, organizational or state channels are unnecessary or unhelpful in principle, but it is to say that these forms of giving and caring need further interrogation and complication. To begin, the heterogeneity and ambiguity of these active forms of response must be amplified: there are more creative and critical ways of being 'practical' than the present official channels recognize. Moreover, such active forms of response must simultaneously recognize and respond to how these 'practical' actions are not the only forms and 'sphere' in which suffering of Others can touch us and stir action. '*Meeting and parting at crossroads, we each walk our own path*': this phrasing by Trinh foregrounds how responding to the suffering of Others is most centrally not just about acting upon suffering but instead being receptive to Otherness more pervasively, intimately and (self-)disruptively. Crucially it does so again, expressively, in a mode that disrupts the site of academic publication.

Action here includes parting ways, walking our separate paths, disrupting the fortunate/unfortunate hierarchy that so firmly structures intercultural encounters in sites of suffering. What this phrase highlights is the need to 'meet' as prevailing channels for intercultural relations moves us (i.e. take creative practical actions), but also at the same time move away from understanding responsible action and responsiveness to suffering as *acting upon* the suffering of Others. There is a difference between action and acting upon. We must meet and part ways to move towards a different way of being in this world that reflects that encounter with suffering and the touch in that site. To borrow Ahmed's phrasing, what needs consideration is how we might 'inhabit' and 'dwell' in this world *differently* – a world where 'suffering North Korea' happens (Ahmed 2002: 29).

The key question here is, having encountered what we have encountered (i.e. suffering North Koreans in its contingency, ungraspability, complexity), how do we inhabit this world differently in such a way that our dwelling disrupts the hierarchy of fortunate/unfortunate, active/passive and abled/disabled along the self/Other binary? What makes asking this question through Trinh different from the way it has been asked by critical thinkers before me, is that it resists being assimilated into a rational project. It is not only a question of thinking, digging deeper, finding a better image, asking harder questions about suffering, atrocities, silences, etc. It is in this context that the haphazard way Area Park's image made its way into this chapter matters. Taking note of the material encounter in the form of a newspaper clipping highlights the circumstantial nature of its meaning and its critical use. Responsibility is also, and more importantly, a matter of changing the instinctual, emotive, modal dimensions of the act of viewing and inhabiting (with) the suffering of Others. It is inescapable that that responsibility and inhabiting (with) suffering makes visible contingent, happenstance order of things.

Conclusion

If 'seeing' is important in responding to suffering (and here a response does not have to be that of acting upon), we have a particularly thorny problem of suffering in the North Korea case. Compounding the general problem of seeing suffering from a privileged position of spectatorship is the problem of access to sites of suffering – or as I conceived in the chapter, 'touching' suffering – which arises from the North Korean state's censorship and control over its territory, people and sources of information. How can suffering be touched, and its contingency attended to, when sites of suffering are patrolled by the very institutions and people that benefit from preventing (intercultural) encounters in these sites?

Choi's *Defectors* understood this as a problem of distance that must be overcome by exploiting the privileged relationship of photography and first-hand accounts to the 'truth' or 'what has been', and putting to use defector images and stories to produce an abject, helpless North Korea. Ri's *Landscape of the Everyday North* understood this problem as secretly documenting the site of suffering (the rural landscape inhabited by ordinary people), and showing how hard their lives are in material deprivation. Chancel's *North Korea* understood the problem as showing how dead, artificial and mechanized North Korean society is and how a repressive state power is behind this. What all these photo books have in common is that they retain the hierarchy of pity (i.e. encounters with suffering as one between fortunate 'us' and unfortunate 'North Korea'). In effect, they produce North Korea as an object for outside action. In short, all fail to attend to the contingency of pain and suffering.

To foreground the contingency of suffering is to recognize that our understanding of suffering always escapes us. It is thus important to foreground alternative images of North Korea that speak to multiplicity of pain, or more accurately, to traces of imaging practices that either get relegated, wished away or reductively appropriated to keep alive a singular image of North Korea as a repressive state causing untold misery and suffering. More importantly, the challenge is to see, be moved and respond, in more ways than one, to the heterogeneity of suffering – in ways that disrupt the privileged ways of seeing and responding to pain. Part of the strength of Area Park's photograph of the North Korean boys is the return gaze and mobility in his image that impregnate it with the potential to move viewers in ways that are irreverent, complex, unruly and tangential. The circumstantial way in which it entered this project adds to the story of its irreverence, complexity, unruliness and tangency. Trinh helps us to point to how this photographic movement must be allowed to unfold in ways that do not feed back into the circuit of rational, intellectual, knowing/thinking projects. The encounter with contingency, the ambivalence of suffering Others, should move us to inhabit the world differently, which is a way of inhabiting and dwelling that most centrally involves meeting and *parting* ways, i.e. privileging the heterogeneity of a world that is not *containable by, or in, the self.*

Notes

1 I do not delve into the relationship between pain and suffering in this chapter because I think characterizing the relationship falls into the trap of differentiating affect from emotion. This privileges pain affect as the rawer version of emotion in

the way Brian Massumi (2002) encourages (for more on this debate see Ahmed 2008; Davis 2009). For the rest of the chapter I use both terms, suffering and pain (as well as misery, injury, harm, etc.), as the context requires.

2 While unacknowledged in the main body, Lauren Berlant's introductory chapter in *Compassion: The Culture and Politics of an Emotion* (2004) has been helpful in formulating this section.

3 For Azoulay, this responsibility is a civic duty in the contractual sense, an obligation of citizenry that, if not exercised, is a breach of one's duties as a citizen towards fellow citizens (defined as the fellow bodies that are governed, not governing) (Azoulay 2008: Chapter 2). I bracket this rationalist turn in her argument, but it is unclear how reifying the hierarchy between rational/affective in her argument for a contractarian understanding of responsibility is defensible in light of the feminist scholarship on citizenship (see Berlant 1997; Ahmed 2004).

4 The Korean title of this book reads, '*Talbukja: Geuduel-ui iyagi*'. All English quotes, including the title of the book, that appear here in relation to Choi and other South Korean photographers are my translation. Choi identifies himself as a photographer and photojournalist interchangeably. He has been working for the South Korean newspaper *Chosun Ilbo* since the 1990s (Choi 2008: dust jacket cover). Choi currently works as an entry-photographer to the Blue House (South Korean presidential palace) for the same newspaper.

5 The Korean title reads *Bukneok Ilsang-eu Pung-gyong*, and the English title is my own translation (as with Choi's *Defectors* and Oh's *Pyongyang Project*, English translations of these works do not yet exist).

6 As mentioned in Chapter 2 (note 12) in discussing Oh, the author of *Pyongyang Project*, KEDO is an intergovernmental energy agency, created as part of the 1995 Agreed Framework, but has stopped its activities since the second 'nuclear crisis'.

7 Often referred to as the Dusseldorf School, these photographers emerged in the 1970s and are appreciated for their large colour photographs of urban landscapes.

Bibliography

Photography websites

Philippe Chancel, www.philippechancel.com (accessed April 2012).
Gary King Photographer Photojournalist, www.garyknightphotography.com (accessed April 2012).
Eric Lafforgue, 'North Korea, DPRK, Bukhan, a set on Flickr', www.flickr.com/photos/mytripsmypics/sets/72157604812751507/?page=5 (accessed March 2012).
Eric Lafforgue Photography, Photographie, www.ericlafforgue.com (accessed April 2012).
Christopher Morris, Photographer, www.christophermorrisphotography.com (accessed April 2012).
Christopher Morris, 'Photo Essay Daily Life in North Korea', www.viiphoto.com/detailStory.php?news_id=443 (accessed April 2012).
Area Park, Photographer, areapark.net (accessed April 2012).
Tomas Van Houtryve, Tomas VH Journal, tomasvanhoutryve.wordpress.com (accessed April 2012).
VII Photo Agency, www.viiphto.com (accessed April 2012).

Books and articles

Ahmed, Sara (2002) 'The Contingency of Pain', *Parallax* 8 (1): 17–34.

——(2004) *The Cultural Politics of Emotion*, Edinburgh: Edinburgh University Press.

——(2008) 'Open Forum Imaginary Prohibitions: Some Preliminary Remarks on the Founding Gestures of the "New Materialism"', *European Journal of Women's Studies* 15 (1): 23–39.

Ahn, Hae-ryong (2005) 'A Documentary of the Daily Life of the North Korean Masses', in Ri, Man-geun (photographer) *Landscape of the Everyday North* (*Bukneok Ilsang-eu Pung-gyong*), text by Ahn, Hae-ryong, Seoul: Hyeonshil Culture Research.

Andrews, Molly (2007) *Shaping History: Narratives of Political Change*, Cambridge: Cambridge University Press.

Azoulay, Ariella (2008) *The Civil Contract of Photography*, New York: Zone Books.

Barthes, Roland (1993) *Camera Lucida*, London: Vintage.

Berlant, Lauren (1997) *Queen of America Goes to Washington City: Essays on Sex and Citizenship*, Durham, NC: Duke University Press.

——(ed.) (2004) *Compassion: The Culture and Politics of an Emotion*, London: Routledge.

Bernstein, J.M. (2004) 'Bare Life, Bearing Witness: Auschwitz and the Pornography of Horror', *Parallax* 10 (1): 2–16.

Bhambra, Gurminder and Shilliam, Robbie (2009) 'Introduction: "Silence" and Human Rights', in Gurminder Bhambra and Robbie Shilliam (eds) *Silencing Human Rights: Critical Engagements with a Contested Project*, Basingstoke: Palgrave Macmillan.

Bleiker, Roland and Kay, Amy (2007) 'Representing HIV/AIDS in Africa: Pluralist Photography and Local Empowerment', *International Studies Quarterly* 51: 139–63.

Boltanski, Luc (1999) *Distant Suffering: Morality, Media and Politics*, Graham Burchell (trans.), Cambridge: Cambridge University Press.

Bonnett, Alastair (2000) '"Alternative" Film or "Other" Film? In and Against the West with Trinh Minh-ha', in Mike Crang and Nigel Thrift (eds) *Thinking Space*, London: Routledge.

Browne, M. Anne (2002) *Human Rights and the Borders of Suffering: The Promotion of Human Rights in International Politics*, Manchester: Manchester University Press.

Campbell, David (2003) 'Salgado and the Sahel: Documentary Photography and the Imaging of Famine', in Francois Debrix and Cynthia Weber (eds) *Rituals of Mediation: International Politics and Social Meaning*, Minneapolis: University of Minnesota Press.

——(2007) 'Geopolitics and Visuality: Sighting the Darfur Conflict', *Political Geography* 26: 357–82.

——(2011) 'Vietnam, Afghanistan and the Sphere of Legitimate Aesthetics: Developing a Critical Photographic Practice', *David Campbell – Photography, Multimedia, Politics*, 13 May, www.david-campbell.org/2011/05/13/vietnam-afghanistan-aesthetics-critical-photography/ (accessed April 2012).

Campbell, David, Clark, David J. and Manzo, Kate (2005) *Imaging Famine Exhibition Catalogue*, www.imaging-famine.org/images/pdfs/famine_catalog.pdf (accessed February 2012).

Chancel, Philippe (n.d.) *Artist Statement for the Moving Walls Exhibition*, Open Society Foundation, www.soros.org/initiatives/photography/movingwalls/15 (accessed September 2011).

——(2006) *North Korea*, texts by Michel Poivert and Jonathan Fenby, London: Thames and Hudson.

Choi, Soon-ho (2008) *Defectors: Their Story* (*Talbukja: Geuduel-ui iyagi*), Seoul: Sigongsa.

Chouliaraki, Lilie (2006) *The Spectatorship of Suffering*, London: Sage.

Chow, Rey (1993) *Writing Diaspora: Tactics of Intervention in Contemporary Cultural Studies*, Bloomington, IN: Indiana University Press.

——(1995) *Primitive Passions: Visuality, Sexuality, Ethnography and Contemporary Chinese Cinema*, New York: Columbia University Press.

——(1999/2000) 'When Whiteness Feminizes ... : Some Consequences of a Supplementary Logic', *Differences: A Journal of Feminist Cultural Studies* 11 (3): 137–68.

Clark, David James (2008) *Representing the MAJORITY WORLD Famine, Photojournalism and the Changing Visual Economy*, doctoral thesis, Durham University, etheses.dur.ac.uk/136 (accessed July 2011).

Clarke, Graham (1997) *The Photograph*, Oxford: Oxford University Press.

Crane, Chris (2007) *Welcome to Pyongyang*, London: Chris Boot Ltd.

Dauphinee, Elizabeth (2007) 'The Politics of the Body in Pain: Reading the Ethics of Imagery', *Security Dialogue* 38: 139–55.

Davis, Noela (2009) 'New Materialism and Feminism's Anti-biologism: A Response to Sara Ahmed', *European Journal of Women's Studies* 16 (1): 67–80.

DLA Piper LLP and US Committee for Human Rights in North Korea (2006) *Failure to Protect: A Call for the UN Security Council to Act in North Korea*, www.dlapiper.com/files/upload/North%20Korea%20Report.pdf (accessed March 2014).

DLA Piper LLP, US Committee for Human Rights in North Korea and Oslo Center for Peace and Human Rights (2008) *Failure to Protect: The Ongoing Challenge of North Korea*, www.dlapiper.com/ ... /NK_Report_F2P_North%20Korea_Sep19_08.pdf (accessed March 2014).

Edwards, Holly (2007) 'Cover to Cover: The Life Cycle of an Image in Contemporary Visual Culture', in Mark Reinhart, Holly Edwards and Erina Duganne (eds) *Beautiful Suffering: Photography and the Traffic in Pain*, Chicago, IL and Williamstown, MA: University of Chicago Press and Williams College Museum of Art.

Fenby, Jonathan (2006) 'A Country Apart', in Philippe Chancel (photographer) *North Korea*, texts by Michel Poivert and Jonathan Fenby, London: Thames and Hudson.

Friday, Jonathan (2002) *Aesthetics and Photography*, Aldershot: Ashgate.

Gandhi, Leela (1998) *Postcolonial Theory: A Critical Introduction*, New York: Columbia University Press.

Haggard, Stephan and Noland, Marcus (eds) (2006) *The North Korean Refugee Crisis: Human Rights and International Response*, Washington, DC: US Committee for Human Rights in North Korea.

——(2011) *Witness to Transformation: Refugee Insights into North Korea*, Washington, DC: Peter G. Peterson Institute for International Economics (PIIE).

Harris, Mark (2007) *Inside North Korea*, San Francisco, CA: Chronicle Books, LLC.

Hirsch, Marianne (2001) 'Surviving Images: Holocaust Photographs and the Work of Postmemory', *The Yale Journal of Criticism* 14 (1): 3–37.

Horstkotte, Silke and Pedri, Nancy (2008) 'Introduction: Photographic Interventions', *Poetry Today* 29 (1): 1–29.

Hutnyk, John (2004) 'Photogenic Poverty: Souvenirs and Infantilism', *Journal of Visual Culture* 3: 77–94.

Imaging Famine (n.d.) 'Imaging Famine Exhibition', www.imaging-famine.org/index.htm (accessed February 2012).

Inayatullah, Naeem and Blaney, David L. (2004) *International Relations and the Problem of Difference*, London: Routledge.

Kang, Chol-hwan (2001) *The Aquariums of Pyongyang: Ten Years in the North Korean Gulag*, Pierre Rigoulot (co-writer), Yair Reiner (trans.), London: Atlantic Books.

Kim, Suk-young (2010) *Illusive Utopia: Theatre, Film and Everyday Performances in North Korea*, Ann Arbor: Michigan University Press.

Kleinman, Arthur, Das, Veena and Lock, Margaret (eds) (1997a) *Social Suffering*, London: University of California Press.

——(1997b) 'Introduction', in Arthur Kleinman, Veena Das and Margaret Lock (eds) *Social Suffering*, London: University of California Press.

Lafforgue, Eric (2008–10) 'North Korea, DPRK, Bukhan, a Set on Flickr', www.flickr.com/photos/mytripsmypics/sets/72157604812751507/?page=5 (accessed March 2012).

Linfield, Susie (2010) *The Cruel Radiance: Photography and Political Violence*, London: University of Chicago Press.

Lisle, Debbie (2006) *Global Politics of Contemporary Travel Writing*, New York: Cambridge University Press.

——(2009) 'The "Potential Mobilities" of Photography', *M/C Journal* 12 (1), journal.media-culture.org.au/index.php/mcjournal/article/viewArticle/125 (accessed February 2012).

——(2011) 'The Surprising Detritus of Leisure: Encountering the Late Photography of War', *Environment and Planning D: Society and Space* 29: 873–90.

Lutz, Catherine A. and Collins, Jane L. (1993) *Reading National Geographic*, Chicago, IL: University of Chicago Press.

Malkki, Liisa H. (1996) 'Speechless Emissaries: Refugees, Humanitarianism, and Dehistoricization', *Cultural Anthropology* 11 (3): 277–404.

Manzo, Kathryn (2008) 'Imaging Humanitarianism: NGO Identity and the Iconography of Childhood', *Antipode* 40 (4): 632–57.

Massumi, Brian (2002) *Parables for the Virtual: Movement, Affect, Sensation*, Durham, NC: Duke University Press.

Miyoshi, Masao (2000) 'Ivory Tower in Escrow', *Boundary 2: An International Journal of Literature and Culture* 27: 7–50.

Moeller, Susan D. (1999) *Compassion Fatigue: How the Media Sell Disease, Famine, War and Death*, London: Routledge.

Morris, Christopher (2006) 'Photo Essay Daily Life in North Korea', VII Photo Agency, www.viiphoto.com/detailStory.php?news_id=443 (accessed March 2012).

Morris, David B. (1997) 'About Suffering: Voice, Genre, and Moral Community', in Arthur Kleinman, Veena Das and Margaret Lock (eds) *Social Suffering*, London: University of California Press.

Nyers, Peter (2006) *Rethinking Refugees: Beyond States of Emergency*, London: Routledge.

Oh, Jean (2008) 'Mix it Up with Vietnamese and Korean Art', *The Korea Herald*, 10 January, Culture section: 16.

Park, Area (n.d.) *Area.Park Photographer*, areapark.net (accessed April 2012).

Park, Hoo-gi (n.d.) 'The Game that Does Not End but Must End' (*Kkeut-naji ahnneun hajiman Kkeut-naya ha-neun Gae-im*), *Area Park Photographer*, areapark.net/text.htm (accessed April 2012).

Pasha, Mustapha (2009) 'How Can We End Poverty?' in Jenny Edkins and Maja Zehfuss (eds) *Global Politics: A New Introduction*, Abingdon: Routledge.

Poivert, Michel (2006) 'Appearances', in Philippe Chancel (photographer) *North Korea*, texts by Michel Poivert and Jonathan Fenby, London: Thames and Hudson.

Poole, Deborah (1997) *Vision, Race, and Modernity: A Visual Economy of the Andean Image World*, Princeton, NJ: Princeton University Press.

Price, Derrick (2004) 'Surveyors and Surveyed: Photography Out and About', in Liz Wells (ed.) *Photography: A Critical Introduction*, Abingdon: Routledge.

Price, Derrick and Wells, Liz (2004) 'Thinking About Photography: Debates, Historically and Now', in Liz Wells (ed.) *Photography: A Critical Introduction*, Abingdon: Routledge.

Prosser, Jay (2005) *Light in the Dark Room: Photography and Loss*, Minneapolis: University of Minnesota Press.

Ramamurthy, Anandi (2004) 'Spectacles and Illusions: Photography and Commodity Culture', in Liz Wells (ed.) *Photography: A Critical Introduction*, London: Routledge.

Reinhart, Mark, Edwards, Holly and Duganne, Erina (eds) (2007) *Beautiful Suffering: Photography and the Traffic in Pain*, Chicago, IL and Williamstown, MA: University of Chicago Press and Williams College Museum of Art.

Ri, Man-geun (2005) *Landscape of the Everyday North* (*Bukneok Ilsang-eu Punggyong*), text by Ahn, Hae-ryong, Seoul: Hyeonshil Culture Research.

Ryan, James (1997) *Picturing Empire: Photography and the Visualization of the British Empire*, Chicago, IL: University of Chicago Press.

Scott, Clive (1999) *The Spoken Image: Photography and Language*, London: Reaktion Books.

Shim, David (2010) 'How Signifying Practices Constitute Food (In)security – The Case of the Democratic People's Republic of Korea', *GIGA Working Papers*, www.giga-hamburg.de (accessed 2011).

Silverstone, Roger (2006) *Media and Morality: On the Rise of the Mediapolis*, Cambridge: Polity.

Sliwinski, Sharon (2004) 'A Painful Labour: Responsibility and Photography', *Visual Studies* 19 (2): 150–62.

——(2006) 'The Childhood of Human Rights: The Kodak on the Congo', *Journal of Visual Culture* 5: 333–63.

Sontag, Susan (1979) *On Photography*, London: Penguin Books.

——(2003) *Regarding the Pain of Others*, London: Penguin Books.

Tagg, John (1988) *The Burden of Representation: Essays on Photographies and Histories*, Basingstoke: Macmillan.

Trinh, T. Minh-ha (2011) *Elsewhere, Within Here: Immigration, Refugeeism and the Boundary Event*, Abingdon: Routledge.

United Nations (2006) 'Failure to Protect: A Call to the UN Security Council to Act in North Korea', 16 November, ECOSOC Special Event, with its sponsors Former President of the Czech Republic, HE Vaclav Havel, Former Prime Minister of Norway, HE Kjell Magne Bondevik and Nobel Prize Laureate, Professor Elie Wiesel, www.un.org/webcast/2006c.html (accessed March 2014).

UN Human Rights Council (2014) 'Report of the Detailed Findings of the Commission of Inquiry on Human Rights in the Democratic People's Republic of Korea', 25th Session, Agenda 4, A/HRC/25/CRP.1, www.ohchr.org/EN/HRBodies/HRC/CoIDPRK/Pages/ReportoftheCommissionofInquiryDPRK.aspx (accessed March 2014).

4 I love you, do you love me?

Conflict, melodrama and reconciliation, South Korean blockbuster style

> Most of all, [the Korean conflict] is excellent material for telling dramatic stories. There is extreme confrontation and then there are moving stories uniquely possible that follow when this extreme confrontation is overcome and the opposing sides come together. And it makes for good battle scenes, high-tech fighting scenes and stories of impossible love. So it is really good material for making commercial films, for creating extreme emotion and entertaining stories that people like.
>
> (Park 2007: 24, my translation)

> No matter how much we may thread the same beaten paths, each love story we live remains unique to us, so how you enter (or don't enter) this love-on-film story is for you to decide.
>
> (Trinh 1999: 197)

Introduction

Previous chapters examined how international problems of human rights, security and humanitarianism are moments that define our norms, values and who 'we' are. International problems like North Korea create us as much as they reflect our moral and aesthetic thresholds and compositions. In this chapter, I take a closer look at inter-Korean dimensions of the international that is constructed through North Korea, in particular South Korea's narratives of national reconciliation and unification. The idea that the two Koreas must be one has structured inter-Korean relations since the inception of the two 'nation-states'. I study one of many possible dimensions of how this idea unfolds and structures the Korean conflict.

Crucially, this study of the international and inter-Korean relations is an effort to study the international dimension of the Korean conflict that sees 'Korea' as part of the international. What is at stake in narratives of national togetherness that the Korean division incites is the positionings and inter-subjective recognition of 'Korea' as a part of, and within, the international community, which are positionings that express desire for *upward mobility* in the international hierarchy through attachment and centring of 'Korea'. This is to say, first, that relations between North and South Korea can be seen as an enactment of the international, or more precisely intercultural; and second, that the Koreas allow the construction of the international not only because they are an Other of the international but also because they *are* part of the international. What is under constant reconstruction, performance and contestation is this second accented 'are-ness' and the terms of this being (international).

The first quote in the epigraph from Park, Chan-wook, a highly acclaimed South Korean film director, serves as a way into another related question that frames the inter-Korean relations in this chapter – the question of love. Explaining why the Korean conflict continues to serve as a popular backdrop for South Korean blockbusters, Park argues that the conflict is a dramatic story that reliably allows commercial filmmakers to do what they do best: weave together a fantasy that produces spectacular economic and technological satisfaction. Love, or more particularly the theme of impossible love, is just one of the ingredients for good filmmaking using the Korean conflict as its stage. I think this is rather a cynically accented acknowledgement of the significance of not only the Korean conflict but also love in popular imagination. Perhaps it is a well-grounded and even a refreshingly honest perspective from a practitioner but this chapter juxtaposes this dose of 'honest realism' with Trinh Minh-ha's urging that we take love and the love stories that we make more seriously and sincerely.

The focus on inter-Korean relations and more specifically on narratives of reconciliation and unification brings to the fore love as an emotion that crucially mediates intercultural relations. As in other national contexts and political issues, love and togetherness feature prominently in narratives of Korean division (see Jager 1998, 2002; Kim 2007; Choi 2010; Ryang 2006; Berlant 1997, 2008; Ahmed 2003; *Positions* 2008, special issue). Love stories everywhere, or so it seems, have long been a site for performing optimism about convergence, togetherness, national unity and resolutions. But why? Why does love become the main way in which narratives about national pain and futures get told? Is it merely the prominence of love in modern storytelling that gets reflected in national narratives? What is the relationship between love and the nation-state? How does love matter – become a matter – in international relations? This chapter seeks to map out what is involved in taking love seriously. Building on currently circulating scholarship on love, I explore the concept as it gains articulation when we look at the Korean conflict and narratives of division and togetherness.

The first section provides one outlining of the entanglement of love, nation and state apparatuses. More specifically, I map out the rough contours of what turns love into hate, bonds into expulsions, life into death in moments when boundaries and borders are in tension. Interrogated here is the particular melodramatic overture of sadness that pervades in South Korea's national narratives of togetherness and the way *han*, an emotion of lamentation that is supposedly unique to Korean culture, structures these narratives. I ask what undoing entanglement of love, nation and state involves, given the sticky, binding order of love as a desire that would not allow easy disentanglement.

The second section reads two quite differently accented films about national division: an action/thriller, *Typhoon* (2007, dir. Kwak, Kyung-taek), and a sugary love melodrama, *Over the Border* (2006, dir. Ahn, Pan-suk). Familial love accomplishes miraculous world-saving and Earth-shattering heroic reconciliation in *Typhoon*, while in *Over the Border*, romantic couple-love ties North and South Koreas together which overcomes the painful separation of impossible love.

My readings of these films focus on how political imaginings in the name of love are constrained by and uncritically serve a particular network of privileged moral communities (South Korea, the West, heteronormative families, etc.), and how these constructions subordinately position 'North Korea', the stand-in perhaps for the outer limits of Otherness in contemporary Asia and beyond. Reading these films as *han* melodramas offer insights for this chapter not because it is a uniquely Korean emotion of sadness and sad love but because it helps to articulate the issue of cultural differences in South Korean imagination of itself, love and how it belongs (at the top) in the international world.

The final section of the chapter begins with the question, what is the problem of love in the 'North Korea problem' when our Korean problematique extends beyond a framework that privileges South Korean narratives? I read a Korean-Japanese film *Our Homeland* (2013, dir. Yang, Yonghi) in relation to the director's other works, documentary films and memoir, to explore this question. Yang's returns to and repetitions of scenes of loving (and hating) North Korea from her specific location in Japan provide a rich text for thinking about alternative ways of expressing commitment to staying attached to the Other.

Love and convention

Sonia Ryang (2006: 2) argues that love, in the case of Japan, is a political technology closely tied to the production of the modern self. Love has become a state apparatus that shapes the Japanese population as self-policing and self-disciplining agents of love-nation. Ryang writes:

> As the nation-state's sophistication as a biopower intensifies, human marriages become yet more important as primary sites through which to control, discipline, and reproduce men and women. However, not just for any men and women – for these are nationals. In this process, love becomes a key institution, both discursively and culturally, making men and women voluntarily subject themselves to state apparatuses, thereby making them into model 'national lovers'. And this is closely related to the notion of the national sovereignty in modernity: if human rights in

the post-WWII [World War II] world – as Arendt noted – were attained only by being a national, and not by being a naked human being, love (the right to legitimately love and be loved) is available only within the boundaries of the nation-state. Unlike what is popularly believed, love knows national borders very well.

(Ryang 2006: 128–29)

In other words, if one wants to love and be loved, which in modernity is synonymous to being an individual with a meaningful life, then individuals must enter the national realm of state discipline in areas of education, reproduction, labour, lifestyle, health and so on. Ryang illustrates the significance of this thesis by contrasting the ways the Japanese public on one hand embraces national women-in-love (who can most bizarrely break many social taboos), but turns non-national women into objects of hate and harassment (for just being visible as such, as foreign).[1] As stated earlier, I want to map out the rough contours of what turns love into hate, bonds into expulsions, life into death in moments when boundaries and borders are in tension. I argue that optimism about pure, unmediated, intimate unity lies at the heart of these contradictory effects of love, bonds and affirmations of life.

Love's optimism and borders

Optimism about pure, unmediated, intimate unity called love has been damned and explored under many banners: romantic love, passionate love, sentimental love, modern love(s), imperial love, neoliberal love (for instantiations see Pearce 2006; Evans 2002; Illouz 1997; Langford 1999; Hendrick and Hendrick 1992; Berlant 2000a, 2008; Shumway 2003; Hirsch and Wardlow 2006; Povinelli 1998, 2006). Love is supposedly benevolent because it takes us outside an 'I' and connects this 'I' to a world, a cause or a way of being that is greater than the individual. Moreover it ushers in a transformation that brings out the truer and a more human self and thus is a form of empowerment since the hero/heroine transcends limits and boundaries through the power of love (Langford 1999: 24–25, 42–63, 143; also Pearce and Stacey 1995: 15–17). Here, love's transformative power speaks the language of truth, transcendence and fundaments. Critics of love, however, point out how such promises of transcendence and transformation ultimately fail to deliver. While the arguments under each banner differ, this scholarship, which is mainly feminist, variously articulates how love's virtue fails because it relies on *demarcating boundaries* of self/other, inside/outside, us/them to sustain the benevolence of two-become-one. Another way to articulate these dynamics is to say that boundaries set up in the name of love mislead us to believe that lines and walls are drawn and erected to keep out strangers, danger, contaminants or intrusive gaze. The history of border-crossers, however, reminds us that walls produce creativity in the sense that they keep (some) undesirable bodies out by producing creative castings (e.g. caricatures), and also create new ways of climbing them. The higher the walls, the taller our ladder: 'You show me a 50-foot wall and I will show you a 51-foot ladder' (Trinh 2011: 3).

Berlant (2007/08) places the accent on cruelty in articulating the limits of love, that such promises are toxic to that which they supposedly give life (also see Choi 2013). To love is to desire conventionality, 'the stand-in for the experience of belonging to a world that welcomes them' (Berlant 2008: 204). Berlant discusses how heroines in love plots are depicted to be successfully engaged in enacting self-transformation (through 'therapeutic talk') which might appear resistive to norms and social conventions but actually affirms conventions, or to be more precise, affirms conventionality rather than any specific social convention. Conventionality is affirmed when one attempts to master this world by better adapting to it and retaining '*the courage to live better clichés*' (Berlant 2008: 193, emphasis in original). In short, the mantra is 'Transform yourself!' rather than problematize the world that makes one unhappy, unfulfilled, unloved, impossible. Love demands that we as individuals and our private thoughts and desires align with certain social conventions (which are changing, but not without continuity) so that we will always somehow *feel* welcome. Central in all these is union and unity in love. Love is about achieving 'oneness with an alterego, one's other self, a man or a woman who would make up one's deficiencies, respond to one's deepest inclinations and serve as possibly the only person with whom one could communicate fully' (Singer, in Hendrick and Hendrick 1992: 40).

This thesis on love, self and nation-state translated into the inter-Korean context brings to the fore other additional areas of (self-)discipline and attributes that follow this emotion. Love in the Korean context is a technology that variously bonds people through feeling sad together. To be clear, this is not to argue for Korean uniqueness because there is nothing unique about historically rooted, sad, melancholic national narratives; they are all too common, for instance in Vietnamese, Chinese and disaporic/immigrant narratives (Trinh 1999; Chow, in Bowman 2010: 181–95; Ahmed 2010: 121–59). Stories that become associated with national Korean division produce this sad togetherness through the suffering that North Korean Otherness supposedly inflicts on 'us', whether this is pain of separation from a blood brother or pain from fear and hate.

What we need to understand better is the complexity of how sad narratives get manufactured, for what end and with what effect. Illustrative is an excerpt from an interview with Park, Chan-wook quoted in the epigraph, which lists impossible love as one of several reasons why the Korean conflict is an engrossing and rewarding material to dramatize cinematically. What is interesting here is that the original print of the interview is curiously followed by an insert that is not part of the interview:

The film [*JSA*] was made in the hopes that we [Koreans] are one nation that should get along and be able to live together. We thought this hope could change the environment and also change the people making the film. This is why many people enjoyed the film and we were able to make a film that could be made uniquely in South Korea but at the same time a film that could be recognized more generally.

(About JSA, Cheung Oram Representative, Choi Yongbae, in
Park 2007: 24, my translation)

This paragraph – highlighted in blue in the original – is an unusual editorial intervention. In the context of the interview transcript, the highlighted paragraph works against and even neuters Park's point that the proliferation of films that deal with Korean division stems from filmmakers' need for material that has a wide appeal. What I am pointing to is how Park's explanation and the unexplained editorial insertion should be taken together to understand the relationship between the political reality of Korean division and the melancholic overture of the Korean self-narration. To begin, it involves differently positioned actors re-writing, writing over, competing and talking past each other in imagining the nation and what our activities of imagination mean.

My larger point is that the construction of the nation is intricately entangled with the imagination of the international in the Korean case, which becomes particularly visible when the Korean division becomes material for films. The prominence of the emotion '*han*' is illustrative of this national-international dynamic. Hye Sung Chung (2005: 121) links tearjerker South Korean melodramas to '*han*', approximated as 'a deep-rooted sadness, bitterness and longing sparked by prolonged injustice and oppression'. '*Han*' gives suffering and oppression an historical particularity that foregrounds Korea's history of suffering under foreign rules and invasions. Chung argues that in this sentimental and melodramatic mode of storytelling, *han* forms a powerful critique or social consciousness about marginalization and historical and social justice.

A similarly optimistic take on *han* is Bleiker and Hoang's (2011) proposal that we understand it as a transformative process of mediation in conflict situations wherein sorrow produces introspection (not a grudge against an external force), which in turn allows forgiveness and reconciliation. The idea is that this reconciliation is transformative rather than assimilative, which brings about subtle change not only in the victims but crucially in everyone and in the very ecology of conflict. Korean tradition is also mobilized by Bleiker and Hoang (2011: 260–65) through the concept of '*sakim*', which roughly translates as fermentation or gestation, and through shamanistic ritual '*gut*', a form of exorcism, to flesh out the emotional structure and process of how *han* is subtly and locally transformative. In this chapter, I interrogate the contours of transformation possible through *han* and highlight the intercultural nature of how it often gets mentioned and is called forth by authors in various genres to make sense of and find hope in the case of Korean division.

To set the stage, I want to outline the genre of melodrama to propose that we understand *han*, and mobilization of 'traditional Korea' as a form of melodrama that gets called forth in intercultural contexts. Rey Chow makes the claim that scenes of melodrama, 'exaggerated grief or dejection or a propensity towards shedding tears', are products of a particular self-consciousness of loss that tries unambiguously and movingly to show that the suffering we see *should not occur* (in Bowman 2010: 193). Unlike classical tragedy where suffering is a fate and thus has no moral significance, melodrama's fundamental interest is in telling moral and emotional truths and producing a story that refuses to reconcile with the inevitability of suffering (Smith 1973: 7–9). Suffering is prolonged, repetitive, virtuous and heroic, with a heavy play on pathos (passive suffering), which delays the gratification of returning to innocence and contrasts with action in the narrative (see Brooks 1976; Neale 2000: 185–87; Gledhill 2000; Smith 1973; McHugh and Abelmann 2005). Moral register is expressed as a desire to begin in, and return to, a space of innocence, an undivided oneness in a 'mode of excess'. As Gledhill put it, 'acknowledging the limitations of the conventions of language and representation, it [melodrama] proceeds to force into aesthetic presence identity, value and plenitude of meaning' (Gledhill, in Williams 1998: 53, also see 54–62).

What is problematic about melodrama is not that it relies on 'exaggerated' emotion that is not authentic, but how togetherness, belonging and convergence are part of a melodramatic worldview that 'begins and wants to end in a space of innocence' (Williams 1998: 65). Melodramatic convention seeks to ascertain what is (im)moral and correct immorality wherein absolute polarities of good and evil cast suffering as an issue of justice. If you have been bad, your suffering is a punishment, but if you have been good, your suffering is an injustice that will be redeemed. This promise of redemption and catharsis is what makes melodrama attractive. Melodrama echoes much of the demand that *han* makes as an affective narrative structure in how it demands justice, a return to a space of innocence and the achievement of belonging. The transformation of victims' pain to reinstitute harmonious relations and achieve reconciliation and justice is the melodrama of *han*. Put differently, *han* is a melodramatic narrative genre that powerfully disciplines Korean nationals and narratives. The persistence of *han* in Korean self-narratives, then, is symptomatic of a longing for a public recognition of the injustice of its suffering, i.e. the certainty that the Korean self – whether this is collective or individual – is good, benevolent and on the right side of history.

Thus, while I agree that (*han*) melodrama can harbour a locally attuned moving critique of injustice and violence, I believe that melodramas must crucially enable critical distance and interrogation of not only its own narrative structure (of innocence) but also national myths such as those that mobilize *han* and other Korean traditional values (a gesture to innocence and redemption). This double gesture to innocence is at the heart of how 'North Korea', or more precisely what can be associated with it, perpetually remains an object at the outer limits of our boundaries. Shared feeling of oneness, however noble or authentic, that is established by and establishing exclusivity cannot be a sound basis for political imagination. Moreover, this 'us' retains a colonial self-fashioning as a formerly colonized subject in relation to the 'international'. That is, the *han* melodrama enacted in relation to North Korea often enables narratives of the (South Korean) self as rightfully belonging to the international where agency and subjectivity are conceived to exist. This desire to belong seeks to correct the terms of this belonging (inclusion rather than exclusion), but in a way that retains the principles of exclusion and hierarchy of some Others. My point is that accepting the terms of existing international hierarchy – its conditions of sovereignty and order, its norms and knowledge claims, its aesthetics – occurs because colonial mentality continues to structure the international. Writing about the colonial logic in the IR discipline, Agathangelou and Ling use the metaphor of the household:

> The House of IR exhibits a similar politics of exclusion and violence [to French colonial relations to Indochina in Stoler's study]. It clearly identifies who's 'in', who's 'out', and who's precariously 'on the border'. It also stratifies who's 'upstairs' and who's 'downstairs'. This hierarchical division of space reflects the house's participation in and complicity with material relations of production and its uneven distribution of social wealth.
>
> (Agathangelou and Ling 2004: 23)

Just as colonial impulse remains in former colonial powers that desire to rule, identify and stratify, so does the impulse to follow, submit and accept existing terms of international order. Material preponderance in production capacities in economic, knowledge, cultural and political realms sustains colonial subject positions. My point is that *han* melodrama finds articulation within this larger reality. A lot can and must be said about the uncanny relationship between *han*, colonial mentality and the maintenance of the international order. All three expressions are optimisms about hierarchy, i.e. that hierarchic relations between the powerful and the powerless, while they might be immoral and must be corrected, are inescapably how the world is organized. Implied in this way of thinking is that the weak must conform, align with power and/or find ways to become more like the powerful. Also part of colonial thinking is its expression of aggression to those who can be labelled 'less developed' and thus 'weaker' than South Korea (Kim 2001: 35). I think this optimism about hierarchy gains expression in films in complex ways. As Kim, Soyoung put it, 'When the weak seek to become strong, the dynamics of desire and anxiety become more complicated. The South Korean blockbuster is one example of this dynamics of desire and anxiety that becomes explosively visible. This is the postcolonial South Korean context under global capitalism' (Kim 2001: 25, my translation). I explore this theme in my reading of the South Korean blockbuster films that stage the Korean conflict.

To sum up, exaggerated sadness and grief produced by sentimentalism and melodramatic convention are entangled with, and entangle, love's optimism in unity, moral truth and conventionality. Love's optimism seriously complicates the above thesis on the social and critical function of sentimental and melodramatic storytelling. If indeed we live in a 'postsacred world' and 'melodrama represents one of the most significant and symptomatic ways we negotiate moral feeling', what needs further interrogation is how love's desire for an intimate space of sameness, security, recognition and togetherness impedes and constrains our negotiations with moral feelings (Williams 1998: 61). This crucially implicates interrogating national myths such as that involving *han* being supposedly untranslatable, shared by nationals and rooted in history, wherein history is understood as a linear progression of events with facts that can be separated from fiction.

Disruptive love

Recognizing cultural locations and differences in articulations of love, intimacy and optimism is a starting point for this rethinking. Elizabeth Povinelli (1998, 2006) does this eloquently in her studies of indigenous and queer intimacy practices of women and men by moving in and out of Belyuen, Australia and the USA, which in effect show how intimacy practices do not necessarily occur with couple at their centre. These stories remind us that there are entirely different ways love and intimacy have been and continue to be organized. Rather than reject conventionality and desire to belong, transcend or become truer, the idea is that we rigorously negotiate how we belong in this world and seek reconciliation. 'To love a thing is not only to embrace its most banal iconic forms, but to work those forms so that individuals and populations can breathe and thrive in them or in proximity to them' (Berlant 2008: 3). This is a tricky business and Ahmed's forceful warning against searching for a better, uncontaminated form of love is useful here:

> There is no good love that, in speaking its name, can change the world into the referent for that name. But in the resistance to speaking *in the name of love*, in the recognition that we do not simply act *out of love*, and in the understanding that love comes with conditions however unconditional it might feel, we can find perhaps a different kind of line or connection between the others we care for, and the world to which we want to give shape.
>
> (Ahmed 2004: 141, emphasis in original)

To love is to move towards something, whether this is an idea, a person or a thing, and to become stuck to this particular constellation of people, things and ideas. In thinking about disruptive love, we have to be concerned with how and what this sticky, fluid labour excludes. Ahmed (2010: 90–120) explains the implications of love = happiness/optimism in her discussion of familial bonds, where she illustrates how love equated with happiness produces happiness scripts, which act as straightening devices to make us share the same happiness-causing objects. Ahmed attempts to separate love from happiness and demonstrates the need for this separation: the equation love = happiness causes unhappiness for those who are designated as unhappiness causes because they refuse to give up their object of love/desire (see ibid.: 100–6). At the same time, because love is sticky (one cannot tell one's desire what to do and what it should be), simply prohibiting or offering 'healthier' prescriptions on love is not an option and we must think harder about how the separation of love from happiness can occur. I would argue that these expressions of everyday desire require a methodology that attends not so much to what we should do about them (a normative framework) but how we can outlive them (an aesthetic). The concern thus is not so much to dis-entangle by means of deconstruction (there is only so much that critical reading understood as deconstruction achieves in a practical sense), but to see what various entanglements are doing and how they may be differently aligned, kept afloat, misappropriated.

However, in seeing multiple ways and effects of entanglements of nation, division and lovers, what also need re-visioning and re-alignment are the way we see and attend to them. Trinh writes:

> Handling 'love in fiction or anthropology' is no easy task for a voyeur who aspires to scientism ... what is put forth is not the interpretive aspect – the gathering of details through gossip – but the observational aspect, which does not fail to give the reader the feeling of being the accomplice of a voyeur hidden, taking delight in seeing and appropriating two lovers' utmost intimate acts.
>
> (Trinh 1989: 69)

One interpretive use of the quote above is to trouble the observational aspects of 'handling love', i.e. how we value and take delight in being in the know and seeing love's most intimate form in action. Translated into the context of films, which mediates love, nation and division in this chapter, observation occurs through how the scene of love is approached by the camera and how the images, sound, action and atmosphere captured through the camera are edited to tell a story. Trinh as a filmmaker and teacher of filmmaking attempts to unmake the filmmaking process. In her various books (e.g. *Framer Framed*, *Cinema Interval* and *Digital Film Event*), Trinh writes how filmic genres, script writing, blueprinting, rituals on film sets, production costs and technologies of editing all have ways of dictating what love is. Disruptive making of love/film, according to Trinh, is not to let filmmaking's potential to create get lost in these processes. Trinh's approach to filmmaking is one of 'jump[ing] into the void' and letting what she sees, hears, feels, witnesses and participates in dictate the form and structure of the film. 'In other words, the subject matter is in the way you record and create it' (Trinh 1999: 69). Put differently, the making of love and of film occur simultaneously. Similarly, in the editing process, Trinh stresses:

> One can say that when you come to the editing table, what you have are: the raw sound, and an unorganized body of verbal fragments (quotations,

reflections, and snatches of conversations). All three materials are equally loose at the cutting stage; neither one of them comes first as a unified whole, and neither is given priority over the other.

(Trinh 1999: 70)

What Trinh is pointing to is the emptiness in the subject matter of love. Thus, love as a disruptive political concept means disrupting the very idea of coherence in love stories or, to be more precise, in stories stemming from a desire to stay attached, to be optimistic about the self, life and the world. The effects, then, of disrupting the alignment of love, nation, state and international are themselves incoherent and we should not demand love's disruption to be otherwise. What theorists/filmmakers of love must do is graft together the multiple-mediated and fragmented disruptions so as to make them visible, audible or perceivable in some other way, but not necessarily to turn them into objects, to clarify, to accumulate unreflectively. As mentioned in Chapter 1, grafting is a non-knowing approach that is a playful joining together of materials and the self which empties out the signifiers involved in makings of meanings. It is an attachment to the medium, to the specific site and to the attachment itself. Or, as Berlant put it in explaining love as a properly transformational political concept, '[it] would open spaces for really dealing with the discomfort of the radical contingency that a genuine democracy – like any attachment – would demand' (Berlant 2011: 690). Love is a commitment to discomfort, radical dizzying openness, jumping, emptying out, being emptied.

To disrupt love and filmmaking is also to disrupt the meaning of Korea. It is to empty out the significance of Korea that weighs it down and makes its sorrow (e.g. the reality of national division) an attractive resource for enacting, in the name of nation, the male fantasy of togetherness and belonging. To do this, Korea, which forms the particular location for this exploration, is better conceptualized performatively, which comes with understanding space as 'a loose entity or mixing of features, movements, energies; ideas, myths, memories, actions; an active ingredient in processes of feeling' (Crouch 2010: 2; also see Thrift and Dewsbury 2000; Wylie 2007). Highlighting looseness and entangled fluidity of space, reality and politics is strategic. It is a strategy that aims to move beyond the essentialist approach to studying nations and states in concrete ways that might open up alternative modes of attending to and disrupting power relations, conflict and divisions. It is to understand Korea transnationally and recognize how the networks that sustain Korea as a signifier extend and even centre on actors, issues and processes beyond peninsular actors, issues and processes. In short, it is to decentre the two Korean states in our conception of the Korean nation, to understand the latter internationally and to recognize that it implicates multiple states and extends beyond the reach of state apparatuses. Trinh's accent on grafting and playing helps us to think through what radical commitment to inter-Korean relations must be, wherein inter-Korean relations can encompass concerns beyond inter-*state* relations involving the two Koreas and beyond states.[2]

Love conflict

If *JSA* and *Shiri* are to be taken as landmark South Korean blockbuster films for the theme of the divided era (see Kim 2004; Parquet 2009; Kim 2007; Choi 2010), a pessimistic reading of the genealogy of the narrative of Korean division would be that not much progress has been made. As I argued elsewhere, the problem with these landmark South Korean blockbuster films is that the terms of Korean reconciliation are hierarchical: the casting of South Korea as high-tech, sleek, orchestrating, and North Korea as lacking, deviant, manipulative, ultimately deploys 'North Korea' to signify what one seeks to exclude from the present Korea (Choi 2013).

Building on Berlant, I argued that such ploys are cruel in the sense that this optimism in the self and togetherness not only kills the object of one's love but the subject that love supposedly empowers, transforms and sustains through a gendered familial narratives. However, one starkly obvious development in the genre over the decade is how the international has increasingly become visible in these films about national division (*bundan*) which references the period since the Korean War that produced the two sovereign Koreas, South and North. Despite how the South Korean blockbuster films' international and domestic successes derived from the idea that the Korean national problem has international relevance, the world in the films in the early 2000s felt as if only Korea(ns) existed. The world that Hollywood techniques and genres enabled for Korean filmmaking was an imagining of Korea that felt enclosed and in a world of its own. Closely reading how (re-)insertions of the international have been occurring on and through the screens that succeed them might allow us to articulate a new way of seeing how cruel desire for togetherness operates in imaginings of the Korean division. Two somewhat different films – *Typhoon* (2007, dir. Kwak, Kyung-taek) and *Over the Border* (2006, dir. Ahn, Pan-suk) – form the main script for this analysis.

The argument here is that the conversation about inter-Korean relations and imaginings of North Korea is simultaneously also a moral assertion of a new South Korean self that is masculinist, heteronormative and nationalist. In other words, South Korea's engagement with the 'North Korean problem' always occurs with one eye, a side glance, at the international. It is a, 'Hey, look at us! Look at what we are doing!' which seeks new terms of attachment to and from the international. This form of inter-Korean relations has an element of instrumentalizing the Other Korea (North Korea) to attach and seek attachment from the 'international', which is to cast South Korea as morally good and aesthetically an equal. What remains unexplored in these narratives is how this international is itself an unstable space and is simultaneously always under construction. Moreover, as indicated earlier, I worry that this elemental move is a form of maintaining colonial mentality as a former colonized subject using 'local', non-Western resources that are supposedly resistive but are actually aggressive towards some Others.

Illustrative is the opening sequence of a recent South Korean blockbuster, *The Front Line* (2011, dir. Jang, Hun), which joins the illustrious – i.e. big-budget, technological spectacular – line of Korean War films, a subgenre of films about the Korean division. The scene is a useful entry point into considering what might be at stake in South Korea's imaginings of the Korean conflict. A camera touchingly (soft, yellow light) pans a re-enactment of the busy streets of Seoul during the war and eventually reaches a scene labelled 'Nolmunri (Panmunjeom)', where a dialogue across the enemy line is taking place around a negotiating table divided by two flags, North Korean on one side and the UN on the other. In one corner, peripheral to the official men in uniform from North Korea and the UN (presumably), South Koreans watch and assist their side of the table (the white UN officials). While the camera enters the scene through a South Korean officer (whom we soon learn is the real protagonist of the film), none in the main camera frame are South Koreans. In other words, while the North Korean side is visibly centre stage, South Korean officials watch from the side lines, occasionally whispering to the (elderly) white man leading the negotiations. As soon as the scene concludes, the film quickly becomes about South Koreans, who are the prime movers and characters battling North Korea, the villain in this war film. This opening sequence of *The Front Line* succinctly visualizes what motivates the *bundan* (national division) films – namely, the rehabilitation of South Korea that got usurped under the international flag of the UN in the 1940s and 1950s.

As mentioned earlier, Kim, Soyoung makes the connection between South Korean blockbuster films more broadly and the issues of desire and anxiety, deeming these films 'a post-IMF [International Monetary Fund]-era political, economic, industrial construction' (Kim 2001: 23, my translation). Referring to the Asian financial crisis of the late 1990s which burst the fantasy of South Korea's rapid development, Kim highlights how the IMF demands for transparency and subordination created another opportunity for the South Korean national imagination to reassert itself against foreign actors. The implications of Kim's analysis, which the disappearance of South Korean women from the screen further supports, is that South Korea's cinematic fantasy seeks to satisfy male desire for Western modernity as a means to gain power (also see Kim 2006; Choi 2010; Yoo 2012). South Korean women mostly disappeared because they are not as effective in satisfying the South Korean male fantasies about power, subjectivity and agency. I am concerned with a subset of South Korean films that use the Korean conflict as its staging material, which I argue magnifies the crucial mediatory role that the idea about the international plays in South Korea's expression of power.

Typhoon at our border

The film *Typhoon* (2007, dir. Kwak, Kyung-taek) stages the narrative of Korean division using sleek, high-contrast cinematography, and travels international waters and landscapes populated by multinational characters. This international staging of the Korean conflict was intentional and was meant to strengthen the resonance of this Korean film with a wider international audience. The director Kwak, Kyung-taek, who also wrote the script, explains:

> The film's title is *Typhoon* so my hope was that countries within the reach of the typhoon [in the film] would enjoy the film, not just Asia since the North Korean nuclear weapon is an important issue in the USA and Europe as well. The plan in the beginning was to create a story that uses this pre-existing interest abroad to draw audiences in. We chose locations under this big framework, for example, one of the characters is a pirate, so locations became places that pirates can go such as Pusan, the Thai coast and port cities like Vladivostok and Hong Kong. This way, during the production planning stage, the Asian audience was identified. In the past, big-budget Korean films did not necessarily lead to box office successes but through these films the Korean film industry has accumulated skills – in cinematography, special effects in filming and in computer graphics. We thought the film would be valuable in integrating the different know-how that has accumulated over the years. The drama of the film centres on the tragedy of the Korean division [*bundan*] but it is also a film with bold action scenes which, I hope, make it worth seeing.
>
> (Kwak 2007: 474, my translation)

This is an excerpt of Kwak's response to an interview question about how the film, while dealing with the *bundan* Korean problem, also has Asia as its stage. Here, we see how South Korean filmmaking is crucially concerned with the international – in expanding its international audience, in succeeding by accumulating skills, in using the international as its stage and so forth. However, Kwak articulates a tension between the national-local problem (the Korean situation) and the Asian-international expansion to which the film aspires. This section explores how the Korean drama necessitates and is deeply concerned with, mediated by and creates the international order *thanks to* the Korean local problem.

When we see *Typhoon* in the context of other *bundan* films of the 2000s, it becomes significant that the back story of the North Korean antagonist, Sin, organizes its plot. Sin is a North Korean orphan who grew up vowing to make South Korea pay for refusing his family a safe refuge. As a powerful pirate in his own right, the grown-up Sin sets out to execute a grand plan to avenge this past by nuclear means, i.e. to release nuclear contaminants, promising that 'the people of Korea will see their flesh splattered everywhere and die in a pool of their own blood'. Crucially, Sin's back story, which is dramatized through flashbacks, allows the villain to be more than an inexplicable evil Other, but a character with a history whose actions can be sympathetically explained. In this respect, *Typhoon* goes further than the landmark blockbuster *JSA*, which has been lauded for portraying North Korean soldiers as likeable, humorous long-lost brothers. It goes deeper into the history of the North Korean character than any other *bundan* film. Indeed, it could be seen to have more in common with defector dramas such as *Over the Border* (examined later) and *Kureosing* (2008, dir. Kim, Tae-gyun), which are concerned entirely with portraying the lives of North Koreans in the outside world.

The opening of *Typhoon* nicely sets up the questions the film tries to answer about North Korea. It first cuts in sepia tones to a 'recounting' of Sin and his family's experience/impression in temporary safety, which cuts immediately to the present day, when Sin with his pirate brothers pretend to be stranded refugees. Enacted in the two scenes of asylum seekers at two different borders is the question: what do we do about these seemingly innocent Others who demand that we bring them into our embrace? What do we do when both options – to accept and to refuse – bring vengeance against us? These questions are further weighed down by the idea of Korean-ness that the opening segment accentuates – that is, what are we to do when we have come to fear and be hated by our own kind, and there is no way out? How do we love our own when our fear and their hate make this impossible? In short, these scenes are performances of anxieties about borders and Otherness which narratives of togetherness produce. One way to cast these questions is to see them as a version of the fortunate/unfortunate binary introduced in the previous chapter. Here in the inter-Korean context, the narratives of responsibility have a strong preoccupation about nationhood. What is curious about *Typhoon* and also about *Over the Border*, examined below, is how this anxiety about fear and being hated (and even hating?) the Other is repressed in South Korean popular imagination of reconciliation and love. I argue that this repression of hate and fear is part of what fails South Korean narratives of love, togetherness and reconciliation.

In short, 'Love, love and then love some more!' seems to be the answer the film proposes, which is theatrically dramatized through Sin's reunion with his long-lost older sister, Myungju. Following the faltering in Sin's voice at his first contact with Myungju is the eventual meeting of the siblings, which brings forth a climax of emotion, or should have done so, from its viewers. The siblings, in tears and anguish, fall into each other's arms; stringed music reaches a crescendo and the rest of the world disappears. What also ensues from this scene is further heart-wrenching scenes of tender togetherness (e.g. a silhouette of the siblings together as one; Sin's utter devotion to his dying sister). Moreover, once Myungju enters the narrative, the film is also able to present more vignettes of the siblings' childhood, which are again dramatized through flashback. To make matters more heart-wrenching, the sister is visibly close to death – emaciated, pale and coughing feverishly – and even in her deathly state, or perhaps because of it, she wants nothing but the safety of her brother and begs the South Korean agent to take her in instead of her younger brother when she realizes that she has become bait to capture Sin.

These filmic and narrative techniques collectively and heavy-handedly explain away the seemingly inexplicable evil we saw in Sin in the beginning. The film leaves no narrative stone unturned and unexposed to convey the power of love.

To return to the character of Myungju for a moment, we see *Typhoon* construct and rely on the figure of the suffering female, and more particularly the suffering older sister ('*nu-eui*'). This is a common figure in modern Korean narratives, as Lee, Young-jae (2001: 47–51) argues in the context of South Korea's rapid modernization in the twentieth century. These women labour in the margins in support of the male mythology of success and arrival, for instance by foregoing their own education to support that of their younger brothers. The older sister triggers male guilt, which at the same time scripts Korean women as innocent, sacrificial and less fortunate. Aesthetics is key in this scripting of innocence; older sisters often have an unsophisticated 'rural aura', which Lee argues triggers *and* functions to shield the modern, wealthier and more fortunate of us from the full weight of the guilt we might have in relation to our older sisters: shield, because after all, the guilt does not transform our relationship with such figures.

To be clear, this is specifically a *male* fantasy because '*nu-eui*' is a honorific form in Korean that is used by the male younger sibling to refer to his older female sibling. The '*nu-eui*' figure shields guilt by portraying suffering of '*nu-eui*' as a self-driven condition that produces a greater good, i.e. the transformation of the brother (who becomes modern) and the greater good of humanity (progress). The Korean nation becomes modern but this modernity occurs by centring the male and at the cost of reifying the idea that women must suffer, sacrifice and remain innocent. Not so puzzling, then, is how Myungju, Sin's older sister, is figured as an angel, a symbolism perhaps intended behind the choice of her garments for most of the film – all-white attire that covers her emaciated body from top to bottom. Not that we ever see her standing long enough to register this fully as she is very ill and mostly lying down, seated or carried in the film. Myungju is an angelic, heroic vehicle for the innocent past and is what re-humanizes Sin for the viewers. Crucially, through the figure of Myungju, South Korean women disappear from the screen, as pointed out earlier by Soyoung Kim (2001). Crucially in *Typhoon*, Sin does not become modern but remains a roguish, unkempt, anguished man, and insofar as he becomes part of the benevolent Korean 'us', does so through his death.

The bond between Sin and the other main (male) character – the South Korean agent, Lieutenant Kang Sejong, who is in pursuit of Sin throughout the film – most obviously explains Sin's death. This male bond across enemy lines exhibits the familiar optimism about reconciliation that we see through the sibling love, as well as in earlier versions of male love in *JSA* and heterosexual love in *Shiri*. The bond between Agent Kang and Sin is one of mutual respect from opposite sides of the melodramatic (read: moral) divide, which in case we missed it all along, is made explicit before it is too late, 76 minutes into the film (the full run is 104 minutes). The voiceover reading

Agent Kang's letter to his mother contains the lines, '[Mother,] I am off to find a person who, 20 years ago, wanted to come to South Korea. I have to risk my life and point my gun at this madman but if I meet him in another lifetime, I would like to be his friend'. This melodramatic voice overlaps with the director's pride and joy, the final visual spectacular of a sinking ship. Here, the Korean melodramatic and action sequences (which aspire to international audience and standards, a point I return to shortly) are intricately knit together into one interspace. Sin mirrors Agent Kang's expression of mutual respect in his final act of self-destruction where the two men face each other, stripped of what separates them (technology, power, society) and each stands on his own with the great equalizer of manhood, a knife. Moments before Sin surprisingly thrusts his knife deep into himself rather than into his nemesis, he bellows over the noise of destruction around them, 'You and I! Understand one another!' Sin, the North Korean Other, verbally reciprocates the film's (and the South Korean agent's) desire for togetherness and understanding which creates a clear sense that the feeling is mutual, our sadness is shared and this symmetry of emotions is natural.[3]

Crucial to the modern Korean male melodrama is the *reciprocation* by the North Korean Other of this desire for togetherness that births the suicide of the North Korean Other. I argue that Sin's death is scripted by anxieties about embracing rogues, which seems to lie outside our skill set. It produces too many anxieties involved in border crossing, encountering Otherness and interruption of the self. In short, *Typhoon* does not seem to have the skills, habits, capacities, disciplines and knowledges to deal with this extreme intercultural encounter. Instead of responding to ambiguities in embracing a 'rogue', it holds fast to the idea that only we, Koreans, understand each other and that love will save the day.

The problem with roguery is that, as the tagline to the film title reads, vengeance – the source of roguery – never dies. The monstrous Sin in our midst has no recourse but death of the Other, not through our technological and material preponderance but by rekindling the human in the Other. The film's narrative implies that this is uniquely possible through familial love and the male bond which allows enactment of the idea of 'only us' at the inter-Korean level. While the narrative of togetherness between Agent Kang and Sin seems to suggest that they stand side by side as equals and as simply men, the aesthetic differentiation between the two retains the modern/traditional hierarchy that sees hope only in the former. Agent Kang is the last man standing and it is his melancholic, heroic, honourable figure that we map on the new Korean nation, while the tormented Korean soul that is Sin sinks to the bottom of the sea. Sin cannot be part of the peaceful, modern Korea because he produces anxieties not only in cross-border love in inter-Korean relations but in the ascendancy of (South) Korea in the international order. I return to this point shortly.

Bleiker and Hoang (2011) might read the narrative of togetherness in *Typhoon* differently, perhaps suggesting that we see *han* function as an introspective way of responding to suffering wherein the victims (Sin and Agent Kang) forgive and are forgiven to achieve reconciliation that transforms the Korean conflict. However, I ask, does this reading of the scene through *han* transform the environment of which the sufferers are part? In other words, the idea here is that we (Koreans) are all victims of the Cold War and the Korean conflict. Who are the villains, then, and what is this environment that needs transformation?

The film points to foreign or foreign-contaminated bodies and the international space: namely, the real villains in the film are the US government and the South Korean statecraft that Agent Kang cannot embrace as his equal (unlike Sin) and has to sever himself from (albeit momentarily) to stop the source of destruction (Sin). However, while the South Korean statecraft in the form of the government officials and high-tech government interior and situation room are visualized, the US government that repeatedly sabotages efforts to stop Sin does so off screen and through destructive technology. In short, the US government's callous actions and commands are the main sabotage, but American human bodies do not appear on screen and are manifested only in the form of compromising requests, intercepted messages, a submarine, and the missile that kills Sin. If anything, the USA enters the film through the South Korean state as the latter's source of disempowerment, i.e. of the latter's inability to act autonomously in the interest of the Korean nation due to its subordinate relation to US interests.

To create a true villain (the USA) that allows a formation of an innocent Korean national inner circle, *Typhoon* reproduces and contributes to anti-Americanism and anti-state sentiment that is part of a larger trend in the South Korean film industry (see Kim 2006: 66). My argument is that the environment that needs transformation is the international order between (South) Korea and the USA (a stand-in for the international) but the logic of *han* melodrama and its potential to transform fails here. How do you assimilate and transform the perpetrator that is not human, not visible, not within the reach of the framework of reconciliation? For *han* melodrama to be transformative in the Korean conflict, it would need to address the international order.

In other words, despite the anti-Americanism that the film espouses, *Typhoon* is an expression of a desire for alignment with the international with the West-modern-masculine at the top and the Asia-traditional-feminine at the bottom. My larger point is that re-centring 'Korea' is a contradictory process of re-centring the Western international, which is an expression of a desire for universality but, for postcolonial cinematic productions, this expression is weighed down by local, national (and masculinist) concerns that perpetually create an Other. As quoted earlier, the director, Kwak, Kyung-taek, values film productions that enable South Korean cinema to catch up with Hollywood by the accumulation of skills in camera work, cinematography and action special effects. In his assessment of Korean blockbusters, Kwak makes the ascendant metaphor for South Korean films even clearer:

The terms Korean blockbuster and masterpieces are used to advertise films but Korean cinema has yet to produce a genuine masterpiece. How could *Typhoon* be a masterpiece blockbuster when compared to *Gladiator*? It's embarrassing that Korean cinema makes claims to these labels simply because they have big budgets. Why can't we just make films using millions with the entire world as our audience? We still have a long way to go and it is too early to call what we have masterpiece blockbusters.

(Kwak 2007: 477, my translation)

For Kwak, having an Asian stage for his film is part of the larger vision of catching up with American films, which in turn would mean an achievement of genuine greatness. What is problematic here is how this catching up that eyes the entire world as its stage occurs concurrently with derogating Other Asia(ns) on the screen.

I point in particular to the multinational bond between Sin and his bandit brothers that remains an inert and underdeveloped side plot despite the film's ambitious opening. As described earlier, the opening sequence sets the stage for problematizing the international problem of refugees through the figure of Sin, which links the plight of North Koreans to the plight of boat people and asylum seekers more generally. For a film with a plotline involving global travel and a multinational cast, *Typhoon* curiously remains a film exclusively about Korean love. Asia is literally just a stage and its people mere props for Sin's grand design of vengeance and the Korean bodies that complicate this plot, namely his sister and the South Korean agent. Just as genuine masterpieces only exist outside Korean cinema, only Koreans genuinely care about the Korean peninsula and have any weight in the narrative of conflict and reconciliation. Importantly, the nuclear North Korean problem gains a different accent in *Typhoon* – the North Korean Other we should fear is not the North Korean state or activities inside North Korea, but rather a free-roaming transnational agent. The 'substance' behind the North Korea that produces fear and anxiety is in Asia, which interestingly is the target audience Kwak wants to secure for Korean cinema through *Typhoon*. It is not very surprising, then, that the film has had limited success abroad. While for the Western international the film might be too much of a national melodrama, for the Asian international the film requires turning their homes into a barbaric, crime-ridden jungle which takes the place of the North Korean state in our popular imagination about evil and suffering.

In sum, despite its international stage (high waters, multinational locations and characters), the film mostly works within the framework of national division where the North–South Korean border becomes the main boundary and obstacle of interest for the plotline. Here, trespassing and transcending the division that separates North and South Korea is linked to the idea of loss and lost wholeness, which is wholly abstract and symbolic in the film. There is no discernible socio-political detail or dramatization that gestures to the kinds of problems that might be solved through Korean unification and reconciliation (wealth disparity? corruption? economic deficit/failures?). Put differently, the film gives Korean viewers a parochial sense of pride in Korea's new ascendant place in a global world, a sense of a 'we' that is glamorous, skilled, technologically equipped to participate and catch up with the West. The idea that the Korean crisis has international implications allows convincing productions with a Hollywood-esque backdrop and a sense that our cultural productions have global appeal, market and post-production lives. However, the re-insertion of the international into South Korean blockbuster films about the Korean division merely props up South Korea and flatters, but does so without disturbing the world view and hierarchic terms of world making that create problems like North Korea or limits its own belonging.

Over the border: their arrival

Over the Border (2006, dir. Ahn, Pan-suk) explores the scene that action/thriller films like *Typhoon* leave out – the scene of arrival, new beginnings and what comes after the North Korean Other enters the loving embrace of the South. It is a comically accented boy-meets-girl melodrama centring on Kim Sun-ho, the protagonist who, unlike Sin, successfully crosses the border out of North Korea and enters the South with all his family intact. However, his fiancée Yeon-hwa does not make the journey, but promises to join him as soon as he sends a broker for her. Sun-ho does not do so (he is conned) and this separation turns Yeon-hwa, as a depository of his longing for home (North Korea) and their relationship, into an allegory of the Korean division. While mostly a tearjerker love story composed of the sickly-sweet stuff of melodramas (e.g. close-ups of happy togetherness or heart-wrenching suffering), the film, in spurts, also dramatically renders the struggles that North Koreans in South Korea commonly experience: impoverishing financial scams; becoming church-goers as a survival tactic; selling out their North Korean-ness; and experiences of homesickness.

The DVD promotional insert casts the film as a production that opens up a new 'melo' dimension of '*bundan*, which is our reality of national division that you cannot ignore if you are a person of our country [*urinara*]'.[4] This text, written in Korean and presumably for Korean viewers, emphasizes an 'us' – our country, our problem of division. For me, what is interesting about the new 'melo' story *Over the Border* is that it is a story about making the North Korean Other melodramatically reciprocate our desire for the North Korean Other. Rather than read the film as a text about the struggles of a North Korean defector couple in South Korea, I consider the film to seek the North Korean love story that mirrors our desire for togetherness. I shall illustrate the contradictory scenes of togetherness and belonging that this desire for reciprocity and an 'us' (*uri*) produces.

If *Typhoon* was a heroic tale of male love in mythical male space with Asia as its stage, then *Over the Border* is a heteronormative domestic tale involving a less-than-heroic but mostly likeable North Korean protagonist, Sun-ho. The story shapes around Sun-ho and his struggles as he resettles in South Korea. The story of resettlement in the film follows a narrative arc of a classic melodrama involving recurring gestures that seek to recover the initial space of innocence and belonging, which for Sun-ho is Pyongyang. Due to the reality of the Korean division, Sun-ho's desire to return to this space of innocence can only be satiated by recreating this space of innocence and belonging in the South, i.e. recreating a home across the border.

It is interesting how this narrative structure required physical recreations of scenes from Pyongyang, which, we learn from the supplementary disc to the DVD, required heroic, bank-breaking commitments from the production team. The head costume designer tells the camera how she was under strict orders from the director to recreate costumes accurately, 'as if [the clothes] were pictures taken from Pyongyang', which even involved 'importing' the real military badges from the North. The film invests in Pyongyang, a North Korean space, to visualize what true happiness looks like (which is hard to find in the South for a man like Sun-ho). However, this investment in creating the spectacle of Pyongyang is to set the stage for the South Korean dream to which Sun-ho and Yeon-hwa aspire. Interestingly, this has the curious effect of uncannily recreating the North Korean government's own propaganda.

The fantasy of the South Korean dream – that if you work hard, you will succeed and become happy – comes to life through the melodramatic love triangle between Sun-ho, Yeon-hwa and a good-natured South Korean, Kyung-ju. I explain the two dyads involving Sun-ho in turn. When Sun-ho does not send for her, Yeon-hwa comes looking for him and they are reunited. For Sun-ho, being with Yeon-hwa is to 'return' home to North Korea where he experienced belonging, fulfilment and happiness. Their first date in Seoul is illustrative: the couple relives their past relationship by going to an amusement park where they are pictured in alternating framings in the past (North) and in the present (South) of a happy youthful couple. There is a snapshot-like quality to the editing of this scene: short cuts of the couple's enjoyment of the rides from the North and the South are edited together, showing how the present scenes closely resemble and build on their past love. Through this process the world and people outside the couple disappear. This editing, for me, highlights how their love comes to stand in allegorically for Sun-ho's past life in North Korea as a citizen, an accomplished musician, a much-loved colleague and an ordinary person. The film does not offer much in terms of the details of his social condition, relations and forms of attachment. If the scenes in Pyongyang are rich ethnographic 'realistic' recreations of North Korea, the social relations do not receive a similar reconstructive research-driven, bank-breaking recreation. As director Ahn is recorded saying in the supplementary disc to the DVD:

> The events we [North and South Koreans] experience look different but the particular emotions that we feel at that very moment are actually more universal. So if we *feel* this, while we cannot help but see this young man [Sun-ho] is a foreigner, we will feel like we're looking at myself [sic].

> There aren't that many opportunities in our lives to be introspective and reflective about our own lives, right? Through these experiences [of introspection], if we mature and learn in small ways, then I think this film *Over the Border* is in its own way a meaningful film.

What I want to highlight in Ahn's statement is how ideas about universality of emotions and the immediacy of emotion overwrite the need for attention to social reality (and the differences we experience). Ahn is wholly concerned about us, or more particularly, with promoting the film on the basis that it is an effective resource for our projects of self-improvement. Realistic rendition of social relations in Pyongyang does help with this self-improvement project; in fact, Ahn is concerned that viewers will find Sun-ho to be foreign and thus get in the way of the viewer's introspection and learning.

Sun-ho's longing finds articulation also through Kyung-ju. On one level, Kyung-ju ushers in a sense of belonging for Sun-ho that is no different from Yeon-hwa. On one of their dates, which takes place not in a glittering, exciting entertainment complex but on a quiet riverbank over drinks, Kyung-ju, still his wife-to-be, acts to aid Sun-ho's recovery and return to this sensitive space. This occurs again through bringing into South Korea the character's happy memories of Pyongyang. If the happy memory of Pyongyang was shared by the North Korean couple, here with Kyung-ju, the memory and experience solely involve and centre on Sun-ho. Kyung-ju acts nonetheless as the instigator; she urges Sun-ho to play his trombone on their date, which allows him to forget himself and his admiring onlooker and be transported, *alone*, to his past as part of Pyongyang's Mansudae Orchestra. This transposition is an effect achieved through the transposition of two sounds from two different times. The present time (trombone) occurs to the rhythm of the past, the orchestra playing the second movement of Mozart's 'Horn Concerto Number 3'. By acting out the scene and pausing to the rhythm set by an imagined orchestra, Sun-ho recreates the sensation of being an integral part of something, of a social body that relies on him, accepts him, makes (sound) space for him. As viewers, we experience this transposition with Sun-ho and enter his inner world through Mozart, first faintly and then at full volume. There should be immediate recognition by viewers of this music from Pyongyang, which was played by Sun-ho and his orchestra earlier in the film.

Thus, both women can be read as instruments for Sun-ho's enactment of longing and desire to belong: Yeon-hwa by being in the picture with him, and Kyung-ju by urging him to indulge and fade into the background as a result. While the visual presence of Yeon-hwa leads us to believe they are together in this scene (and that this is a good thing), I question this togetherness that visual representation of presence leads us to believe. What both women keep afloat for Sun-ho is a cluster of promises of acceptance in intimate and labour relations while leaving much of the women's experiences and desires underdramatized. In short, *Over the Border* is a story about how heterosexual union enables a man like Sun-ho to feel welcome, to experience belonging and to be happy. These scenes are also scenes that tie together spaces – the present and the past, South Korea and North Korea, male and female – in a melodramatic mode. In a way, they repair the Korean division by editing and piecing together snapshots and soundscapes from the North and South. They enact – bring into presence – the national fantasy of togetherness, albeit momentarily, and by so doing, map out the hierarchy of this longing for togetherness. Despite the thick descriptive portrayal of North Korea and North Koreans, a fantasy that transplants promises of happiness to South Korea is at work through North Korean bodies, in particular through the figure of Sun-ho, with his devoted female supporters and onlookers.

Sun-ho is loyal to his circumstances. He acts out his faith in togetherness wherever he is and at no point in the film does he express opinions critical of either societies, North or South. Both are merely different sites for achieving belonging. However, there is a hierarchy in this seemingly apolitical, neutral positioning. We see this in how the love triangle is disbanded. While the North Korean couple run away for a night, not only does Sun-ho return to his South Korean wife, and become a father, but we learn that Yeon-hwa has also married a truly decent South Korean man who is above her social station (her husband is one of the government counsellors in charge of the North Korean resettlers). In their separation, the North Korean couple Sun-ho and Yeon-hwa separately find their places and new sites of happiness with their respective 'good' South Korean partners.

I would argue that this de-coupling of North Koreans and re-coupling them separately with 'good' South Koreans is a demand that the North Korean Other mirror our desires in not only becoming like us, but liking, i.e. *desiring* us. Moreover, the film's ending clarifies what has been at stake all along: becoming South Korean is synonymous with reproducing heteronormative nuclear families and working hard to achieve better positions in life.

Parenthetically, *Over the Border* is a testament to how the sickly-sweet nature of love has been technically 'perfected' by South Korean cultural producers. This technical 'perfection' – the constant harping back to a beautified past, the flashbacks that dramatize memory, the scenes of coming together and parting ways accompanied by stringed music, lashing rain, glistening water, soft lighting, eye-meets-eye editing – theatrically produces the attachments that drive and arise from border crossings. South Koreans call this genre 'melo', which dominates the terrestrial waves in the form of popular TV dramas. Director Ahn, Pan-suk is much more established and successful in television as a producer than he is in film as a director. In fact, this film is his only work on the big screen and for those interested in the finer details of *Over the Border*, one might feel that the film can be read as a TV melodrama on the big screen (rather than a film). It resembles – in editing, story material, camera work – the South Korean fantasy of the good life established through the drama of life's trials and tribulations, scandals and affairs. As quoted earlier, Ahn promotes the idea that watching this drama could be a form of self-improvement; here, the Korean division and a North Korean young man are merely cultural material to bring a fresh and new space to enact domestic drama about family, love and everyday life.

However, if we are to continue reading *Over the Border* as a national melodrama, I would read it in relation to the picture mentioned in the previous chapter of a dismembered North Korean defector in Choi, Soonho's *Defectors: Their Stories*. In Chapter 3, I read the picture of a headless body and leg stump in the foreground as a passive, abject and objectifying photographic encounter with the North Korean Other. Another reading of this image might be as an expression of a sense of national dismemberment; in other words, the picture is distressing not only because it functions as evidence of North Korean state violence but also because it symbolizes the Korean division. Korea is a dismembered nation that needs re-piecing together. The de-coupling of the North Korean pair (Sun-ho and Yeon-hwa) and re-coupling of the South–North Korean pairing (Sun-ho and Kyung-ju, and Yeon-hwa and her South Korean case worker) can be read as a positive expression of the anxiety about separation and the passive, abject position this separation creates for the 'Korean nation'. In other words, if a dismembered figure can be read as anxiety in the form of showing negation (i.e. what's not whole, there, normal) about the Korean division, then the multilayered, heavy-handed coupling of North and South Korea in this present film can be read as a positive expression of a unified Korea. My point is that this positive form is just another expression of anxiety about being the only divided nation in the post-Cold War era. Both expressions re-centre Korean agency which assumes that a unified North and South Korea would allow the full realization of Korea as a true agent of its own destiny and a more normal member of the international community. Here, at the risk of sounding repetitive, I stress how selling the Korean conflict and relying on the conflict for filmmaking and ascendancy internationally does not mean that anxieties and a sense of disempowerment/dismemberment are not with us. The dynamics of desire and anxiety in formerly colonized spaces is complicated.

To sum up, the theme music of *Over the Border* and *Typhoon* differs (quiet versus apocalyptic), as do their locations (inland and seashore versus high seas) and love (between a woman and a man versus between two heterosexual men), but they are singing the same song of consummation, reciprocity and mirroring as the only ways out of the problem of North Korean Otherness. In short, centring North Koreans in our melodrama does not necessarily change the terms of our melodrama which seek to re-centre South Korea in how the international is imagined.

Finally, I want to touch on an adjacent theme that *Over the Border* melodramatically brings to fore: borders and, in particular, border crossing. The film's enactment of what happens after crossing borders allows us to experience how border crossings are acts that weigh down border crossers to a wider network of people and lives rather than experiences that are freeing, redemptive or resistive. I am here pointing to how *bundan* 'melo' narrative helps us to revise critical engagements with border crossings that remain preoccupied with how trespassers and transgressions resist and erode borders and statecraft (see Soguk 1999, 2006; Rajaram 2004; Rajaram and Grundy-Warr 2007; Dillon 1999; Shapiro and Alker 1996). They often do not. The way Yeon-hwa disappears at the film's end is illustrative in the wake of Sun-ho's proposal that they run away together and leave South Korea 'to America or China; if they don't let us in, to wherever will'. Anywhere that is outside the Korean peninsula offers possibilities for the couple to be together and on the night before she disappears, Yeon-hwa passionately reciprocates this desire to be together:

> I am not going to let you leave my side. A century, a millennium, I am going to be here right by you. If you can't leave that other woman, then I will just become your mistress. I'll hold on to you if you try to leave and not let you go and follow you around. Like it or not I am not going to let you leave me. Not much you can do. Be prepared.

In this monologue about staying together – bravado, perhaps, knowing all too well that Comrade Sun-ho does not have it in him – the camera closes up on the tearful couple. The stringed music plays to a crescendo as the couple collapse into each other's arms, acting out with their bodies their verbal promise to never let go, to belong together. Yeon-hwa disappears the next morning without explanation, and the film cuts to their lives apart through Sun-ho's painful (or is it relieved?) chance encounter of news of her in a photo studio, a hotbed for familial reproduction (family portrait photos and wedding photoshoots are must-haves for middle-class South Koreans). Yeon-hwa's unexplained act of disappearance helps to register the difficulty of starting anew and cutting existing ties even when these are corrective acts of past mistakes and circumstantial parting. While breaking off ties and opening up new possibilities, they also multiply how one is attached and oriented in this world. Old ties are not cut off and forgotten, but instead linger on as just that: mysterious, haunting attachments. Moreover, following border crossing, inclusion and embrace through a genre that dramatizes the entangling effects of mobility has a way of attaching us, the viewers, to this by way of through images, music and settings. The coupling of Yeon-hwa and Sun-ho with their respective South Korean partners also points to the limits of our imagination when it comes to irreconcilable love, starting anew and what comes after crossing borders. *Over the Border* opens up a new realm of 'melo' to imagine and engage the realities of border crossing and the problem of Korean division and the North Korean Other, but it does not necessarily produce disruptive forms of imagination and engagement.

Reformulating (Korea) love

South Korean filmmakers make and need the Korean conflict as much as the problem of Korean conflict might benefit from filmic interventions. *Our Homeland* (2013) is different in this sense. To begin with, it locates *bundan* (national division) and attendant emotions, conflicts and attachments beyond the geographic North and South Koreas. More crucially, the problem of North Korean Otherness is understood as a problem that no amount of national love and togetherness can (dis)solve. Nations fail and national projects of capacity building (e.g. blockbuster films) do not interest Yang, the director of *Our Homeland*. In part, this is because Yang and the characters in her film gain articulation of their identities as Koreans from outside the Koreas, in Japan. National love takes on a more complicated form when the nation-state alignment is not taken for granted but is a failure of alignment that needs constant negotiation and renegotiation.

Our Homeland forms part of director Yang, Yonghi's larger attempt to tell her family's story – which she does through her films and memoir – of how her three brothers, under parental influence or even pressure (her father was a Chongryun activist, an arm of North Korean government) moved to Pyongyang during the 1959–84 large-scale 'repatriation' of Koreans to North Korea from Japan. Her feature film is based on one small event in this family history: a miraculous visit by her brother from Pyongyang to their family home in Osaka. While based on a real-life visit in 1999, Yang is fictionally looking from the inside out, as somebody entangled in the history and future of North Korea. The intimate distance from which this film is written and directed is visually captured in her first documentary, *Dear Pyongyang* (2006). In one of her numerous interviews with her parents, a naked foot, which can only be the cameraperson's, appears in the frame. Given that the scene takes place inside their family home in Osaka and because her family is seated on the tatami floor, we can perhaps assume that Yang, too, is lying down, just like her father, whom we can see in the frame – comfortably and probably in her house clothes like her parents in the footage. This intimate relationship with her subject gains articulation in all her productions, which crucially mediates how North Korea as an object of love is encountered and imagined.

Complicating relations

Our Homeland is an expression of horror with North Korea that cannot simply stay there. It expresses a complicated awareness of fearing and rejecting North Korea that does not then turn into a matter of national reconciliation and relationship of innocence. The film is also an effort that aims to go where the documentary form of Yang's previous efforts could not. These efforts produce an interesting criss-crossing version of emotional truths when read together. Yang explains the difference between documentary and feature films as one of camera work. Documentary films point the camera at the people or scene that one seeks to understand while feature films take the camera inside and see and hear what cannot be shown or said in front of the camera (Yang 2013b). In other words, *Our Homeland* tries to say and see what her brothers could not communicate to the world in her documentary camera. In her memoir, Yang makes this exact point, describing how the camera affected her brothers and that many of her questions were dodged or remained unasked out of respect for her brothers and their relationship (Yang 2013a: 270–73). My concerns here revolve around how her use of the fictional genre that supposedly opens up a dimension unavailable to the documentary form benefits politically transformative attachment. How does it disrupt conventionality? What comes after the disruption of the narrative of Korean division that centres South Korea? In what sense is it transformative?

I appreciate how the camera travels to and from different subject positions in *Our Homeland*, though I am not sure that this mobility we see in the film is necessarily possible only through fiction and not in the documentary form. I return to this point later, highlighting the film's disruptive effect from its ambiguous relation to her documentary and nonfiction productions; I argue it is her repetitive return to the questions that haunt her family which produces alternative ways of loving. For now, I want to stress how the different directions in which the characters travel in the fiction (her alter ego Li-ae, her brother Seung-ho, the mother, father and even the North Korean minder) help us to approach North Korea in a mode that is weighed down by having imagined what it feels, looks or sounds like to be intimately entangled with a place like North Korea. The complicated emotion and communication that this entanglement produces are dramatized in a scene where Li-ae confronts the North Korean minder assigned to her brother:

LI-AE: [in Japanese] What is this about? Why are you following us around? [Comrade Yang gets out of his car.] You should be able to tell me yourself. Tell me yourself. Don't hide behind my brother and tell me yourself. I know you know Japanese. You're listening to everything that is said in that house. Say something! I hate you and I hate your country!

COMRADE YANG: [in Korean] Your brother lives with me in this country that you hate and we will continue to live together like this until we die. [Leaves the scene.]

LI-AE: [Wordless tantrum.]

Li-ae hits herself as she angrily walks around in circles in an empty, darkened street. To begin with, the expression of hate is a complicated emotional act that emerges, not least, from ambiguity about what this emotion actually is. Thus, masking this hate with harmony, fondness and love, as we saw in the South Korean blockbuster, is just asking for trouble. The outburst is steeped in pent-up anger and disgust at the meaning that North Korea has in her life. For Li-ae/Yang, North Korea has been nothing but a source of pain, aggravation and oppression. It is interesting how even in Yang's fantasy of fighting back, she loses.

In an interview, Yang explains the object of her/Li-ae's hate: 'I really hate that country but country doesn't mean the people right? The government, uh, the social system' (Yang 2013b). Searching for what the North Korea that she hates means, Yang hesitates between the words 'country' and 'government', and finally settles on 'social system'. Unlike 'the government', which allows us to point fingers at particular individuals (e.g. the government officials, rulers) as the culprits, the idea of a 'social system' as an object of hate and criticism acknowledges how her brothers and people in North Korea whom she does not want to hate have a more ambiguous relationship with what she does hate. Individuals are social beings who are shaped by and shape the social system even in a coercive, authoritarian country like North Korea (also see Kim 2010; Ryang 1997). In short, contrary to Yang's efforts to separate out the people she loves and the nation-state she hates, the two appear inescapably intertwined, making ambiguous the relationship between the individual who is oppressed and the nation-state apparatus that oppresses. Perhaps it is this ambiguity that suffocates Yang and drives the angry dance that Li-ae performs in the dark.

Also significant is the complicated process of communicating hate and disgust in Li-ae's confrontation with the North Korean minder, Comrade Yang. Li-ae speaks in Japanese, which is the language of Yang's feature film. This stands in significant contrast to her earlier documentary films, which more prominently include exchanges and conversations in Korean (mainly the parts that are filmed in Pyongyang with her brothers and their families). In short, when Yang's filmic engagement becomes fictional, her film speaks Japanese which shifts the terms of the intercultural encounter between Yang/Li-ae and North Korea. In part, this is because the plot of the film takes place in Osaka, Japan, but this plot is a circumstance of production that highlights the position from which this family story is told/fictionalized. A plotline that takes place in Pyongyang probably was not an option since the film had a very small budget, making the kind of recreation we see in *Over the Border* impossible, and very few outside filmmakers can even dream of making a film inside North Korea. In short, it reflects Yang's position in relation to North Korea – as Japanese and an outsider.

This exchange is one of the two important bilingual scenes (the other is between the mother and the North Korean minder, which I discuss below). The language difference allows the characters to speak past each other yet understand all too well what the Other is saying. It is a moment that makes plain the different incommensurable but intimately interlinked planes that each character occupies: Li-ae dwells in the hyphenated Japanese–Korean plane, which is the main plane on which the film itself operates, and Comrade Yang operates in the plane organized by forces, desires and decisions that lie beyond the former, North Korea, which sits in the outer layers of the film. The film assumes that the latter is organized by North Korea (and perhaps it is) but this is something we cannot know, or to be precise, we can only sense as it comes into form in our imagination.

It is not the incommensurability of the planes of reality that is the cause of tension here, but the *inescapably interlinked* nature of their separate worldviews and commitments. Li-ae is committed to her brother – she loves her brother – and Comrade Yang is committed to the world in which her brother and he belong together. In other words, while their objects of love differ (this is not a love triangle), their separate but analogously pursued unconditional, internally driven, total commitment to an Other greater than oneself (which is what we mean when we call something love) produces this confrontation. My point is that the problem of hate here is inescapably part of the problem of love, and moreover that this is an intercultural problem which the inter-lingual character of the scene makes visible for our ears (I am here pointing out how we actually do see with our ears as Trinh encourages!).

In Yang's memoir, the focus is on the limits of loving North Korea within her own family, and not Comrade Yang, who is not in the book. This shift in focus on the object of the protagonist's hate is worth reading closely for how it further complicates the love/hate dynamics involving the North Korea Other. In the memoir, which shares the same title as her feature film, the author struggles with her unruly emotions towards the youngest of her three older brothers in Pyongyang, Gen-jjang, whom the character Seung-ho roughly resembles.[5]

The problem of 'hating the country' is framed in Yang's memoir as the pain of distance. In the final chapter, which narrates the event that forms the basis for the film, Yang writes about Gen-jjang, who was only 14 when he left for Pyongyang: 'Gen-jjang always maintains his usual self, standing apart from the two other older brothers who look [at me] sympathetically. Sometimes he laughs to himself. He never says what is on his mind. He does not show his real face. This was my impression of Gen-jjang' (Yang 2013a: 273, my translation; also 243–49). Now an elite in North Korea (he works in international trade), Gen-jjang was the most reluctant participant in the making of her documentary films and is indeed barely in either *Dear Pyongyang* (2006) or *Goodbye Pyongyang* (2011). Moreover, Gen-jjang does not let her in, even when he visits Osaka, even though Yang still relishes how the visit allowed her to see a different side of him. She also reluctantly admits how, upon reflection, she tried everything not to hate Gen-jjang during the visit, and upon further reflection she wonders if she was actually trying to be not hated by him (ibid.: 275).

The problem of hate in her film gains articulation as a problem of distance in her book, which leads her to doubt who is driving the relationship. Is she hated or does she do the hating? Yang is painfully aware that she does not know the object of her emotion (though she should, he is her brother), and her emotions vacillate between attachment, fear (of rejection), rejection and hate. There is also a sense of helplessness, i.e. a sense of being an object of another's emotions and actions, in her awareness, which might be under-girding the ambiguity with which she is grappling. Her relationship with Gen-jjang makes her uneasy, unsure and unhinges the presuppositions with which she operates (e.g. to love not hate one's family; either you are the subject or the object; and what it means to know someone).

A few pages later, Yang's story about her brother and his visit home ends with the sentiment, 'The brother to whom I spoke in Kansai dialect is no longer in front of me. Just like the [North Korean] minder, he is a North Korean' (Yang 2013a: 280, my translation). While, once again, North Korea is deposited as the outer limit of what she can understand, relate to and love, there is a sense of uncertainty about herself and how she stands, related to her brother.

The minder becomes a fully fleshed-out character in the film *Our Homeland*, which differs from how the memoir maps out the commitment to loving North Korea. An evaluative reading of this remapping would be to highlight how the fictional mode of the film enables an affective mapping that can position Gen-jjang/Seung-ho closer in proximity to Li-ae/Yang by erasing the ambiguity that arises in the distance between them. In place of Seung-ho, the scene of confrontation in the film makes the figure of Comrade Yang, the minder, demarcate a new outermost limit of Yang/Li-ae's attachment. This is a work of fiction in the sense that the character of the minder is fictional, used as a target for hate, fear, repulsion. Moreover, fiction also plays a hand in how the film character of Seung-ho significantly differs from Gen-jjang, the brother she struggles the hardest to love, with ambiguous results.

Not only might the character of Seung-ho be a product of Yang's hypothesis and impressions of her brother Gen-jjang, but Seung-ho is also better understood as a character composite of her three brothers as she imagines them. Most notably, the heart-to-heart talk, which forms an important moment of excess and togetherness, closely resembles the conversation Yang recounts having not with Gen-jjang but with her middle brother, Geun-ah, to whom in her memoir and her documentaries she appears to be closest (Yang 2013a: 198–99). In the heart-to-heart talk, the brother tells Li-ae to live her life and not become like him, 'a person whose mind has been put on pause'. Together with Seung-ho's confrontation with the father, the talk draws a figure in conflict, unhappy and dying inside, positioned as a more sympathetic character to whom Li-ae can more easily express attachment; he is one of us – he feels, speaks and sees the world as we do. Seung-ho remains mysterious, but we get a better glimpse of his inner thoughts through such scenes, which makes him easier to love.

Language also plays an important role in constructing the inner familial circle: Seung-ho only speaks Japanese and Comrade Yang only speaks Korean on screen, though supposedly both characters speak both languages. In sum, familial love that is supposedly natural, unconditional and demands mutual reciprocation, causes anxiety that the filmic rendition seeks to remedy by constructing an us-versus-them boundary which retains the boundaries of our difficult familial love.

The fiction of Comrade Yang

At the same time, the presence of the character of Comrade Yang, the outsider, in the film also allows a scene that centres, however momentarily, him and his world as a total outsider in this tale of a family rooted in two countries, North Korea and Japan. This occurs not through Li-ae's encounters with Comrade Yang, but by foregrounding her mother's approach to him, which remains foreshadowed in most of the film.

The scene I have in mind occurs towards the end of the film, when the camera follows Comrade Yang into a room where he is shown the gifts that the mother has prepared – a new suit, a letter written in her 'awkward' Korean, a bag filled with a stack of clothes, and lastly money, which is not pictured but mentioned. In a way, it is a scene of bribery and of the power of foreign currency to safeguard her son in North Korea, but it is also a scene of attachment and staying attached to North Korea which travels to a world that remains off the screen in *Our Homeland*. I would argue that only Comrade Yang is in view but it is a scene of an intimate encounter between the mother and the North Korean minder that ties the two (and the viewer) together into one. It is a scene that brings together and maps onto each other divided worlds/characters.

The mother's presence is in the form of a voice, or to be more precise, in the common film technique of a voiceover, presumably by her, reading her letter to Comrade Yang in Korean. It begins apologetically: 'I write to you in my less than perfect "*urimal*" (our language).' This opening sentence establishes their common shared culture that positions her in an outer margin of the cultural circle, a humbler position as an inadequate speaker/member. The letter delicately goes on to establish further connection, talking about her worries as a mother, and mentions Comrade Yang's three children, while the camera pans the room full of family photographs and paraphernalia. She expresses hope that the money that is included, while minimal, could be used for his children. Hanging over the scene are her words in the letter, 'Living apart from my sick son, there is nothing I can do for him but have faith in our country [North Korea]'. Comrade Yang understands this more than anyone in the film since he has no attachments and connections outside the North Korean state and society to keep promises of happiness afloat for him. I would argue that the mother echoes the idea coldly expressed by the comrade to Li-ae earlier – whether we love or hate them for it, his and her families' past, present and future are *with* North Korea. While Li-ae rejects this and wants to be freed from it, the mother accepts this reality and responds practically. If the figure of Seung-ho pulled him into our embrace (the outside) as somebody we can more easily love, which was achieved crucially through the figure of Comrade Yang in the film, then the encounter with the figure of Comrade Yang here pulls us toward North Korea by establishing common grounds that require us to be, for the lack of a better word, humble about our abilities not only to speak but also to care and act.

I cannot stress enough the complexity of this latter move as well as the former move that 'hates' North Korea. The derogatively but widely used categorization of 'pro-North Korea' and 'anti-North Korea' to cast our *choice* of relations with North Korea is of little use here, other than as derogations of course. The form of attachment that is opened up through the mother's way of not hating (but not necessarily loving either) dwells on the object that lies at the outermost limit of what we can fathom loving, understanding and not hating. Is this an example of how *han* structure brings about transformation in the Korean conflict? Is this the reconciliation structure that Bleiker and Hoang, Chung and many Korean scholars advocate, as discussed earlier? Perhaps, although I do not personally see the critical/disruptive value of reading this scene using the *han* structure. One can read in this scene, if one wants, the *han* structure of resignation → introspection about one's suffering → pronounce-ment of the suffering female figure → forgiveness asked and/or given → mutual transformation → new relations. Even so, this structure does not align neatly with the state and the South Korean national allegory of togetherness because the film has Japan as its location for the family drama of love, hate and separation. When talking about an 'us', even in these pages, the substance of this 'us' is not clear. If I had to say something about this 'us', it is probably a transnational overseas Korean 'us' that mobilizes multiple, incommensurable cultural planes and dissonant linguistic and bodily experiences.

Yang, Yonghi is a master of repetition. She repeats her family story over three films (two documentaries and one feature film), one memoir and in multiple interviews and the press coverage of her work. Stories are repeated in fiction and non-fiction as well as in filmic and textual media. Through Yang's engagement, we learn about relations, ways of relating and negotiating rela-tionships by travelling to and as different specific subject positions. I think more than the problem of love/distance that Yang explores in relation to her brothers, what is interesting in her iterative love stories is her treatment of the figure of Comrade Yang, whom as an individual she cannot love, but as a scriptwriter and director she can stretch her imagination and fictively inhabit. If director Kwak of *Typhoon* creates a technological masculinist spectacle in staging the Korean division (*bundan*), and director Ahn of *Over the Border* creates a nationalist fantasy of togetherness through the spectacle of North Korean figures, then Yang as filmmaker and cultural producer creates a tale of relations. Yang, through repetition, explores issues of relations between us and them (i.e. problems of relationality), but also uses fiction and non-fiction, film and text alongside, to offer thicker, self-contradictory findings that take our imagination to quarters we are averse to entering or relating to.

Yang also tells relational stories in that her engagement highlights the problem of relationality in South Korean blockbuster films, which seem to be driven crucially by an ascendant project of re-centring the Korean nation-state (and a whole un-divided Korean peninsula would be helpful) which has been humiliated, colonized and manipulated by outside forces (mainly the USA). Yang is not part of this filmmaking culture in South Korea and her commitment is not to the film industry but to the filmmaking at hand – a commitment to the story she has to tell as a Korean in Japan, a daughter of a Chongryun official, a sister to brothers who live in Pyongyang, an aunt with niece and nephews in Pyongyang whom she loves dearly. Admirably, Yang's articulation of her family story goes beyond the basic South Korean narratives in the 2000s that revolve around the North Korean threat, national reconciliation and unification. While Yang tells a sad story about divided Korea, its location (Osaka), its language (Japanese) and its actors (also Japanese, with the exception of the actor who plays Comrade Yang) make the *bundan* and *han* narratives strange to themselves.

I want to return to the epigraph of this chapter, 'No matter how much we may thread the same beaten paths, each love story we live remains unique to us, so how you enter (or don't enter) this love-on-film story is for you to decide' (Trinh 1999: 197). In Trinh's film *A Tale of Love*, she opens up a slightly different approach to love when she seeks to understand it as a state of being rather than an action-driven plotline. Trinh is not interested in the storyline or the plot of the poem but in the story of the state of being in love, the radical openness to which those who find hope in love as a political concept repeatedly point. As quoted earlier, 'In other words, the subject matter is in the way you record and create it' (Trinh 1999: 69). In contrast, Yang is interested in love's plotline, in the political message (North Korea is nowhere for humans) that she reiterates in her interviews and media appearances. At the same time, I think Yang's multiple attempts to love North Korea, which for her means staying attached to what she cannot but reject, which makes her a vocal critic of North Korean society and seeks to transform it, can also be read as an expression of love as a state of being. The point is not to seek to *observe* and *assess* her intimate engagement with North Korea but to understand the contradictions in her intimate entanglement in a way that enables ours. Lauren Berlant writes how love's 'normative utility is that love allows one to want something, to want a world, amid the noise of the ambivalence and anxieties about having and losing that merely wanting an object generates' (Berlant 2011: 687). The destabilizing effect of love, and its production of 'willingness' to bear the weight of ambivalence and contradiction, makes scenes of love potentially useful for political transformation. There is an openness in Yang's engagement, however flawed, and openness in how to stay attached, since shaking herself free of North Korea is not an option.

I want to end with a puzzle. For me what is odd, perhaps predictably given my training as a student of politics, is how Yang is completely silent about Japan, where she and her parents live, or South Korea, which she now frequents, having secured South Korean citizenship, and where her cultural productions find an audience. She is also disturbingly silent about the international audiences of her films (she has toured widely in the USA and Europe). For me, Yang's filmic engagements are insightful examples of politically transformative commitment in relation to North Korea (though her films and book are banned in North Korea) but they do not have a similar critical relationship with the other sites of belonging in which Yang participates through her work, in particular the international 'free' world.

As I argued for narratives of inter-Korean relations, I believe that Yang's critique of North Korea and her family tale are crucially negotiations of belonging and identity in the site of her production (the same is true of my book and authorship of course). Her silence leaves an impression that the world minus a place like North Korea is unambiguously better because somebody like Li-ae can travel and do as she wishes. This impression is reinforced by how the film ends with Li-ae returning to a luggage shop she visited with her brother and purchasing the suitcase she looked at with him before his abrupt departure.

For me, exploring love as a politically transformative concept crucially requires, in our contemporary context, interrogating multiple configurations of nations and states, national love and the international, which includes one's site of production, engagement and identity. Yang is a filmmaker and her films work because she responds to her artistic and affective/ed instincts. I understand that it is unfair to criticize Yang for not dealing with the larger international politics within which she forms a critical relationship with North Korea. This is where we as scriptwriters, directors and creators come in. It is our task as consumers from our different positions to enact attachments that are questioning, troubling and disruptive of the international, South Korea or Japan. What Yang does particularly well is demonstrate what capacity building for dealing with incommensurable – even aggressive – differences entails: repetition, returning and more repetition.

Conclusion

Commentaries from politicians and pundits abound in South Korea about the apathy of the South Korean public, especially the younger generation, towards North Korea and Korean unification. Such commentaries frame this apathy as a social problem, a major hindrance that will only get worse with time. My analysis of *Typhoon* and *Over the Border* examined the terms of embrace and togetherness to see how we are failing if this apathy (which itself is a questionable description of South Korean public sentiment given the popularity of *bundan* films) is allowed to run rampant. *Typhoon* and *Over the Border* differ in how they embrace North Korea and go about dramatizing crossings of, and meetings at, the border that divides the two Koreas, but both share the optimism about togetherness through gendered love. *Typhoon* achieves this through masculine bonding and a feminine suffering angel; *Over the Border* relies on heteronormative love. *Typhoon* brings to centre stage a North Korean villain determined to bring havoc to the peninsula and shows how love, in particular a return to childhood innocence through an angelic sister's embrace, could turn even a demon into a reasonable human being. The bond between Sin, the villain, and the South Korean agent, our hero, cement the ideals in a human being: clever, principled, heroic. It is not so much that these ideals in themselves are problematic (although they are), but that this notion of the ideal human being imagines unification in seemingly 'equal' terms but, lest we forget, it is not. It also privileges national imagining that homogenizes how the film casts Sin and the agent as if they could have been the same kind of man if it were not for the Korean division. In sum, *Typhoon*'s story of the transformative effects of sibling love is part of a larger modern Korean script, a script that the director of *Typhoon*, Kwak, Kyung-taek, helped to cement in film with his earlier, much more highly acclaimed male-bonding film *Friends* (2001).

Over the Border travels where *Typhoon* leaves off and follows a North Korean into the South. Sun-ho, our main protagonist, strives to belong, to *possess* love, which means finding happiness in marriage, a good successful livelihood and acceptance as an ordinary person (a resident) wherever he resides. His border crossing that produces new affective ties complicates this struggle to belong rather than enabling its successful closure. Women in both films are mere instruments for the male actor who drives the plotline. Both filmic enactments also see their engagements with the divided Korea problem as transgressive, but ultimately close the circle of love, of belonging and the contours of a fulfilling liveable life.

A parallel and related argument made in this chapter is that South Korean blockbusters, a phenomenon of the 2000s, call into presence 'the international', which is a form of 'gazing back' by bodies objectified by privileged subjectivities for their self-realization. In other words, one way of reading the disparate South Korean filmic imaginations is as a world and network of subjectivities located in interconnected cultural, economic and political institutions – this is important in film, a powerful corporate industry – which were acted upon and gazed at, gazing back to create their own narratives, images and constellations of worlds.

Yang's film, *Our Homeland*, is technically not part of this South Korean film industry (her film was funded by a small Japanese production company), but similar uncritical alignment with the international can be seen expressed in not only her film, but also her public engagements. Throughout this chapter I tried to show how gazing back is not, first, an oppositional practice, and second, is not talking back from a more authentic or moral outside.

Nonetheless, Yang's three films and book about her family's homeland, or more accurately about the intimate relationships entangled with and by North Korea, are iterative love stories that articulate what remains mostly repressed in the first two films. Most significantly, Yang traverses the problem of hate that the national narrative of togetherness masks over; in my reading of Yang's engagement as a collection, I foreground the ambiguous, unstable order of hate and the implications of this to our understanding of love as a politically transformative concept. My reading of Yang's work is not to claim that it in itself ushers in political transformation. Transformation of the world takes the form of a promise held out to the viewer and remains off screen. Yang's engagement nonetheless offers an alternative site for rethinking how we can be drama queens about love, nation and North Korea without re-enclosing the radical contingency and discomfort that love opens up.

Yang is a drama queen, not the kind who succeeds in closure but in opening up contradictions, tensions and wounds and staying there. In her various press engagements in relation to *Our Homeland*, I have seen Yang cast herself as 'the trouble child' of her family and now of North Korea. She speaks about how she used to be afraid of how her work would harm her family in North Korea, but how she has *decided* to think differently – that it is her job to become more notorious. She does not expect the ban on her travel to North Korea to be lifted, which means that it is hard to imagine how she is to meet her family again, especially the affable niece and nephews we meet in her two documentaries. However, she continues in her ways. Her mischief is an expression of her love, of her radical attachment. She does not own her family in Pyongyang and they do not own her. I think this particular rupture is a potent site from which to pursue our negotiations with the sticky, binding nature of love/desire.

Notes

1 Controversy over kidnappings of Japanese residents by North Korea spurred a series of attacks and harassment of young Korean schoolgirls in Japan by Japanese men. These girls attended Korean schools and wore school uniforms of black and white Korean traditional wear which made their foreignness and connection to North Korea visible (the schools with this uniform were run by a citizen organization with ties to North Korea). They were targeted because they exhibited signs that allowed some to render these female bodies as worthless or stand-ins for what was threatening to the Japanese nation.

2 One important implication of this would be that Korean unification is de-centred as the most important task for Koreans, which is a position widely professed by Koreans in various promptings about the current state of affairs. I fail to unpack this issue fully in this chapter but my hunch is that it would produce a rich area for critical/alternative interventions.

3 Underexplored here is how the male bond across the enemy line also demands equality. In this final spectacular action sequence, Agent Kang becomes his own man and defies the chain of command (which is corrupt from US pressure) and prepares to intercept Sin on his own accord. Just like Sin, Agent Kang has become a rogue agent for his own cause, detached from statecraft. They are men who understand each other as humans, men, autonomous agents. This might be worth exploring further in future readings.

4 The insert has four pages of images from the film with in-laid texts about the film, the characters and the director. The quotation is my translation.

5 Yang's memoir is not available in English, so technically her book's title remains untranslated. The Korean title of the film *Our Homeland* translates as 'the country of my family', which is also the title of her memoir in Korean.

Bibliography

Films

Dear Pyongyang (2006) Directed by Yang, Yonghi, 134 minutes, Video Travel, DVD.
Friends (Chingu) (2001) Directed by Kwak, Kyung-taek, 113 minutes, Cineline 2.
The Front Line (2011) Directed by Jang, Hun, 133 minutes, Showbox Mediaplay, DVD.
Goodbye Pyongyang (2011) Directed by Yang, Yonghi, 81 minutes, Video Travel.

JSA: Joint Security Area (*Gongdong Gyeongbi Guyeok JSA*) (2000) Directed by Park, Chan-wook, 110 minutes, Myung Films, DVD.

Kureosing (2008) Directed by Kim, Tae-gyun, 107 minutes, Vantage Holdings, DVD.

Our Homeland (*Gajok-ui nara*) (2013) Directed by Yang, Yonghi, 100 minutes, DS Media and Miro Vision, DVD.

Over the Border (*Gukgyeing-ui namjok*) (2006) Directed by Ahn, Pan-suk, 109 minutes, Sidius Pictures, DVD.

Shiri (1999) Directed by Kang, Je-gyu, 121 minutes, Kang, Je-Kyu Film Co. Ltd. and Samsung Entertainment, DVD.

Typhoon (*Tae-poong*) (2007) Directed by Kwak, Kyung-taek, 124 minutes, Zininsa Film Production, DVD.

Books and articles

Agathangelou, Anna and Ling, L.M.H. (2004) 'The House of IR: From Family Power Politics to the Poisies of Worldism', *International Studies Review* 6: 21–49.

Ahmed, Sara (2000) *Strange Encounter: Embodied Others in Post-coloniality*, London: Routledge.

——(2003) 'In the Name of Love', *Borderlands e-journal* 2 (3), www.borderlands.net. au/vol2no3_2003/ahmed_love.htm (accessed April 2012).

——(2004) *The Cultural Politics of Emotion*, Edinburgh: Edinburgh University Press.

——(2010) *The Promise of Happiness*, Durham, NC: Duke University Press.

Berlant, Lauren (1997) *Queen of America Goes to Washington City: Essays on Sex and Citizenship*, Durham, NC: Duke University Press.

——(2000a) 'Love (a Queer Feeling)', in Tim Dean and Christopher Lane (eds) *Psychoanalysis and Homosexuality*, Chicago, IL: Chicago University Press.

——(2000b) 'The Subject of True Feeling: Pain, Privacy and Politics', in Maureen McNeil (ed.) *Transformations: Thinking Through Feminism*, Florence, KY: Routledge.

——(2007/08) 'Cruel Optimism: On Marx, Loss and the Senses', *New Formations* 63: 33–50.

——(2008) *The Female Complaint: The Unfinished Business of Sentimentality in American Culture*, Durham, NC: Duke University Press.

——(2011) 'A Properly Political Concept of Love: Three Approaches in Ten Pages', *Cultural Anthropology* 26 (4): 683–91.

Bleiker, Roland (2005) *Divided Korea: Toward a Culture of Reconciliation*, Minneapolis: University of Minnesota Press.

Bleiker, Roland and Hoang, Young-ju (2011) 'Korean Sources of Conflict Resolution: An Inquiry into the Concept of Han', in Morgan Brigg and Roland Bleiker (eds) *Mediating Across Difference: Oceanic and Asian Approaches to Conflict Resolution*, Honolulu: University of Hawai'i.

Bowman, Paul (ed.) (2010) *The Rey Chow Reader*, New York: Columbia University Press.

Brooks, Peter (1976) *The Melodramatic Imagination: Balzac, Henry James, Melodrama, and the Mode of Excess*, New Haven, CT: Yale University Press.

Choi, Jinhee (2010) *The South Korean Film Renaissance: Local Hitmakers, Global Provocateurs*, Middletown, CT: Wesleyan University Press.

Choi, Shine (2013) 'Love's Cruel Promises: Love, Unity and North Korea', *International Feminist Journal of Politics*, www.tandfonline.com/doi/abs/10.1080/14616742.2013. 790656#.Uz4syPmSxPM.

Chung, Hye Sung (2005) 'Toward a Strategic Korean Cinephilia: A Transnational Detournement of Hollywood Melodrama', in Kathleen McHugh and Nancy Abelman (eds) *South Korean Golden Age Melodrama*, Detroit, MI: Wayne State University Press.

Crouch, David (2010) *Flirting with Space: Journeys and Creativity*, Surrey: Ashgate.

Dillon, Michael (1999) 'The Scandal of the Refugee: Some Reflections on the "Inter" of the International Relations and Continental Thought', in David Campbell and Michael J. Shapiro (eds) *Global Ethics*, Minneapolis: Minnesota University Press.

Evans, Mary (2002) *Love: An Unromantic Discussion*, Cambridge: Polity.

Gledhill, Christine (2000) 'Rethinking Genre', in Christine Gledhill and Linda Williams (eds) *Rethinking Film Studies*, London: Edward Arnold.

Hendrick, Susan and Hendrick, Clyde (1992) *Romantic Love*, London: Sage.

Hirsch, Jennifer and Wardlow, Holly (eds) (2006) *Modern Loves: The Anthropology of Romantic Courtship and Companionate Marriage*, Ann Arbor: University of Michigan Press.

Illouz, Eva (1997) *Consuming the Romantic Utopia: Love and the Cultural Contradictions of Capitalism*, Berkeley, CA: University of California Press.

Inayatullah, Naeem and Blaney, David L. (2004) *International Relations and the Problem of Difference*, London: Routledge.

Jager, Sheila Miyoshi (1998) 'Woman and the Promise of Modernity: Sign of Love for the Nation in Korea', *New Literary History* 29: 121–34.

——(2002) 'Monumental Histories: Manliness, the Military, and the War Memorial', *Public Culture* 14 (2): 387–409.

Kim, Kyung Hyun (2004) *The Remasculinization of Korean Cinema*, Durham, NC: Duke University Press.

Kim, Samuel S. (ed.) (2004b) *Inter-Korea Relations: Problems and Prospects*, New York: Palgrave Macmillan.

Kim, Soyoung (2001) 'Introduction' (*Somun*), in Kim, Soyoung (ed.) *Korean Blockbuster: Atlantis or Perhaps America* (*Hanguk-hyeong Blockbuster: Atlantis hok-eun America*), Seoul: Hyeonshil Culture Research.

Kim, Suk-young (2010) *Illusive Utopia: Theatre, Film and Everyday Performances in North Korea*, Ann Arbor: Michigan University Press.

Kim, Suna (2006) *South Korean Cinema, A Strange Boundary: The Korean New Wave and State, Sexuality, Translation and Cinema in an Era of Korean Blockbusters* (*Hanguk Yeonghwa ra-neun Natsun Gyeong-gae: Korean New Wave-wa Hanguk-hyeong Blockbuster Sidae-eui Gukga, Sexuality, Beun-yeok, Yeonghwa*), Seoul: Communication Books.

Kim, Sun-Young (2007) 'Crossing the Border to the "Other" Side: Dynamics of Interaction between North and South Koreans in *Spy Li Cheol-jin* and *Joint Security Area*', in Frances Gateward (ed,) *Seoul Searching: Culture and Identity in Contemporary Korean Cinema*, Albany, NY: State University of New York Press.

Kwak, Kyung-taek (2007) 'Cinema that Shows Humans: Film Director Kwang, Kyung-taek' (*Saram-eul boyojuneun Yonghwa: yonghwa gamdok Kwak Kyung Taek*), in Indiecom Cinema, Kim, Young-seok, Cho, Jin, Cho, Tae-young, Lee, Mijin (eds) *Cinema Factory of Hope: The Journey of Korean Cinema* (*Cinema-gongjang-eui Hwimang: Hanguk-yonghwa Gil-eul Naseoda*), Paju: Hangilsa.

Langford, Wendy (1999) *Revolutions of the Heart: Gender, Power and the Delusions of Love*, London: Routledge.

Lee, Young-jae (2001) 'Alibis of Male Mythology, Nostalgia in the Shade of Yellow' (*Namsong Shinhwa-eui Alibi, Guribit Nostalgia*), in Kim, Soyoung (ed.) *Korean*

Blockbuster: Atlantis or Perhaps America (Hanguk-hyeong Blockbuster: Atlantis hok-eun America), Seoul: Hyeonshil Culture Research.

Lie, John (2008) *Zainichi (Koreans in Japan): Diasporic Nationalism and Postcolonial Identity*, Berkeley, CA: Global, Area, and International Archive, University of California.

Lopez, Alfred (2005) *Postcolonial Whiteness: A Critical Reader on Race and Empire*, Albany, NY: State University of New York.

McHugh, Kathleen and Abelmann, Nancy (eds) (2005) *South Korean Golden Age Melodrama: Gender, Genre, and National Cinema*, Detroit, MI: Wayne State University Press.

Neale, Stephen (2000) *Genre and Hollywood*, London: Routledge.

Park, Chan-wook (2007) 'The Stylist that Does Not Change: Film Director Park Chan-wook' (*Byeonhwa-ji an-eun stylist: yonghwa-gamdok Park Chan-wook*), in Indiecom Cinema, Kim, Young-seok, Cho, Jin, Cho, Tae-young, Lee, Mijin (eds) *Cinema Factory of Hope: The Journey of Korean Cinema* (*Cinema-gongjang-eui Hwimang: Hanguk-yonghwa Gil-eul Naseoda*), Paju: Hangilsa.

Parquet, Darcy (2009) *New Korean Cinema: Breaking the Waves*, London: Wallflower.

Pearce, Lynne (2006) *Romance Writing*, Cambridge: Polity Press.

Pearce, Lynne and Stacey, Jackie (eds) (1995) *Romance Revisited*, London: Lawrence and Wishart.

Positions (2008) 'Taking it to Heart: Emotion, Modernity, Asia', special issue 16 (2).

Povinelli, Elizabeth (1998) 'The State of Shame: Australian Multiculturalism and the Crisis of Indigenous Citizenship', *Critical Inquiry* 24 (2): 575–610.

——(2006) *The Empire of Love: Toward a Theory of Intimacy, Genealogy, and Carnality*, Durham, NC: Duke University Press.

Pratt, Mary Louise (1992) *Imperial Eyes: Travel Writing and Transculturation*, London: Routledge.

Rajaram, Prem K. (2004) 'Disruptive Writing and a Critique of Territoriality', *Review of International Studies* 30: 201–28.

Rajaram, Prem and Grundy-Warr, Carl (2007) *Borderscapes: Hidden Geographies and Politics at Territory's Edge*, Minneapolis: University of Minnesota Press.

Ryang, Sonia (1997) *North Koreans in Japan: Language, Ideology and Identity*, Oxford: Westview Press.

——(2006) *Love in Modern Japan: Its Estrangement from Self, Sex and Society*, London: Routledge.

Shapiro, Michael J. and Alker, Hayward R. (eds) (1996) *Challenging Boundaries: Global Flows, Territorial Identities*, Minneapolis: University of Minnesota Press.

Shumway, David (2003) *Modern Love: Romance, Intimacy, and the Marriage Crisis*, New York: New York University Press.

Smith, James L. (1973) *Melodrama*, London: Methuen.

Soguk, Nevzak (1999) *States and Strangers: Refugees and Displacements of Statecraft*, Minneapolis: University of Minnesota Press.

——(2006) 'Splinters of Hegemony: Ontopoetical Visions in International Relations', *Alternatives: Global, Local, Political* 31: 377–404.

Thrift, Nigel and Dewsbury, John-David (2000) 'Dead Geographies – and How to Make them Live', *Environment and Planning D: Society and Space* 18: 411–32.

Trinh, Minh-ha (1989) *Woman, Native, Other: Writing Postcoloniality and Feminism*, Bloomington and Indianapolis: Indiana University Press.

——(1992) *Framer Framed*, London: Routledge.

——(1999) *Cinema Interval*, London: Routledge.

——(2005) *Digital Film Event*, London: Routledge.

——(2011) *Elsewhere Within Here: Immigration, Refugeeism and the Boundary Event*, Abingdon: Routledge.

Walker, R.B.J. (1993) *Inside/Outside: International Relations as Political Theory*, Cambridge: Cambridge University Press.

Williams, Linda (1998) 'Melodrama Revised', in Nick Browne (ed.) *Refiguring American Film Genres: History and Theory*, Berkeley, CA: University of California Press.

Wylie, John (2007) *Landscape*, London: Routledge.

Yang, Yonghi (2013a) *The Country of My Family* (*Gajok-ui Nara*), Jang, Minju (trans.), Seoul: Hankyore.

——(2013b) 'Our Homeland', Post-Screening Q&A in Asia Society, 3 August, asiasociety.org/video/arts/our-homeland-post-screening-q-complete (accessed January 2014).

Yoo, Hyon Joo (2012) *Cinema at the Crossroads: Nation and the Subject in East Asian Cinema*, Plymouth: Lexington Books.

5 Objecting objects
Be(com)ing North Koreans in an affective world

And I find that I am actively avoiding learning more about North Korea because I feel like that if I become the expert on it then suddenly I'll become the disembodied voice on CNN over the map of the country like, [switches to a voice with an 'Asian accent'] 'Situation very dire. We're very concerned about the Demilitarisation [sic] Zone'.

(Margaret Cho: Assassin, 2005)

Introduction

Previous chapters questioned narratives and images that construct 'North Korea' as a problem that compelled exclusion and extermination of that which could not be transformed, embraced or accepted into our prevailing conceptions of the world and the self. These chapters also introduced examples that contradict, complicate and even shift away from the dominant framings that construct North Korea as an object of 'our' knowledge and action. The argument has been that alternative frameworks and points of departure, modes and preoccupations can potentially have transformative effects on intercultural encounters that value coevality and co-presence. This chapter more explicitly turns to narratives produced by North Koreans themselves to interrogate how survival as a 'North Korean defector' is negotiated in sites of self-representation: memoir writing and autobiography.[1] As the Korean-American comedian Margaret Cho performatively demonstrates, expertise and authentic voice in sites of self-representation are disembodying and alienating subject positions that require creative, nonsensical and contradictory manoeuvres to outsmart and outlive experiences of disembodiment and alienation.

As I began discussing in previous chapters, turning to 'North Koreans themselves' is a difficult and deeply fraught move. When we turn to North Korean productions 'themselves', they powerfully mobilize narratives of authenticity and claim by some – often those with first-hand experience – to a privileged relationship with authority and knowledge. Efforts to distinguish the authentic 'real' from the manipulated/ing North Korean(ns) often effectively constrains how North Koreans speak, act and become political subjects. Desire to overcome the mediated nature of North Korean voices always and inescapably opens up another dimension of mediation. In short, authenticity and the real are ways of disciplining how North Korean agency is possible; they are ways of allowing 'North Korea' to exist in this world on 'our' terms. While fraught, I believe this turn to North Korean self-representation is also necessary. After all, the goal of this critical examination of 'our' construction of North Korea – as enigmatic, dangerous and suffering – which reveals how it does violence to North Korea(ns) 'themselves' is ultimately to foreground the agency of the Other. This foregrounding is a strategy of heterogenizing and recognizing multiplicity, plural agencies and contingency from a perspective that takes issues of positions, relations and intercultural differences seriously. While North Korean agency has been a concern in previous chapters (e.g. in privileging heterogeneity and co-survival of both the 'we' and the 'Other'), this chapter is an effort to foreground North Korean narratives more concertedly to understand processes of mediation, translation and creation in these particular sites of politics.

I argue that defector memoirs are sites of intercultural communication and understanding, which demand change in, and reformulation of, existing political reality both inside and outside North Korea. Mindful of how such demands for change and reformulation can have depoliticizing effects, the first section examines the survivor-and-witness subjectivity in self-representational practices that engage in cross-cultural communication. I suggest that survivor-witness memoirs are necessarily acts of translation which (re)create their stories of hardship to make demands on publics and publicity on behalf of those who suffered and continue to suffer. Building on previous chapters, I problematize empathy as the object that organizes these intercultural communications. I show how seeking empathy from outsiders and the emphasis placed on outsider action create pain and loss of their own. To trouble this dominance of empathy as an object that structures intercultural communicative encounters, I introduce the concept of 'third scenarios' to expand on what North Korean agency means and how alternative terms of demanding and inciting change take form.

The second section begins by showing how testimonials of survival, namely Kang, Chol-hwan's *The Aquariums of Pyongyang* (2001) and Hwang, Jang-yop's *The Memoir of Hwang, Jang-yop* (2006) are narratives that attempt to secure the Western and South Korean public's empathy. They do this to secure redemption and recovery, not only in relation to the political situation of North Korea(ns), but also in their personal lives. I examine the problematic ways in which narratives of redemption, salvation and rescue foreclose efforts to recover what was lost and recover from the trauma of that loss.

My turn to Choi, Zini's *The Woman who Crossed the Border Thrice* (2005) in the last section attempts to show how her story of survival helps us to re-imagine the rather narrowly constructed intercultural encounter that survivor memoirs traditionally allow. Thus, I read Choi's memoir for its effectiveness as a translative act that critically and creatively negotiates not only loss and suffering in intercultural contexts, but also the site of her action. I examine how Choi's engagements produce 'new' political subjectivities that generate 'third scenarios' for the 'North Korea problem'.

'Speak out'

In his memoir, Kang, Chol-hwan makes an urgent appeal that we 'speak out against barbarity [taking place inside North Korea]' (Kang 2001: xii). The strength of Kang's plea is its mode – the speaking out about North Korea through the telling of his personal story as a victim-survivor of atrocities. It points to how memoirs are vehicles and spaces for generating publicity. Here I am using publicity as Lauren Berlant uses the term to emphasize how 'the public' is not a stable space or social entity (understood in opposition to 'the private sphere' and 'the individual') that establishes a community or identity through politics of inclusion and exclusion (Berlant 2008; Berlant and Warner 1998). Rather, it is a social or collective 'world-making project' that binds 'more people together than can be identified, more spaces than can be mapped beyond a few reference points, modes of feeling that can be learned rather than experienced as a birthright' (Berlant and Warner 1998: 558). A social 'world-making project' mediates, and is significantly mediated by, attachments, promises and affect. While creating a sense of feeling that the prevailing norms and infrastructures express a pre-existing shared common-ality, in actuality publicity and publics are collective productions-always-in-process. They are always in the process of expressing and being expressed, and of producing and being produced, driven by desires to belong, to be social, to be 'good', to live a 'good life', to live. In other words, the public figure of the victim-witness and the empathic stories that serve as evidence of human rights violations are involved in a mediated and mediating *affective* network. This affective network is less of a locatable space and more a set of imaginary worlds that are always on the move. It makes sense then that publicity, i.e. the public-ness of a social context, of stories of survival and of a subject position, is emotionally charged and seeks to attach and be attached. It also makes sense that storytelling and narratives are central to the public and political.

However, perhaps because of their always-in-process form, these affective networks are 'enter[ed] without a high bar of self-consistency but with enor-mous needs to hammer out bearable and just principles of convergence' (Berlant and Prosser 2011: 185). This enormous need for normative con-vergence means that claiming public-ness involves translating personal his-tories of lived and embodied experiences of social harm into collective injustices that constrain, discipline and demand homologous stories (Baxi 2000: 38–39). North Korean defectors must tell their personal stories in a mediated and mediating language of human rights or national solidarity to claim value, for example as subjects of human rights. This is to assert the public-ness of their lives as a matter of collective redress rather than just a private problem or a product of individual circumstances. My point is that the identity 'North Korean defector' – the public figure and bearer of suffering – is constructed through the performance of telling one's story. This performance itself effects a complex network of publicity or publics that does not have 'a high bar of self-consistency' or coherence (Berlant and Prosser 2011: 185). The question, then, is how can stories enlisting and enlisted by human rights or other political frameworks that demand intervention from 'over here' to change the reality 'over there' politicize the manner in which they produce and become a 'public' in this intercultural context? How and why do these stories often fail to translate their survival stories into the stuff that can transform and create a social that reflects the in-between-ness that results in such storytelling and receiving? What lessons can we learn from such failures, and how can we identify more promising performances of survival?

Speaking out across cultures

Gillian Whitlock (2007: 13) makes the point that autobiography, couched in terms of human rights and social justice campaigns, is the 'transit lane for these life narratives to move from East to West rapidly'. For me, this statement invites the question, why should this be the case? Why are autobiography and, more broadly, life narratives 'couched' in human rights and social justice frameworks so popular and powerful in shaping the terms of intercultural relations?[2] Where can I go to see this transit lane from East to West, and why does it seem a one-way road?

The movement from 'East' to 'West' trades in pain, suffering and loss that exist 'over there', which 'the public' located 'over here' can supposedly do something about. Because political memoirs are life narratives driven by the desire to communicate and induce understanding *across cultures* about experiences of unjust treatment and degradation, it is useful to understand them centrally as translations of suffering and the self. As discussed in previous chapters, translations are creative manoeuvres of survival and continuation of life in a postcolonial world, where multiple worlds and cultures demand simultaneous presence, visibility and articulation. Acts of translation use the 'original' to create things that are neither new nor the same as the 'original'. They are acts of creating anew in a different medium and for a different end which privilege the transmission process (the form), rather than what is transmitted (the content). However, as also argued in Chapter 3 for photographic encounters, the dichotomous and reductive enactment of suffering – as something that exists over there that non-suffering people over here can alleviate – in intercultural communications produces a perennial hierarchy between the West and the East (or, in my formulation, the international and North Korea). Self-narration can produce particular versions of translations of suffering, survival and loss that enact this dichotomy in a way that is uniquely possible in the autobiographic convention centred on authenticity and truth. In other words, particular cultural resources available in self-narration might be behind the smooth trade in pain from 'East' to 'West'.

To begin, the 'original' in political memoirs is the 'true' suffering experience of the memoirist that supposedly demands a particular kind of response. As Schaffer and Smith (2004a: 6) put it, '[storytellers] hope for an audience willing to acknowledge the truthfulness of the story and to accept an ethical responsibility to both story and teller'. My question here is, what if truthfulness that stakes claims on the narrative and identity of the sufferer constrains this 'ethical responsibility to both story and teller'? This question especially arises in the widespread collaboration between a charismatic member of a collective and an empathetic professional writer to enable the transit from 'East' to 'West' (Smith and Watson 2001: 54; Goldman 1993; Whitlock 2007; Schaffer and Smith 2004b: 60–62; Eakin 1999: 172–75). These collaborations use a particular 'journalistic' convention of telling truths, or rather, of storytelling and representation of the self. Here, first-person narratives, even when the 'collaboration' is acknowledged in the periphery of the book (usually in the form of a 'behind the scenes story' by the professional writer in an introductory essay), are produced to effect singularity and deliver a coherent experience of survival, social harm and injustice. In short, for life narratives to function 'as persuasive global carriers of the "rights discourse"', experiences must be presented as things that are owned by persons. They operate with the assumption that experiences are best recounted by the person who has lived through the experience (Whitlock 2007: 117; also Smith and Watson 2001: 30).

Part of what powerfully structures the unfolding of life narratives in human rights discourse is the legacy of the Holocaust as the 'limit case' for representation, thought and memory (Felman and Laub 1992; Langer 1991, 1996; Liss 1998; Smith and Watson 2001; Bennett and Kennedy 2003; *Poetics Today* 2006, special issue; Peters 2001). As Felman and Laub (1992: 57) put it, 'The victim's narrative – the very process of bearing witness to massive trauma – does indeed begin with someone who testifies to an absence, to an event that has not yet come into existence, in spite of the overwhelming and compelling nature of the reality of its occurrence'. Important here is how trauma is the 'limit', i.e. the impossible experience or absence that testimonies bear witness to, and we listen to witness testimonials for this 'limit'. However, two elements are privileged in these studies despite their attention to fragments, silences and margins. These are, first, the foundational victim/perpetrator dichotomy and the attendant binaries of protector/protected, innocence/guilt, action/inaction that enable a coherent political strategy and narrative to emerge; and second, the idea that telling and listening to testimonies helps survivors and listeners to *rehabilitate, recover and heal*. Centred on the victim status of the storyteller, translations about survival in intercultural communications predominantly occur with *empathy* as the object of translations, where the authenticity of the story and storyteller is intertwined with the innocence of the communicative vehicles. This is to assume *some other rehabilitative space for those who enter the testimonial circle*, composed solely of subject positions that are either victims or bystanders, and survivor-witness or audience of the witness testimony. It is a circle that firmly excludes or condemns the 'perpetrator' and the 'guilty' to achieve rehabilitation of the victim in the collective processes of remembrance, recognition and mourning. Here, through the idea of testimony, an empathetic circle around the testimony is formed. Empathy is the affective glue that holds together this new collective formation of innocent people who condemn the perpetrators and embrace the victims.

The problem of empathy

Translation and intercultural communication that seek to incite and demand empathetic responses are limiting because they mostly empower the addressee and the addressed but with questionable effects on those in whose name empathy is evoked. This is partly a problem that accompanies the idea of testimony, which seeks to render survivor stories and memoirs sacred and beyond dispute. This reverence leads to an authoritarianism of the victim-survivor-suffering subject position that casts certain questions as off-limits.[3] While an empathetic relationship between survivor and listener privileges the idea of 'sharing' the experience of pain, the political achievement of 'sharing' the experience of pain needs a more sustained interrogation. Many scholars have discussed the limits and risks of empathetic listening and have examined the problem of substitution and identification with the victim-survivor that is at the heart of empathetic reading and listening (e.g. Boler 1997; Bennett 2003; Whitlock 2007; Heckner 2008; Liss 1998). These critics recognize that empathy often has a way of empowering the privileged consumer of life narratives and making us as readers and viewers feel good about ourselves (through donations, signing petitions, etc.). Their critical concern nonetheless solely remains with empathy arguing that it can lead to a more reflective and transformative encounter and can occur without usurping the place of the testimony and the historical referent the speaker and listener come together to remember. For instance, Heckner (2008) suggests that a 'postmemory' that avoids identification with victims (which too easily leads to 'identity theft') holds out a form of empathetic remembering that is pedagogical and attentive to the otherness of the remembered. Liss (1998) argues that part of what needs to occur is the creation of more space (in museum exhibitions among others) to acknowledge the guardians and translators involved in representing the Shoah. These postmodern approaches that recognize the impossibilities in representation of trauma, horror and pain are echoed in studies of women's life writing and postcolonial autobiography (e.g. Miller 2007; Hornung and Ruhe 1998).

In short, the assumption in much of the scholarship on testimonials and memorializing is that remembering and mourning in more ethical ways, i.e. making empathy more ethical, are our main tasks. Here, rehabilitation, social change and learning from history and suffering occur from sites of *our* agency which do not do enough to pluralize the source of agency and attend to the agency of what/who were lost in seeking alternative terms of enacting publics. The hierarchic terms of a testimonial world-making project that unwittingly privileges 'over here' above 'over there' does not attend to the agency of the object of the public's empathy.

In Chapter 3 I discussed how empathy has a way of constraining the stories of suffering and reifying the agency and space of those who enter the public. What concerns me here is what happens to the object of the public's empathy. While survivors can enact this public, and this enactment can be rewarding and 'rehabilitative' for them, I ask what the effect of this public is on those who continue to suffer or lost their lives. I am not asking what this testimonial public does for the lost lives, which would be to assume that the public can and must save the damned, i.e. act upon what is deemed the Other. Instead, my question relates to how this public – the publicity of the survival stories – can be enacted nearby, in relation to and together with the Other. In other words, how can survival stories effect change without reifying the easy hierarchic, world-making practices? At the heart of the problem is that lost lives, and the loss that the stories try to recover by bringing the survivor and listener together in the first place, remain that: a loss, an object of our action. The narrative and the socio-political structures that create this sense of loss – and indeed *require* this sense of loss in order to experience mourning and empathy – remain untransformed. My point is that when we stay within the idea of empathy in responding to North Korean defector memoirs, it is a way of staying attached to, and in proximity with, a limited framework of change. All the while, it is to maintain and expand 'our' thinking-acting space, rather than pluralizing the spaces of thinking, acting, identity construction and the sources of change and meaning. Importantly, suffering again remains underdeveloped as a site, a practice, an enactment that can disrupt the hierarchies of storytelling and pluralize the direction, form and mode of world-making projects.

Just because empathy is corrupt does not mean it must be withheld. Feelings are sticky, clustered, attached and attaching, as argued most concertedly in Chapter 4, on love (also, Berlant 2007/08; Ahmed 2010), and for this reason my argument is not directed at what *we* – those who demand empathy as well as those who give it – should do to control, discipline and re-appropriate our empathetic responses. My argument concerns how alternative practices of world making must recognize the intercultural dimensions of such world-making projects. Reshaping empathy and its effects is only one dimension and world making is composed of much larger tasks. Here, I am here arguing for *pluralizing* world-making as a foundational dimension of world making. To pluralize world making and foreground how world making is a pluralizing project, we must fully attend to issues of multiplicity, in-between-ness and other issues of intercultural relations. Trinh's articulation of the void serves as a useful inroad:

> I would make the difference between the negative notion of the void, which is so typical of the kind of dualist thinking pervasively encountered

in the West, and the spiritual Void thanks to which possibilities keep on renewing, hence nothing can be simply classified, arrested, and reified. There is this incredible fear of nonaction in modern society, and every empty space has to be filled up, blocked, occupied, talked about.

(Trinh 1999: 222)

For Trinh, the void is not emptiness and absence, nor is it associated with ideas of inertness and death. In using the term 'spiritual Void', Trinh wants to introduce dynamism, creativity and vitality of the void and, for that matter, emptiness, inertness and other states of being that are associated with 'the end' and 'nothingness'. More useful than Trinh's re-appropriation of the void, however, is how her resistance to dualist thinking – this playful construction ('spiritual Void') – is then deployed to keep the referent of her theory (in this specific case, 'China') open, plural and pluralizing. In a way, the referent is merely a point of departure, a site from which specifically and tactilely to empty out representations that mediate world making. It is to recognize and put to use the ways in which representations are always in process, always in the making, being experienced, being emptied out, continually (re)constituted and re-appropriated for transformative projects.

Void, voiding, pluralizing, emptying out: these are the stuff of the 'third scenario' (Trinh 1991: 153). The 'third' here gestures to an important shift in which the site of theory moves from the self, the visible and the appropriate, *not* to its binary opposite (i.e. the other, the invisible, the inappropriate), but rather to an in-between where conventional rules and binaries do not apply. Trinh writes, 'The challenge of the hyphenated reality lies in the hyphen itself: the *becoming* Asian-American; the realm in-between, where predetermined rules cannot fully apply' (Trinh 1991: 157, emphasis in original). This freedom from rules is important to Trinh because it allows her both to challenge the established rules that ensure the West's 'global domination' (i.e. it allows her to be critical and follow her own critical stance), but it also allows her the space and freedom to create worlds that are not beholden to or bound by this domination. Trinh here is highlighting the power asymmetry between 'Asia' ('East') and 'America' ('West') which disciplines *how* cross-cultural mixing takes place and reinstates the West's privileged position as rule maker, cultural connoisseur and beacon of all that is good. To displace this hierarchy, what is needed is not so much a critical attitude towards the emerging hyphenated Others, but a becoming and inhabitation of the hyphen itself. Becoming a hyphen is the third scenario that marks a shift in the terms of reality making, and from which alternative terms of intercultural realities, encounters and relations come into being. This is not an entrance of a new reality or space; rather, the third scenario is a constant becoming without ever having arrived or been created. Edward Soja's discussion of Lefebvre's *The Production of Space* puts the idea of 'third' this way:

Thirding introduces a critical 'other-than' choice that speaks and critiques through its otherness. That is to say, it does not derive simply from an additive combination of its binary antecedents but rather from a disordering, deconstruction, and tentative reconstitution of their presumed totalization producing an open alternative that is both similar and strikingly different.

(Soja 1996: 61)

Particularly resonant here is how 'and-ness' and 'otherness' of 'the other-than choice' are not actually additive to what is presided as their 'antecedents', but are simultaneous and both similar to and different from in their inappropriateness, disorder, critique and tentatively created alternative scenarios. Trinh's and Soja's articulations can be read to resonate with each other, but turning to Trinh's idea of the third scenario is significant for the particular images, stories and bodies that she brings into focus – images, stories and bodies that are often occluded even by the critical thinkers with whom she has an affinity. For example, Trinh trains her attention on various Asian-American poetry and artist woes, Vietnamese proverbs, African novelists, and is focused on these various forms *simultaneously*. The focus of her theory and her theorizing – the site of intercultural encounter – is a contingent ground from which multiple voices speak that signal more pluralist directions and modes that world making should and can travel.

'Help us to save our North Korean compatriots'

North Korean defectors Kang, Chol-hwan and Hwang, Jang-yop made their personal stories public to galvanize the world to act and help to alleviate the plight of the North Korean people. Both believe this to be possible only with the deposing of the Kim regime and the opening up of North Korea.[4] I look at these two memoirs for what they have in common, namely, how they are tales of defection from North Korea in search of liberation (though how this is defined differs). In both memoirs, narratives of loss and recovery foreground the need to remember loss and recount suffering. Kang, Chol-hwan's *The Aquariums in Pyongyang* is one of the earliest defector memoirs and is the most widely 'invoked' of all North Korean survivor accounts, which serves as an illustrative example to centre the discussion in this chapter.[5] I turn to Hwang, Jang-yop's *The Memoir of Hwang, Jang-yop* (*Hwang Jang-yop Hwe-gorok*) for how it allows us to see the basic survival narrative structure play out in an elite North Korean philosopher/politician's communicative act. In contrast to Kang, Hwang presents his story and the terms of achieving his goal to liberate North Korea in a language that emphasizes his autonomy and position as a highly respected political actor and insider.

Telling life stories

While written in the first-person voice of Kang the survivor, *The Aquariums* is a collaborative project with the French journalist Pierre Rigoulot,[6] who reconstructed the story from his long drawn-out and intimate interview with Kang. The memoir speaks – in Kang's voice – of surviving ten years in a 're-education labour camp'. His family banished when he was nine years old for the mysterious 'sins' of his grandfather, Kang survives starvation, abuse, cruelty and an inhumane existence. Once released from the camp, he again gets in trouble with the authorities, forcing him either to defect or face a return to the camps. This was a life or death decision: staying and going back to the labour camps meant death, a point Kang makes through explicit analogies to the gulags of the former USSR and the concentration camps of Nazi Germany (Kang 2001: xii, also 40, 100).

In contrast, Hwang, Jang-yop's *The Memoir* tells a story of suffering and cruelty from the other end of power, as a former member of the ruling elite who has grown morally disgusted by his circle. Hwang's memoir can be seen as a conventional political memoir, in the sense that the narrator portrays himself to be 'a well-placed political diarist ... [providing] information on contemporary history long before the official documentation becomes accessible' (Egerton 1994b: 344; also see Egan 1987).[7] Echoing this emphasis on accessing elite history, Hwang narrates the development and decay of North Korean society from his insider position as chancellor of the Kim Il Sung University and in Party machinery as chairman of the Supreme People's Assembly and secretary of international affairs for the Korea Worker's Party. Hwang narrates how he decides to turn his dissent into political action which, for him, necessitated taking the unstable and immoral situation in the North 'to a bigger arena and try[ing] to work with our South Korean compatriots by leaving the North to save our nation from its misery' (Hwang 2006: 21). Hwang defected to South Korea in 1997 at the age of 74 and received much attention from the South Korean and international public (see Federation of American Scientists 1997). Hwang published his eponymous memoir in 1998, and a revised version, which this chapter examines, was published in 2006 with a new preface and a chapter reflecting on his ten years in exile.

While the two memoirs similarly see the North Korean state as a source of oppression and suffering and tell coherent life stories that support this vision, they impose coherence in different ways. Moreover, by giving coherent accounts of what they survived and/or witnessed in North Korea, the lives of these authors are intimately linked to their survival as defectors. The argument I put forward is that these coherent narratives about North Korea and their personal pasts perform the double function of mobilizing support to save other North Koreans *and* justifying their decisions to defect as *unambiguous*. My reading of these memoirs is that telling their North Korean life stories is an effort to come to terms with their own defection as much as it is an effort to make people care about the suffering in North Korea.

His family forms an integral part of Kang's testimonial against North Korea: his grandparents were duped into emigrating from Japan by the North Korean authorities and the process of their slow disillusionment, with their banishment, turns into bitter resentment. Kang sees the creation of communist North Korea as a sham and writes, 'Like its counterparts all over the world, the KWP [Korean Worker's Party] showed a formidable knack for creating associations with the allure of democracy and openness to the general public' (Kang 2001: 16). For Kang, North Korea's ideology was a fascist lie from the very beginning that 'everyone' in his family came to denounce, even his grandmother, who was the most fervent believer in communism and was the force behind the family's emigration from Japan. Kang admits that his grandmother never denounced communist ideals but she did not think North Korea embodied them. Kang writes, 'I think it was only then [when they were banished] that she truly realized she'd been had ... She now saw the regime as closer to Hitler's world than anything Marx or Lenin had envisioned' (ibid.: 101). A slight difference in position between Kang and his grandmother opens up here, but Kang does not explore this or the ambiguity that emerges through the other 'minor' characters in his family story such as his younger sister, Mi-ho, whom he 'abandons' when he defects, his mother, who was not sent with the rest of the family to banishment in Yodok because she was a daughter of a revolutionary, and his father. While Kang expresses guilt for leaving Mi-ho behind in North Korea, she remains largely silent in the memoir, never expressing any opinions about North Korea that could explain Kang's guilt. His mother, with whom he re-establishes a good relationship after his release, is an equally mysterious figure whom Kang admits he does not understand. Kang writes, 'I hope my mother isn't angry with me now for having left the country, and I hope she understands me better than I understand her' (ibid.: 169). When writing about his father's peaceful death not long after their release, Kang contradicts his larger narrative and reflects, 'The ten years he spent in the camp were lost years, no question about it – full of hardship and longing for his wife – but they were also strangely peaceful' (ibid.: 165). An interesting statement, but Kang's narrative barely pauses.

The larger narrative is that North Korea's communist project is deceptive and misery producing, just like every other communist project that has come to an end. Pronouncements to this effect occur numerous times, for instance in Kang's explanation of the Japanese residents who volunteered to be 'repatriated' to North Korea, which:

> mostly demonstrates the force of human illusion and its awesome power to render us utterly blind. I have since learned that at other latitudes and at other times, the same Communist powers created similar traps for making people believe and hope in illusions. This led to the misery of countless peoples: in France, in America, in Egypt, and perhaps most notably, in Armenia.
>
> (Kang 2001: 24)

I am not suggesting that these historic examples and the case of repatriated Koreans from Japan did not produce misery, false hope and blindness. However, I am suggesting that there are more nuanced and contingent histories to be told of these events and lives than the triumphalist neoliberal rewriting of communist history deployed by Kang, which sees communism as the product of a mass delusional euphoria which has produced nothing but suffering (see for instance Chen 2010).

The narrative coherence of Hwang's story comes from his identity as a philosopher. Hwang left North Korea after much philosophical reflection. As an intellectual it was his duty to act upon his conviction and voice his dissent against Kim Jong-il and his acolytes. For Hwang, North Korea began to crumble when politicians stopped caring about the people, stopped listening to intellectuals, and failed to seek philosophical rigour for their political project (Hwang 2006: 219, 228). Instead of due political processes, North Korea was ruled by 'Kim Jong-il who, with a mindset of a feudal lord, judged people solely by how much power someone had' (ibid.: 340). In Hwang's humanist philosophy (explained later), he speaks of the political project of democratizing a unified Korea and sees the problem of North Korea to require genuine democratization as its solution. Oddly, Hwang's book ends on the question of what makes a great man. Titled, 'Independent mind and creative wisdom', in the chapter, Hwang tries to explain what makes a man great by way of historical examples. What is behind this chapter in a memoir about his life in North Korea and his defection? What is behind the privileging of independence, creativity and great men? The chapter is especially interesting for Hwang's exaggerated authoritative tone. In the pages that follow, I argue that this unambiguous narrative reveals an anxiety regarding his inability to ensure that his preferred interpretation of his defection, or his account of the North Korean regime – in effect, his legacy – will prevail. My point is that the critique of the North Korean political elite and justification for his personal decision to defect are inescapably linked. Hwang brushes over this through the use of philosophical language to explain his decision.

Claims by Hwang and Kang that they acted in fear of history's judgement, or out of necessity, imply that their decisions were clearly 'right' and not optional. Yet, Leigh Gilmore points out:

> An autobiography is a monument to the idea of personhood, the notion that one could leave behind a memorial to oneself (just in case no one else ever gets around to it) and that the memorial would perform the work of permanence that the person never can ... But the fantasy of autobiography, like the fantasy of nationalism, never quite fulfils its promise in local terms.
>
> (Gilmore 2001: 12–13)

In other words, these defector memoirs perform a double function of publicizing the plight of the North Koreans and justifying the narrators' decision to 'defect'. Kang presents his story as a clear case of survival: to stay would have meant death so he took the only option available to him: he defected. In a sense, Kang's defection was a product of necessity rather than an active decision. Hwang's defection is painted in more heroic terms wherein the author sees his personal journey as one taken 'on behalf of mankind' (Egan 1987: 22). However, even here his story is a matter of survival, of fighting off death by finding a reason to continue living. In other words, for Hwang to find the will to continue living, he had to do the right thing and act on what was making his continued life in the North impossible. He had to find a way to save North Korea.

By portraying their decisions not as choices but necessities, these two narratives seek to cast the decision to defect as something that is opposed to choice, but decision making is always deciding between options and multiple other possibilities, despite the impossibility of decision. My point is that both memoirs are efforts to set the record straight, perhaps even to clear their names and reputations by presenting justifications for their decision to leave. In other words, presenting a coherent story of suffering and loss in North Korea, and portraying their defection as necessity, not choice, are also ways of dealing with the ambiguity surrounding their decision to leave. A nagging ambiguity around the necessity of their decision might be driving them to try to explain – clearly and explicitly – why they had no option but to defect.

A clearly delineated justification for defection is important in both memoirs because, among other reasons, it secures the subject position of survivor and/ or witness that is so effective in getting the message across that 'North Korea needs rescuing'. Testimonials and victim-survivor-witness memoirs are sites of translation that endow agency through self-representation. As much feminist, minority and postcolonial scholarship has amply documented and argued, they are representational sites where the formerly marginalized, silenced or ignored bodies and voices gain public status, i.e. participate in the public and take on identities as political actors (see Miller 2007; Smith and Watson 1992, 2001; Whitlock 2007; Hornung and Ruhe 1998; Reesman 1997). However, what is already beginning to emerge here are constraints on how their agency is enacted. The cross-cultural communication here has to work within the confines of a North Korean survivor-victim subject position, i.e. the subject position of an outsider making an appeal, through telling coherent stories of personal experience, to be heard and heeded. As examined next, the principal constraint on agency is self-imposed, i.e. anxiety about the inescapable ambiguity, contradictions and uncertainties regarding their decision to defect. In other words, part of what is constraining self-representation as a site of publicity and agency is the self's desire to erase ambiguity through narratives of redemption and recovery.

Narratives of loss and recovery

As discussed earlier, the idea of recovery is central to trauma literature and this is certainly the case for accounts of trauma in memoir. Janet Gunn (1992: 75) goes so far as to argue that autobiography is a rehabilitative activity, i.e. a way of recovering from a loss and fighting destruction from loss, thus 'a fundamental gesture of resistance against mutilation'. As we will see shortly, however, the objects that they seek to recover and their experiences with loss differ even when they are expressed for the same political goal.

Recovery in Kang's story operates in two ways: it is partly the recovery *of* his innocent childhood and the happiness that exists in his memory, but it is also explicitly the recovery *from* a feeling of not being home, and the need to heal an unsettling sense of uprootedness. This is to say that, on one level, the loss that Kang mourns in his memoir, and what his defection tries to recover, is his childhood innocence, captured in the title of his book – i.e. the numerous aquariums he kept in Pyongyang prior to the family's banishment to Yodok. The road to recovery from an experience of loss is a generic trajectory in memoirs and autobiographies which often rummages through childhood experiences in expressing loss before launching the journey (Huyssen 2003; Biddle 2003; Eakin 1999: 102–23). Thus it is not surprising that Kang's narrative recalls his childhood as a rich, resettled family from Japan and points to an experience of faith that he lived in a good world where he was valuable and cared for by Kim Il-sung, the Great Leader. Imprisonment in Yodok was a life- and faith-shattering experience and his recovery has been a journey to regain his life and sense of self-worth, which he grew to realize was impossible in North Korea. Kang realizes that the world as it appeared, i.e. the Pyongyang of his youth, was a fabrication, but retains the idea that this sense of perfect belonging exists somewhere. Moreover, a complex experience of loss and what needs recovery emerges when Kang turns to his family story: their search for feeling 'at home' (a feeling that was denied to them as ethnic Koreans living in Japan, despite their family wealth; Kang 2001: 19, 34). Similar to the narrative of national unification and reconciliation that longs for the (mythic) oneness examined in Chapter 4, we see in Kang's narrative of recovery a desire to 'get back' that sense of belonging that he believes he had as a child and feels he deserves as an adult.

When Kang has the freedom and the means to do so in South Korea, he sets out to recover the happiness he knew from youth. Interestingly, Kang professes that his effort to recover from his past in Yodok/North Korea and recover the happiness he lost is not possible unless the North Koreans in North Korea, or those abandoned and lost in China, are saved. Kang writes about how he almost 'lost himself' in his newfound wealth and freedom but recovered a sense of purpose by refocusing his goals: 'I made a clean break with that life [nightlife]. The desire to drown my sorrows didn't run as deep as other longings: to create stability in my life, to tell the world of the situation in North Korea, to help unfortunate refugees, and to find a wife to share the rest of my life' (Kang 2001: 230). Helping other 'renegades' in need, telling his story and bearing witness to the suffering in North Korea are not matters of choice for Kang but an integral part of his recovery. Redemption is figured as an arrival in the promised land, where his present identity (a 'North Korean defector') and social reality (a world where 'North Korean defectors' must exist) have been washed away and a new Korea without division, suffering or unbelonging is established.

This redemptive narrative that Kang enacts establishes clear dichotomies between those who save and those who need to be saved, and between the state of wholeness, happiness and being home, and the state of longing, suffering and unbelonging. We see this even more clearly in the preface to the revised edition of his memoir, when writing about meeting then US President George W. Bush:

> Throughout the meeting with President Bush, it dawned on me that my God was, after all, a living God. I now realize that the Lord wanted to use President Bush to let the blind world see what is happening to His people in North Korea. With one simple stroke of God's finger, the bleak reality, in which nearly no one cared about the ghost of three million famished souls and hundreds of thousands more in the concentration camps in my home country, was instantly changed.
>
> (Kang 2001: x–xi)

Kang believes he has just experienced a miracle when he meets and 'shares sincere opinions on how to save them [the North Korean people]' with 'the president of the world's most powerful nation' (Kang 2001: x). He writes prophetically that this is the beginning of a real, visible change that could liberate the North Koreans imprisoned by the Kim regime. Redemption is possible only with salvation and rescue, which are conceptions of change that require absolute upward (heavenly) movement and the enactment of the binaries saviour/saved, giver/receiver and active/passive.

The above passage also highlights how redemption is always, even when it feels otherwise, almost within one's grasp. Miracles happen. God works in miraculous and mysterious ways. It is important to keep faith. In Kang's *The Aquariums*, we get a glimpse of the important position that Christian faith, theology, narratives and missionaries occupy when North Koreans defect. Through the use of Christian liberation theology, Kang's memoir defers to the ultimate authority of 'outside North Korea', reifies 'North Koreans' as subjects of empathy, and constructs 'inside North Korea' as an irredeemably evil place where 'North Koreans' passively await rescue. Kang's memoir tries to smooth out the contradictions and tensions that come to the fore in one's pursuit of recovery and belonging. Crucially, Kang's main concern in the memoir is the apathy of South Koreans. He wants to speak to the Western public, the reading public of *The Aquariums* (though the book has since been republished in Korean for the South Korean market) about South Korean apathy, in order to get South Koreans to care more and do more for North Korean human rights. He identifies this as the cause of his and other North Koreans' homelessness, of their sense of not being understood, settled or at home. Kang's book speaks out about North Korean suffering in order to speak out about South Korean apathy which alienates him and stands in the way of his arrival in (God's) paradise.

Unlike Kang, who saw the foundation of the North Korean state to be flawed, deceptive and corrupt, Hwang mourns the failure of North Korea to realize humanity's potential to progress: a potential that was there in the foundation of the North Korean state. Hwang believes that the socialist commitment in the state's founding was genuine and had real potential to create a society that increased productivity by valuing communal rather than individual gain (Hwang 2006: 163–66). This potential was squandered by the political elite at the helm of the country when they stopped paying heed to philosophy and reason. As a result, the North Korean people became prisoners of a repressive ruling class. While lamenting the lost lives and the continuing losses in North Korea, Hwang also grieves the lost historical moment for human progress contained in the inception of the North Korean state.

Given the autobiographical nature of the writing, the story of lost opportunity is intertwined with Hwang's life. This story begins in post-liberated Korea, freed from Japanese colonial rule, a period of discovery, development and dedication in both public (North Korean) and private (Hwang's) history. Hwang recounts his personal history as a young, impassioned man of education who wanted to be useful in the rebuilding of Korea. Hwang dedicates himself to teaching and caring for impoverished students until he is sent by the Party to continue his studies in Moscow. When given a lectureship post in Kim Il-sung University, he tirelessly works to develop the philosophical foundations of Juche ideology (Hwang 2006: 83–117, 183–200). When Hwang laments the lost historical moment, he is also lamenting his life's work, squandered by the corrupt elite. What Hwang wants to recover through his defection and the writing of his memoir is this lost historical moment for enlightened politics ('humane politics') with at least three levels of loss: personal, national and universal potential for higher and greater things. To recover this lost opportunity and numerous lost lives, Hwang believes he has to give up his life as an individual for the greater cause: the North Korean people and Korea's progress. His philosophy dictates this conclusion.

I focus on a narrow dimension of Hwang's philosophy that is particularly relevant to his decision to defect. Rejecting a Marxist interpretation of history as class struggle, Hwang's philosophy advocates a focus on the human in history and development as an issue of the realization of humanity's destiny. Hwang develops this idea at length in his numerous publications, but I want to focus on a basic version of his idea that humans and humanity make their own destiny and how he delineates the relationship between the individual human and the collective human (humanity). These two tenets are central to how Hwang explains and justifies his decision to defect. Here, I read Hwang's text for how it testifies not only to the desire to recover the lost *national* opportunity but to recover from the trauma of his *private* loss, i.e. the loss of his family and the loss he might have caused them by his defection. A selection of stanzas from a poem he composes on this theme is illustrative:

Mankind!
You, the omnipotent power
Master of the universe,

Only you conquered the long arduous march
Took fate into your own hands,
Only you, to this lonely world,
Brought happiness and hope
And gave eternal life to this world without worth
                    (Hwang 2006: 190–91)

To live a life of worth
Is to abandon the small 'I'
And live by your will, the great 'I';
To live a life of happiness
Is to abandon the small 'I'
And live in the embrace of your love, the great 'I'.
To abandon the small 'I'
And become one through you, the great 'I'
Is to discover truth through the eyes of greatness,
Find the way forward through the power of greatness,
Feel the joy through the heart of greatness.
                              (Hwang 2006: 192)

Hwang tells us that this poem was written while struggling to develop his humanist philosophy. It captures the worldview Hwang's philosophy promotes: 'mankind' should and can master the world that he inhabits, a world that is nothing without what man brings into it. Hwang thinks that to realize the destiny of humanity, the individual must abandon the small 'I' and act with, and dwell in, the great 'I'. Thus, the chapter that recounts the final leg of his public life in North Korea is titled 'To serve the big "I", not the small "I"'. Importantly, this chapter ends with a return to the scene that began the memoir: Hwang's experience of difficulty and pain in making the decision to defect. In this narrative return to his decision to defect, Hwang explicitly frames the decision as one arrived at through philosophical reflection and justifies it as a decision taken to realize the destiny of mankind – it is a step taken for human development rather than personal gain. In his account of how he took asylum in the South Korean embassy in Beijing in 1997, Hwang puts it unambiguously, 'I killed the small "I" to enter the new road to save the big "I"' (Hwang 2006: 358).

Both Kang and Hwang are engaged in a rehabilitation from their experiences of loss that is utopian, nostalgic and masculine. It produces a heroic self-image and, in Hwang's case, deeply problematic either/or binaries of big/small, communal/individual, ideal/concrete, grand/trivial. While it is important that Hwang's attachment to recovery sees 'North Korea' as very much part of this project of mankind, what gets foregrounded in Hwang's memoir is his private loss. In other words, Hwang's narrative is explicitly an effort to realize the destiny of mankind, but it is also a narrative of a man attempting to recover from a private loss. To begin, the final lines of the chapter, 'To serve the big "I" not the small "I'" speaks of the pain of abandoning the small 'I':

> Separation in death could come to an end by crying to the heart's content but the longing and restlessness of separation in life stays with you and continues to strike. 'That's right, continue the assault so I can turn this hurt into strength and die having washed away even a fraction of ten-thousandth of the sin I have committed against my family and friends ...'
>
> (Hwang 2006: 358)

This monologue concludes a chapter that heroically narrates his pursuit of the great 'I' of his poem, and speaks to the pain involved in following his philosophical conviction. Passages such as this allow a reading of Hwang's memoir as a product of grief involving a private loss and a confession in how it admits the author's guilt about the cost of his defection personally and to his family.

The pain of abandoning the small 'I' is unshakeable, even when the decision was taken with full awareness of this cost. It opens up another dimension of loss that the narrative of recovery can and must traverse: that is, a displacement that keeps the loss (as wound) alive and in circulation. Contrary to what he professes,[8] the pain of that personal loss of the 'small I' lies exposed in the outer layers of the main narrative, as Hwang returns to it again and again in fragments long and short. In writing so vividly and recurrently about this pain, guilt and longing in the outer layers of his memoir, Hwang unwittingly invites us to bear witness to this pain and grieve the death of his small 'I'. My point is that Hwang's memoir contains Hwang, the individual, who experienced a traumatic private loss in a way that does not allow his philosophy about fulfilment in the embrace of the great 'I' to flourish. His memoir testifies to the trauma of putting the great 'I' into practice, impeding the process of bringing about this flourishing. Indeed, it impedes it just as forcefully, and in an equally complicated and layered manner, as other obstacles that stand in the way of recovering the lost national opportunity. The idea of subordinating and sacrificing the individual for the service of 'greater' happiness, hope, truth, life and love ultimately unravels. Like redemption in Kang's narrative, the happiness, truth and meaning promised by human progress, for Hwang, are ideas that in practice produce effects that cannot be logically ordered and tamed. No amount of self-discipline, awareness and willpower can so neatly subordinate the small 'I' under the big 'I'. The rigorous philosophical insights that underpin his dogged pursuit of Korean unification unravel in his life story and in his everyday practice of this philosophy. It serves as a painful lesson that demands we rethink the fundamental binaries that structure his philosophy.

Hwang passed away in 2010, four years after the publication of the revised edition of his memoir. Besides the insider's insight into how the North Korean ruling elites operate and a testimony of his political commitment, the memoir can also and perhaps more compellingly be read as a confession of intimate pain. It is a testimony of a loss he inflicted on himself through his philosophy, a wound that is worsened by the fact that he has caused pain to those he loves. Hwang's memoir elicits our empathy, but what does our empathetic reading of, our second-hand witnessing through Hwang's memoir do? Advocates for 'active empathy' talk about the transformative effect of empathetic reading of testimonials, how it makes us question our role, examine similar social relations around us and try to change their exploitative nature (e.g. Boler 1997; Bennett 2003; Rentschler 2004). This active-reflective effect of empathy could take many forms in the case of Hwang's memoir,[9] but the danger remains of viewing 'our' actions as outsiders, as non-North Koreans and as 'the international community' as necessary to 'solve' the problem. Moreover, it repeats the fantasy of Hwang's philosophy: of singularly pursuing redemptive action in the name of suffering, unification and humanity's progress that produces a new arena of pain (and narrative of recovery). What also remains untouched by the concept of testimony and empathetic responses to survivor-witness testimonials is how Hwang's memoir is a testimony of the production of wounds and pain in his own life. It does not even begin to testify to the pain he has caused his family and his social circle.

However, more damningly, Hwang's and Kang's stories return us to the hierarchical structure of empathy by creating an either/or relationship where to disagree with their message is somehow to dishonour their personal loss and suffering. In other words, because political memoirs give meaning to the narrator's personal life through his/her political message, and the political message is seen to be arrived at through the course of the narrator's personal life, to withhold empathy or disagree with the political message amounts to denying and silencing the survivor's personal life. To disagree with the narrator's politics becomes a form of 'withholding' empathy. Moreover, this formation of a testimonial public assumes a creation of a new space of innocence between survivors, victims and listeners of the testimony, which in turn assumes that only innocence achieved by the exclusion of perpetrator and absence of guilt can be the basis for empathetic encounters. While the larger argument in this chapter is that empathy is just one affective mode (and an especially slippery one) in intercultural production of publicity, what I am pointing to here is the limited way in which empathy, politics and intercultural encounters are allowed to intermingle, unfold and create in these two cases of self-representation.

In short, sites of self-presentation are constrained by intersecting narratives of redemption, recovery, salvation and rescue that the idea of testimony – bearing witness to suffering as a victim-survivor – mobilizes. The dividing lines between victim/perpetrator, saviour/saved and innocent/guilty that are enabled and produced by the conventions of testimony assume that the creation of a respectful, mournful public would enable rehabilitation, redemption and recovery. There is an assumption that a purer collective, one which excludes perpetrators and evil, can and has been established from which actions can be taken to address the problem of suffering and loss. My contention is that some questions to consider in regard to this position include: how does empathy that supposedly leads to the empowerment and increased agency of those who enter the testimonial-memoir pact (i.e. the survivor-witness and the addressee) work to efface the possibilities of on what or whose behalf the testimony speaks? Must life narratives of pain and suffering necessarily incite empathy? How else can North Korean defector memoirs function to speak out about suffering and speak back to power but in a way that also opens up the creativity and agency of loss, 'North Korea' and 'North Koreans'?

In-between space

Self-representation in the context of intercultural communication involves occupying what in postcolonial literature has been variously termed the 'in-between' space, third space, or hybridity that is neither an 'inside' nor an 'outside' (Bhabha 1994; Trinh 1991). While these North Korean defector memoirs attempt to mask over this in-between-ness by reifying the inside/outside binary (thereby securing their position as authentic North Korean voices), it is also possible to identify and explore the in-between spaces that these expressions necessarily open up.

A 'North Korean defector' is someone who left North Korea and stands outside it, but is viewed as an insider when he or she speaks about what he or she has abandoned and now stands outside. A 'North Korean defector' is a North Korean insider who now stands outside North Korea to tell us about what is going on inside North Korea. Moreover, a 'North Korean defector' could be someone who has always been, or has at some point become, an outsider within North Korea even before they leave. Aligning the authentic North Korea with that of the outsider North Korean, i.e. those from marginalized positions in its society, is to read this 'outsider within North Korea' as providing the genuine insider perspective: it supposedly reveals, from a position of authenticity, what life was 'really' like inside North Korea. In effect, a 'North Korean defector' is an insider whose outsider position within North Korea allows the telling of the 'authentic' North Korean story. Ambiguity also exists at the other end, where a 'North Korean defector' is seen by those to whom he/she addresses his/her story as an outsider telling a story about over there. The story is received as that of an outsider because it is about problems and experiences that are supposedly not part of the life worlds of the addressees. The separateness of the world to which the addressee and the addresser belong is assumed in part because the reader (the addressee) wants to read stories about those who are different from them, those who supposedly inhabit different worlds.

For the memoirs examined in this chapter, including Choi, Zini's *The Woman who Crossed the Border Thrice*, which I look at in the next section, the outsider positions and experiences of exclusion in North Korea are important components of their identities as reliable narrators of the authentic North Korea. For Kang, the former child prisoner, and Choi, the former Writer's Federation poet, this process of becoming an outsider was not their own decision; for reasons that were no fault of their own they were pushed out 'unjustly' to positions of poverty and insecurity. They had no other choice but to leave if they did not want to die or be sent back to prison.

For Hwang, his outsider status within North Korea was only 'conferred' with his defection because he was never banished from the elite circle to which he belonged whilst inside North Korea. Hwang, however, presents his position in a way that allows us to see his process of becoming an outsider inside North Korea through the mental process of distancing himself from other elites. This outsider position allows him to speak authentically as an 'insider' informant to the world bigger than North Korea. My point is not that Hwang's outsider position is 'inauthentic' because he was always part of the elite within North Korea; rather, it is that there is something equally ambiguous about the outsider positions that Kang and Choi claim. After all, by crying injustice for the 'unjust' way they were pushed to the outskirts of North Korean society, are they somehow saying they would not have defected if they were allowed to stay closer to the centre of power? Can Kang and Choi really claim they were outsiders within North Korea when they numer- ously confess to having desired to become insiders within North Korea and begrudged being denied inclusion? What matters here is not that we unearth what makes all defector positions ultimately inauthentic (indeed, the entire notion of authenticity is problematic here), but to recognize how the ambi- guity about standing inside/outside is always present in both kinds of 'out- sider' position in relation to North Korea that allow access to the authentic North Korean society.

Similarly, the outsider position of North Korean defectors inside South Korea is misleading since as South Korean citizens, the North Korean defec- tors are in effect part of this so-called international community. I am not advocating the position that we consider defectors as insiders within South Korea and the international community through the flawed citizenship logics of the nation (we are one) and cosmopolitanism (we are humanity). Rather, I want to read these North Korean defector memoirs by positioning them as potential sites of what Trinh calls 'third scenarios'. North Korean defector memoirs enact 'contact zones of *oppositional* logic and power'; they are 'a magnetized, tension-taught space of contestation' which constantly traffics between inside and outside (York 2011: 192, 202). In other words, speaking out about suffering and speaking back to (the official) North Korea cannot simply be understood as unilateral, unidirectional or univocal resistance to the North Korean regime. Speaking out about and back to North Korea are acts that bring into tension the oppositional logic (e.g. inside/outside, good/ evil, authentic/inauthentic, normal/deviant, same/different) and the power at play in the construction of North Korea as an international problem. I return to the significance of the tension that this movement produces through the idea of a 'third scenario' in my analysis of Choi's memoir. However, in pointing to the in-between space that 'North Korean defectors' can occupy and enact, what I am hinting at is how this in-between is collapsed in the approach to intercultural communication that Kang's and Hwang's memoirs take in speaking out about suffering. In the memoirs of Kang and Hwang, the in-between subsides.

The term 'North Korean defector' has undergone various revision and critical rethinking in South Korean public debate. It is considered an outdated term, a term one should be careful when using, especially in the presence of North Koreans. Other more appropriate terms suggested include 'new settlers', 'migrants' and 'escapees' as being more politically correct, neutral or accurate than the term 'defector', which implies a conscious rejection of North Korea and emphasizes the individual's relationship to the place they have left (i.e. North Korea). Each of these terms has its own logic of inside/outside: escapee, which seeks to take the political edge out of leaving North Korea, or new settler, which seeks to emphasize the new outsider position of North Koreans in the South that gestures to becoming part of the new Korea. None of these terms has shifted the politics of authenticity that I mapped out above: we are still seeking access to the authentic North Korea through the life narratives of overseas North Koreans who denounce their former selves, lives and allegiances. We still want them to be defectors albeit while adding other dimensions to what being (overseas) North Korean means.

'I will not write my memoir'

Choi, Zini's memoir, *The Woman who Crossed the Border Thrice* (*Guk-gyung-eul Sae-bon Gut-neun Yeoja Chae Zini*), resembles Kang's memoir in that it is a survival tale. It also has something in common with Hwang's memoir in that her social position in North Korea as an intellectual and a former poet in Pyongyang colours her narrative.

Choi belongs to the Writer's Federation (the official association of writers based in Pyongyang) until she is forced to leave Pyongyang when her husband is banished to a mining village for reasons that never become clear. Facing the status of a divorced woman without work at a time of mass food shortages, Choi crosses the border into China, vowing never to return and keeps this vow despite the desperate and violent turns her life takes. Choi returns to retrieve her son, hence the title of the book, but her story of survival and border crossings, like Kang's and Hwang's stories, ends in South Korea. Upon reading memoirs written by other defectors in South Korea, Choi tells herself that she will not write a memoir. She explains:

> Books that North Korean defectors have written are limited to a small range of topics: the arduous march [famine years], political prisons and the problem of the ruling elite. The problem with them is that they dry

out any possibility for the [South Korean] public's ability to gain a balanced understanding of the North Korean society and people.

(Choi 2005: 349)[10]

Her hopes in publishing what she feels is 'a premature and flawed work' is that it would help to overcome 'the tendency in South Korean NGOs and individuals that work with North Korea of viewing North Korea in whatever way they want to see it' (Choi 2005: 349). Choi wants to improve understanding among South Koreans who, through their work or other engagements, need to know North Korea better – or rather, they need to know that they do not know North Korea very well. Choi wants to communicate with these South Koreans and share her stories in order to disrupt the smooth way that the North Korean society and its people are understood and engaged from self-driven and self-centred positions.

Disruptive translation

The translation that *The Woman* conducts does not have empathy as its object. The survivor memoir that Choi writes is not written to fight apathy, which was a major concern in Kang's *The Aquariums*. In many ways Choi's memoir is a critical response to the empathy with which she as a defector was greeted and helped. *The Woman* can be read as a text that talks back, not so much to the North Korean regime that has forced the author to abandon her homeland, but to the prevailing structure of empathy that shapes relations between North and South Koreans. In telling her survival story, Choi talks back to the empathetic South Korea(ns) whose views of North Korean society and people she finds 'unbalanced'. The testimonial project here is not about improving or increasing South Korean empathy for North Koreans, but rather about disrupting the easy and unilateral way in which empathy flows when stories are told about suffering, injustice and human endurance in the face of insurmountable difficulties in North Korea.

To begin, Choi, Zini the victim-survivor-witness in *The Woman*, is not an entirely easy victim-survivor with whom to empathize. There are softer, moving moments and stories in the book, but also memorable are sudden surges of hate and suicidal impulses that disrupt any comfortable or easy desire to identify with Choi as a reliable, honourable narrator. The author, for instance, expresses her wish to 'explode the kitchen gas tank and kill that hateful family and my family and put a clean end to it all', in reference to the other defector family with which she was in hiding in China (Choi 2005: 309). The other family's infractions – she does not like how they hoard treats for themselves and are brash with her son – seem minor and trivial in comparison to the horror and violence she experienced and witnessed before reaching the safe house. Moreover, Choi not only has violent thoughts, but exhibits inexplicable approaches to dealing with hardship. Illustrative here is how Choi makes sense of her survival plan to 'marry' a Chinese man across the border. She explains how she decided to view her sale to a Chinese man like a 'study abroad programme', as an opportunity to learn Chinese and, if the situation allowed, even start her own small-scale cultural revolution (ibid.: 203). Choi never offers justification or expression of shame in accepting the silent exchange that women defectors enter when they cross the river and step onto the Chinese side, simply stating that 'Chosun [Korean] women have to be ready to offer sex whenever it is required' (ibid.: 205). Her story of this sexual contract becomes more explicit when another man she agrees to marry turns out to be violent and abusive (she ran away from the first marriage, something she does not explain). Choi does not shy away from describing the brutal sexual acts her 'husband' forces upon her and her unashamed explicit treatment of these events shows no concern for the sexual purity expected of a proper Korean woman.

More pointedly, Choi complains about the help she received from various South Korean institutions. Most scathing is the passage on the (unnamed) South Korean missionaries who helped her to travel safely out of China to South Korea. She complains of the delays, changes, and worse, how impractical the organized help was:

> I was beginning to resent the journey organizers (the churches that were funding this crossing wanted to make a video recording of the ordeal for their benefit). I was beginning to feel betrayed by them because they had assured us that this route was nothing in comparison to the Tumen River we had crossed. I would have been grateful for their practical and humanistic concern if they had said something to those of us who had to carry a child on our backs. Like about preparing a piece of string [to keep the child in place] instead they were busy of thinking about the machine to record this border crossing!
>
> (Choi 2005: 291)

Her message here and elsewhere in the narrative is that she cannot and will not be a grateful, deserving recipient of help (though she needs it), and more importantly, she lets those in positions to help her or others like her, know that their help was and continues to be incompetent and deficient. This message and its critical tone reverberate in her criticism of the South Korean resettlement programme run by the government. Again, her focus is on the practical and logistical elements such as how the donation of household furniture should be organized to provide for the new arrivals (Choi 2005: 317). Here, Choi's concern is with newly arrived North Koreans making big purchases that they might regret later. It is a relatively minor concern but her point is that these small issues matter to the people who live 'resettlement' every day and more must be done to help the 'resettling' North Koreans become, for lack of a better word, 'independent'. In short, rather than telling her stories to strengthen the bond between her and her empathetic readers, Choi's manner and critical attitude towards the help she received disrupts the easy way that stories of suffering from North Korea make us feel (benevolent, powerful, in control).

We are used to feeling sorry for the victims and viewing survivors as innocent, helpless, sympathetic or even admirable characters. Choi will not let us take this self-aggrandizing posture. She writes her memoir to disrupt this easy empathy, but the translation Choi conducts as a survivor is interested in turning her experience of suffering into something of value in a broader sense. Choi expresses the need to turn her suffering and experiences into 'a piece of literature that will last in this world' (Choi 2005: 310). The memoir is a way in which Choi 'moulds her life, thoughts and opinions into sentences', i.e. into something else that lasts, as something other than 'just' suffering (ibid.: 349). While the memoir is a way in which she does this, it is not the book she wanted to write from her experience. She wants to turn her suffering into literature that lasts and the memoir does not quite meet her conception, as a poet, of lasting literature. Choi casts her memoir as what she was able to write given her circumstances and opportunities as a *North* Korean poet in South Korea without the right tools and circumstances to write what is in her. As limitations and circumstances, Choi lists the Korean language used in South Korea, knowledge of wider society (given that she was a poet in North Korea with little understanding of the larger events surrounding her life), and the time to devote to writing, given her status as a single mother (ibid.: 310, 347–49). What I am pointing to here is not Choi's sorrows as a poet but her desire to turn suffering, experience, and the experience of suffering into some*thing*. For Choi, experiences of suffering have no value (they only hurt and remain signifiers of loss, destruction or wounds) unless they are transformed into a thing that fights destruction and creates something in an order that is entirely other to suffering. It needs to have a life of its own and outlive her and her past.

Transforming something from one form, order or medium into another is a way of understanding creation as a practice of translation. It is a process whereby something old, unformed or, in the case of suffering, destructive is reshaped through a particular medium (language, genre) that brings newness, life and value to otherwise dying, painful or not-quite-existing things that thoughts, experiences and 'North Korea' inevitably are. Taking this a step further, we can even, perhaps, understand loss and suffering as 'productive rather than pathological, abundant rather than lacking, social rather than solipsistic, militant rather than reactionary' (Eng and Kazanjian 2003: ix). Through sharing her suffering with the South Korean public (in which writing her memoir is only one component), Choi becomes a speaking individual who exercises her own agency, expresses desire, demands space and bitingly insists that we improve our intercultural understanding and communication skills.

Third scenarios

Since the publication of *The Woman*, Choi has not published *the* book or poem she has confessed to want to write. Instead, her commitment and need to create something new from her experiences of suffering have shifted focus. She has now turned to another kind of activity, the publication of *Rimjin-gang*, a magazine established in 2007, run by North Koreans for North Koreans inside and outside North Korea. In an interview, Choi explains that the magazines are smuggled into North Korea through a third country and distributed to key organizations in Pyongyang to target intellectual and government worker classes (Kim 2011).[11] Its reporters (all of whom remain anonymous except Choi) include North Koreans who have escaped from the North and North Koreans occasionally visiting China with legitimate passports. Choi's shift in focus importantly turns to 'North Korea' as a *source* of change and 'salvation' by working to enable North Koreans to act for themselves. In other words, rather than direct one's energy, loss and life to convincing, mobilizing and pressuring South Korean and Western publics to care about North Korea (like Kang and Hwang in their memoirs), or to do a better job of helping North Korea (Choi in her memoir), Choi's *Rimjin-gang* activities are directed at empowering North Koreans.

This shift in the direction of empowerment, agency and action produces tensions and contradictions that make Choi's activities in the magazine an object of criticism. For instance, it can be read as working within the binary choices of the redemptive salvation and recovery narratives where the inside/outside, over here/over there, saviour/saved perennially construct and shape the horizons of the defector experience. Choi's memoir – in her essay chapters – certainly slips into narratives resonant with Kang's and Hwang's calls for salvation. For example, in the chapter titled 'The unification we have to realize today', Choi expresses a deeply problematic logic:

> The unification we have to realize today is one where people in North Korea learn that there is something wrong with a society where there is no work for people who want to work and where people who work still starve. It is to enlighten them with the truth that a ruler who does not care about his dying people cannot be allowed to stay in power … It is to pull the North Korean people out into the world and let them taste the value of life, to experience with their whole body the enormous truth that they are valuable beings born into this world for themselves and not for Kim Jong-il or Kim Il-sung.
>
> (Choi 2005: 235)

In this part of the memoir, Choi willingly and uncritically occupies a position outside North Korea and finds redemption in being on the outside and acting upon an objectified North Korea. Choi positions herself pedagogically, appearing to teach North Koreans the truth as a now-outsider and demonstrating that she has gained a kind of 'enlightenment' as a result of her defection. In this sense, she exhibits a deeply problematic relation to 'North Korea' which is shared by all three memoir writers.

Founded in 2007 around the same time that *Rimjin-gang* was started, Kang, Chol-hwan's North Korean Strategy Center (NKSC) analogously channels his commitment to reforming North Korea and helping North Korean defectors. In his message as the executive-director, Kang, too, speaks the language of empowerment of North Korean defectors who are useful resources for the international community and for North Korean people who are still 'left in the dark' (see Kang in the English version of the NKSC, nksc.co.kr/english/sub1a.php). In the Korean version of the message, Kang expresses this idea of empowerment more actively, highlighting in particular the youth and elites of the North Korean defector community and their role in bringing about democratization and Korean unification (see Kang in the Korean version, nksc.co.kr/sub1a.php). Hwang was an important figure in this organization's activities, and his legacy remains visible in its activities today. While Kang's NKSC engages in a broader range of activities (and is bigger and more proximately located to important South Korean, European and US institutions), the NKSC and *Rimjin-gang*, as well as their respective project figureheads, have in common their shared mission of democratizing North Korea and their faith in their own usefulness to their North Korean compatriots.

Or do they? Elsewhere in her memoir, Choi explicitly recognizes the problem of power between North Koreans overseas and those in North Korea. She makes a firm distinction between inside/outside North Korea and argues that defectors have left so they should remain away from the North Korean society and politics for the sake of the development of the country. Choi draws lessons from the history of returnees in post-liberation North Korea which welcomed those who abandoned it during difficult times as heroes because of their newfound wealth. North Korean defectors' return would be a repeat of this history. She understands the various psychological reasons for why defectors would want to return (e.g. marginalization in South Korea, a desire to flaunt wealth at those who turned their backs on them in times of difficulty), but ultimately Choi believes that 'for the genuine development of North Korea, people who left should stay as people who left' (Choi 2005: 302). This passage presents a problem for the survivor-witness-saviour position which assumes that redemption can be brought to North Korea by outsiders like the North Korean defectors. In sum, North Korean defectors' translation of suffering is better directed not at seeking or making empathy more 'effective', but in pluralizing sources of change. However, if this centrally involves seeing 'North Korea' *as* the source of change, and they are to stay outsiders so as to let North Korean people who stayed (and suffered) determine North Korea's future, what forms can North Korean defector actions take?

Choi's distinction between inside/outside delimits the form and significance that 'North Korea' takes in the project of pluralizing world making. Here, the encounter between North Korean defectors and 'North Korea' is *inter*cultural; at the same time, North Koreans who stayed are just one part of 'North Korea' that makes the relations also *intra*cultural, i.e. intra-'North Korea'. What we must attend to is how the inside/outside boundaries are traversed to challenge, reify, complicate and even perhaps open out existing power relations. Trinh's ideas of the void and third scenario are useful here for how they pluralize the 'referent', i.e. conceive of 'North Korea' as a multiple-location (geographically speaking) *site* of intercultural encounter which requires translation, creativity, suspension and disruption. In other words, 'North Korea' is not a singular geographically located referent, i.e. it does not correspond to the idea of either over there or over here, nor to the idea that we can refer to it in the indexical, literal manner. 'North Korea' is a site of conceiving change wherein it is the *focus* of publicity and world-making projects, and is at the same time seen to be *emptying out* meaning, becoming a void. To conceptualize 'North Korea' as a site of intercultural encounter is to pluralize 'North Korea' and keep it moving, creating, open but at the same time keep it as the focal point of creativity, agency and change. It is to see 'North Korea' as a site of third scenarios – making use of Otherness, movement, emptiness, voiding, thirding. It is to turn to a located, specific Other as a critical source of agency, change and creativity which understands that intercultural relations have no destination, no arrival and no promises of resolution. It is politics without destination.

North Korean-led activities in the 2000s such as Choi's turn to publishing and disseminating news to North Korea are interesting as sites of intercultural encounter, as is Kang's work with the international community and organization of North Korean defector youth and elites. In other words, they are fairly new sites of enacting third scenarios that shift away from where many other intercultural sites and encounters that I examined in this book have taken place (i.e. between 'North Korea' and 'South Korea', or between 'North Korea' and 'the West'). One can imagine how Choi's *Rimjin-gang* activities, and more obviously Kang's mission to help the North Koreans 'left in the dark', can slip into problematic narratives of redemption and salvation in practice, smoothing over the tensions and contradictions that their acts of creation and translation (of their own suffering) bring forth. This is not only a critical conjecture directed at North Korean defector discourse but also gravely points to the constrained intercultural channels that such descriptions must travel (e.g. journalism, academic conventions, NGO reports).

However, one can also imagine otherwise: that is, imagine the 'North Korea' of these defector activities in ways that are not handcuffed to narratives with constitutive binaries of over here and over there, especially when headed by someone like Choi, Zini, who is sensitive to issues of power. More importantly, given how the idea of the third scenario, as articulated by Trinh, foregrounds voiding and emptying out that is embedded in a political theory which attends with non-knowingness, we might also want to ask for something other than descriptions from this new site of third scenarios which we can then critically assess. We might want to ask a different set of questions about this site that is more reflective and disruptive of our desires to know, to grasp, to act.

Conclusion

Empathy as an object of intercultural communication and the enactment of narratives of recovery, redemption and salvation in North Korean defector memoirs constrains subjects from *creatively* translating experiences of suffering. I began this chapter by showing how empathy centrally and problematically structures the conventional survivor stories that enact publics cross-culturally, i.e. from East to West, North Korea to the international, and North Korea to South Korea. This point becomes most obvious when terms such as 'testimony', 'trauma' or 'Holocaust' enter the picture, but it is also closely linked to memoir writing and autobiography more broadly. Narratives of recovery and salvation in memoirs about experiences of loss further reify the inside/outside, victim/perpetrator, sufferer/spectator, saviour/saved binaries that structure our understanding of the 'problem' of North Korea and its 'solution'. Reading Kang's *The Aquariums* and Hwang's *The Memoir* together presents one picture of how these narratives and intercultural communications based on the premise of (a reductively conceived) empathy work to constrain alternative stories of suffering and loss from emerging. They also crucially prevent survival stories from transforming the publics whom they enact through their stories to induce change in North Korea.

Whitlock (2007: 117) and others (mostly feminists, given their sustained engagement with the autobiographic genre) argue for pushing the limits of the autobiography and memoir genre. The idea is that cross-cultural sensationalist production of life narratives can be reformed. My turn to Choi's memoir, *The Woman who Crossed the Border Thrice*, has not been to subvert the limiting effects of the genre of life narratives. In many ways, Choi's memoir is a conventional life narrative that remains problematic in the way it privileges a coherent and authentic self with definable memories and experiences. My interest in Choi, Zini's memoir has been the way in which it disrupts the prevailing assumptions in Kang's and Hwang's narratives about how hope, agency and change come from *outside* North Korea, and that salvation, rescue, recovery and redemption are possible when individuals align with the right side (whether this be history, ideology, religion or power).

Choi is useful here because she understands the politics of testimonial public, i.e. the empathetic circle that promises healing, redemption and transformation. She understands that this circle must itself be transformed. Choi's engagement becomes problematic when we read her memoir for how her work with critical distance to publicity and world making stands in relation to effecting change in North Korea. She – like Kang and Hwang – slips into the privileged position of a now outside, free individual who has travelled that road from subservience to defiance and has reached enlightenment. In this sense, she assumes an authoritative position of an enlightened individual who can proclaim that to solve the 'North Korean problem', all North Koreans must travel to the outside world.

My contention was that this fixes the meaning of 'North Korea' that predetermines the terms of intercultural reality making. Choi's new project as an editor of *Rimjin-gang*, as well as Kang's think tank, the NKSC, can be seen as doing exactly this: of bringing enlightenment from the outside world to North Koreans remaining in North Korea. However, it is a claim that needs further reflection and I stop short of making a full critique of the *Rimjin-gang* project or other defector engagements that follow from the success of their memoirs. Rather than offer a critical reading of these activities, I instead believe that this new site of intercultural encounter (and possible scene of a third scenario) is an exciting area of further research and reflection on what third scenarios demand of academic engagements.

Notes

1 While literary critics distinguish memoirs from autobiography and, moreover, distinguish the subgenres in them (survivor story, growing pain narrative, coming-out story and so on), I use the terms interchangeably. At the same time, I conceptualize sites of representation in the plural form to acknowledge the generic differences between memoirs, autobiography and other life narratives (see Smith and Watson 2001: 1–5; Egerton 1994a, 1994b). This is to say that while the specific differences are not particularly significant in this chapter, the plurality of sites of self-representation and heterogeneity of life narratives, broadly speaking, are.

2 Schaffer and Smith (2004a: 7–8) use the term 'life narrative', which encompasses a broader array and modes of personal storytelling.

3 Gross and Hoffman (2004: 37), for instance, asks what Holocaust testimonies actually accomplish and how the reverence that surrounds such first-hand accounts limits the questions that can be asked. They ask this question as historians concerned that the recognition of unrepresentability of the Shoah in survivor testimony, and the function of the Holocaust in Western culture and politics, impede historical investigation.

4 Kang writes about how he decided to publish his story to 'tell the Western world what it was like to live under the rule of Kim Il-sung and his son, Kim Jong-il' (Kang 2001: xxii). Similarly, Hwang writes: 'I came to the conclusion that if I am going to die, my death would be more useful if I died while fighting to save our North Korean compatriots by aligning with the South' (Hwang 2006: 353). All quotes from Hwang's *The Memoir of Hwang, Jang-yop* are my own translations.

5 Kang's *The Aquariums in Pyongyang* is widely cited not only in other cultural productions discussed in this book, such as Kwon, Lee's *Left-handed Mr Lee* (2007) and Guy Delisle's *Pyongyang* (2004), but also in human rights reports and in academic studies such as Jiyoung Song's *Human Rights Discourse in North Korea* (2010), David Hawk's *The Hidden Gulag* (2003), Bruce Cumings's *North Korea* (2004), and Stephen Haggard and Marcus Noland's *Witness to Transformation* (2011).

6 In the introduction to the book, Rigoulot further admits that it 'results from the efforts of three people, working together as friends, with the common hope of raising international awareness', and acknowledges their interpreter (Kang 2001: xxiv). The interpreter's name nonetheless does not appear on the book cover and the interpreter never speaks directly in the book.

7 Egerton rightly points out that the memoirist is exercising 'the capacity for retrospection and reflection and the application of literary style in crafting a unified narrative out of personal political experience', but he argues, wrongly in my opinion, that this does not take away from the fact that memoirs still provide important historical sources (Egerton 1994b: 344). Egerton (1994a: xiii) defines political

memoir to encompass military, diplomatic and bureaucratic spheres. Political memoir is defined more broadly later in this chapter.

8 While Hwang admits that in retrospect it was naive of him to think that he could realize unification in five years, he remains adamant that it was the right decision. He insists, 'the fundamentals of our [Hwang and his companion defector] unification strategy remain unchanged until today' (Hwang 2006: 354–55).

9 It could take the form of turning our eyes to the pain of other separated families in Korea, reflecting on our apathy towards the situation in North Korea, and acknowledging our complicity in keeping unification always in a near but distant future in our passivity. Even if one does not agree with Hwang or Kang's unification strategies (e.g. deposing the Kim Jong-il regime with the help of the US president, or allying with those in power of strategic importance such as the conservative power base in South Korea, churches, Korean-American Christian NGOs), there are ways in which empathetic readings of their memoirs act upon readers and transform them into active participants in addressing, reflecting on and solving the problem of 'the plight of North Koreans'.

10 All quotes from Choi's *The Woman who Crossed the Border Thrice* are my own translation.

11 The magazine is also in circulation in South Korea and Japan. Its articles' topics have ranged from the North's missile and nuclear testing in 2006, to the 'Jasmine Revolution' in the Middle East and North Africa. For reviews and interviews regarding the magazine, see Kwon 2007; Kim 2011.

Bibliography

Film

Margaret Cho: Assassin (2005) Directed by Kerry Asmussen and Konda Mason, 90 minutes, Cho Taussig Productions, Autonomy Inc., Little Men Entertainment, DVD.

Books and articles

Ahmed, Sara (2010) *The Promise of Happiness*, Durham, NC: Duke University Press.

Baxi, Upendra (2000) 'Human Rights: Suffering between Movements and Markets', in Robin Cohen and Shirin M. Rai (eds) *Global Social Movements*, London: Athlone.

Bennett, Jill (2003) '*Tenebre* after September 11: Art, Empathy, and the Global Politics of Belonging', in Jill Bennett and Rosanne Kennedy (eds) *World Memory: Personal Trajectories in Global Times*, Basingstoke: Palgrave Macmillan.

Bennett, Jill and Kennedy, Rosanne (eds) (2003) *World Memory: Personal Trajectories in Global Times*, Basingstoke: Palgrave Macmillan.

Berlant, Lauren (2007/08) 'Cruel Optimism: On Marx, Loss and the Senses', *New Formations* 63: 33–50.

——(2008) *The Female Complaint: The Unfinished Business of Sentimentality in American Culture*, Durham, NC: Duke University Press.

Berlant, Lauren and Prosser, Jay (2011) 'Life Writing and Intimate Publics: A Conversation with Lauren Berlant', *Biography* 34 (1): 180–87.

Berlant, Lauren and Warner, Michael (1998) 'Sex in Public', *Critical Inquiry* 24 (2): 547–66.

Bhabha, Homi (1994) *The Location of Culture*, London: Routledge.

Biddle, Jennifer Loureide (2003) 'Anthropology as Eulogy: On Loss, Lies and License', in Jill Bennett and Rosanne Kennedy (eds) *World Memory: Personal Trajectories in Global Times*, Basingstoke: Palgrave Macmillan.

Boler, Megan (1997) 'The Risks of Empathy: Interrogating Multiculturalism's Gaze', *Cultural Studies* 11 (2): 253–73.

Chen, Kuan-Hsing (2010) *Asia as Method: Toward Deimperalization*, Durham, NC: Duke University Press.

Choi, Zini (2005) *The Woman who Crossed the Border Thrice* (*Guk-gyung-eul Sae-bon Gut-neun Yeoja Chae Zini*), Paju: Book House.

Cumings, Bruce (2004) *North Korea: Another Country*, New York: New Press.

Delisle, Guy (2004) *Pyongyang: A French Cartoonist's Crash-bang Journey in North Korea* (*Pyongyang: Peu-rang-sue Manhwa-ga-eui Jwa-chung-woo-dol Pyongyang iyagi*), Seung-jae Lee (trans.), Seoul: Munhak-saegae-sa.

Eakin, Paul John (1999) *How Our Lives Become Stories: Making Selves*, Ithaca, NY: Cornell University Press.

Egan, Susanna (1987) 'Changing Faces of Heroism: Some Questions Raised by Contemporary Autobiography', *Biography* 10 (1): 20–38.

Egerton, George (1994a) 'Introduction', in George Egerton (ed.) *Political Memoir: Essays on the Politics of Memory*, Portland, OR: Frank Cass.

——(1994b) 'The Anatomy of Political Memoir: Findings and Conclusions', in George Egerton (ed.) *Political Memoir: Essays on the Politics of Memory*, Portland, OR: Frank Cass.

Eng, David L. and Kazanjian, David (2003) 'Introduction: Mourning Remains', in David L. Eng and David Kazanjian (eds) *Loss: The Politics of Mourning*, Berkeley, CA: University of California Press.

Federation of American Scientists (1997) '1997 North Korea Special Weapons Nuclear, Biological Chemical and Missile Proliferation News', July, www.fas.org/news/dprk/1997/index.html (accessed March 2012).

Feldman, Allen (2004) 'Memory Theaters, Virtual Witnessing, and the Trauma-aesthetic', *Biography* 27 (1): 163–202.

Felman, Shoshana and Laub, Dori (1992) *Testimony: Crises of Witnessing in Literature, Psychoanalysis and History*, London: Routledge.

Gilmore, Leigh (2001) *The Limits of Autobiography: Trauma and Testimony*, Ithaca, NY: Cornell University Press.

Goldman, Anne E. (1993) 'Is that what she Said? The Politics of Collaborative Autobiography', *Cultural Critique* 25: 177–204.

Gross, Andrew S. and Hoffman, Michael (2004) 'Memory, Authority, and Identity: Holocaust Studies in Light of the Wilkomirski Debate', *Biography* 27 (1): 25–47.

Gunn, Janet Varner (1992) 'A Politics of Experience: Leila Khaled's *My People Shall Live: The Autobiography of a Revolutionary*', in Sidonie Smith and Julia Watson (eds) *De/Colonizing the Subject: The Politics of Gender in Women's Autobiography*, Minneapolis: University of Minnesota Press.

Haggard, Stephan and Noland, Marcus (2011) *Witness to Transformation: Refugee Insights into North Korea*, Washington, DC: Peter G. Peterson Institute for International Economics (PIIE).

Hawk, David (2003) *The Hidden Gulag: Exposing North Korea's Prison Camps, Prisoners' Testimonies and Satellite Photographs*, Washington, DC: US Committee for Human Rights in North Korea, www.hrnk.org (accessed January 2009).

Heckner, Elke (2008) 'Whose Trauma is it? Identification and Secondary Witnessing in the Age of Postmemory', in David Bathrick, Brad Prager and Michael D. Richardson (eds) *Visualising the Holocaust: Documents, Aesthetics, Memory*, Rochester, NY: Camden House.

Hesford, Wendy S. (2004) 'Documenting Violations: Rhetorical Witnessing and the Spectacle of Distant Suffering', *Biography* 27 (1): 104–44.

Hornung, Alfred and Ruhe, Ernstpeter (1998) *Postcolonialism and Autobiography*, Amsterdam: Rodopi.

Huyssen, Andreas (2003) 'Trauma and Memory: A New Imaginary of Temporality', in Jill Bennett and Rosanne Kennedy (eds) *World Memory: Personal Trajectories in Global Times*, Basingstoke: Palgrave Macmillan.

Hwang, Jang-yop (2006) *The Memoir of Hwang, Jang-yop (Hwang Jang-yop Hwegorok)*, Seoul: Sidae-jongshin.

Kang, Chol-hwan (2001) *The Aquariums of Pyongyang: Ten Years in the North Korean Gulag*, Pierre Rigoulot (co-writer), Yair Reiner (interpreter), London: Atlantic Books.

——(2013) 'Executive Director's Message', in North Korea Strategy Center, nksc.co.kr/english/sub1a.php (accessed April 2014).

Kim, Yun-duk (2011) 'Why Kim Yoon-duk's People: The Woman who Crossed the Tumen Border Thrice' (*Why Kim Yoon-duk-eui Saram Tuman-gang-eul Saebon Gunneun Yeoja*), *Chosun Ilbo*, 9 April, news.chosun.com/site/data/html_dir/2011/04/08/2011040801582.html (accessed April 2012).

Kwon, Heok-chul (2007) '[Person] "Real North Korean Citizen Reporters Write Them"' (*[Isaram] 'Jeongmal Bukhan Jumin Gija-deuli Sseupnida'*), *Hangyore*, 20 November, www.hani.co.kr/arti/culture/culture_general/251459.html (accessed April 2012).

Kwon, Lee (2007) *Left-handed Mr Lee (Wenson-jabi Mister Lee)*, Paju: Moonhak.

Langer, Lawrence L. (1991) *Holocaust Testimonies: The Ruins of Memory*, New Haven, CT: Yale University Press.

——(1996) 'The Alarmed Vision: Social Suffering and Holocaust Atrocity', *Daedalus* 125 (1): 47–65.

Liss, Andrea (1998) *Trespassing Through Shadows: Memory, Photography, and the Holocaust*, Minneapolis: University of Minnesota Press.

Miller, Nancy K. (2007) 'The Entangled Self: Genre Bondage in the Age of Memoir', *PMLA* 122 (2): 537–48.

North Korea Strategy Center (2013) *North Korea Strategy Center*, nksc.co.kr/index.php (accessed March 2014).

Peters, John Durham (2001) 'Witnessing', *Media Culture Society* 23: 707–23.

Poetics Today (2006) 'The Humanities of Testimony', special issue 27: 2.

Reesman, Jeanne Campbell (ed.) (1997) *Speaking the Other Self: American Women Writers*, Athens, GA: University of Georgia Press.

Rentschler, Carrie A. (2004) 'Witnessing: US Citizenship and the Vicarious Experience of Suffering', *Media Culture and Society* 26 (2): 296–304.

Schaffer, Kay and Smith, Sidonie (2004a) 'Conjunctions: Life Narratives in the Field of Human Rights', *Biography* 27 (1): 1–24.

——(2004b) *Human Rights and Narrated Lives: The Ethics of Recognition*, Basingstoke: Palgrave Macmillan.

Smith, Sidonie and Watson (eds) (1992) *De/Colonizing the Subject: The Politics of Gender in Women's Autobiography*, Minneapolis: University of Minnesota Press.

——(2001) *Reading Autobiography: A Guide for Interpreting Life Narratives*, Minneapolis: University of Minnesota Press.

Soja, Edward W. (1996) *Thirdspace: Journeys to Los Angeles and Other Real-and-Imagined Places*, Oxford: Blackwell Publishers.

Song, Jiyoung (2010) *Human Rights Discourse in North Korea: Post-Colonial, Marxist and Confucian Perspectives*, Abingdon: Routledge.

Trinh, T. Minh-ha (1991) *When the Moon Waxes Red: Representation, Gender and Cultural Politics*, London: Routledge.

——(1999) *Cinema Interval*, London: Routledge.

Whitlock, Gillian (2007) *Soft Weapons: Autobiography in Transit*, Chicago, IL: University of Chicago Press.

York, Lydia (2011) 'Not Quite Not Agents of Oppression: Liberal Praxis for North American White Woman', in Stephen D. Moore and Mayra Rivera (eds) *Planetary Loves: Spivak, Postcoloniality, and Theology*, New York: Fordham University Press.

Conclusion
How do you solve a problem like North Korea? It depends on who you are

> In the light of cultural studies, it becomes possible to realize that 'critical theory' is, after all, a process of cultivation, a process which, despite its claim to radical alterity and heterogeneity, operates by demanding of its adherents a certain conformity with its unspoken rules, rules that have gone without saying until they were revealed for what they are: 'deconstruct the best you can – but continue to center on the West!'
>
> (Chow 1998: xviii)

> The White Left could best contribute to the inter-minority dialogue by getting out of the way and becoming an active listener rather than a patronizing participant.
>
> (Lavie and Swedenburg 1996: 164)

An underexplored dimension of the commonly implied question, 'How do you solve a problem like North Korea?' in discussions about North Korea, is a series of broader questions about those in positions to ask this question and be heard. My own non-exhaustive list of these questions includes: Whose problem is North Korea? Who gets to solve a problem like North Korea? What is the basis for determining this? What is our problem with North Korea? Why does the international community – Right, Left and Centre – feel the need to solve a problem like North Korea in the first place? These questions all variously point out how the international problem of North Korea also requires thinking about who composes the questions, from where, for what ends, through what means, and to what effect and effectiveness.

I here indicate how the problem of North Korea is also inextricably and variously – though not only – a problem of the international self. The 'international' that emerges in this book is a loose network of desires, attachments and ambitions that are both personal and public; global and geographically specific; fearful of and compassionate towards the North Korean Other. Here, too, I do not aspire to an exhaustive list - there are probably other attachments and emotions lurking around somewhere in these pages (and beyond) which did not receive the engagement they deserve. This international self is articulated in diverse cultural sites by producers and productions that are variously positioned in terms of ethnicity, nationality, profession and, to a lesser extent, gender. While loosely networked and variously located and motivated, the international is an *expression* of aligning with 'the top' of the global hierarchy that centres on the West, heteronormativity, masculinity, logocentrism and neoliberal redemption. These descriptors of centring have complex and contradictory attachments and workings, and are not easily defined through their binary oppositions. I have tried to foreground this complexity throughout the book.

Part of my aim here has been to conceptualize and scrutinize the ways in which, the locations of and the directions that dissent expressed against the international hierarchy travels. This emphasis has been an effort to interrogate reflectively and thoroughly, as Spivak (2004: 524) put it, 'the agenda of a kind of social Darwinism – the fittest must shoulder the burden of righting the wrongs of the unfit – and the possibility of an alibi [for domination and intervention]'. I believe that 'the agenda of a kind of social Darwinism' is pervasive and integral in intercultural relations involving problems like North Korea, and complicit here are the critical and dissident engagements. I want to know how displacements of the hierarchy that structures relations between the international and North Korea can occur without reifications of this hierarchy, for instance through transference of the hierarchy in some other domain. The epigraphs register the need for a more reflexive attention to issues of positionality and location in how critical interventions are conceived. While I do not agree with Lavie and Swedenburg that the critical issue is one of inter-minority dialogue, what their argument expresses is the need for shifts in the location, mode and direction that agency and political action take.

The international/North Korea problem

I have argued in this book that to 'solve' a problem like North Korea, the problem of the international also needs examination. I have shown in my cultural engagement how North Korea is constructed as a rogue, out-of-place and out-of-date dictatorial state which, while much is 'unknown', is understood as a misery-producing, dysfunctional and crisis-prone hotspot that continually requires outside surveillance, monitoring and intervention. Cultural engagements echo the solutions in existing international diplomatic, humanitarian, human rights and economic literatures that begin from a position of superiority that reify and rely on the hierarchy of 'the international' over 'North Korea'. The only way to solve the problem of North Korea is through outside intervention. My main contention has been that the subject/object binary is perhaps the most important divide that enables the international to constitute itself through the figure of the Other – a divide that is continually reproduced and entrenched through the problematization of North Korea. This hierarchy of problem solver/problem object enables the naturalization and normalization of a privileged image of the self.

The focus of my analysis has been to show how a community of diverse do-gooders who are democratic, better off, free thinking and free moving – that is, genuinely international (read: universal and ordinary) – is possible only through the construction of a problem like North Korea which allows the enactment and reification of this self-image. In short, the superior international self is achieved through rendering Others like North Korea as spaces, people or ideas that must be kept as objects of the self's supposedly autonomous action and imagination. Here, the Other constitutes the very subjectivity of the international self, which the hierarchy enables. This is maintained by reifying the differences between the (idealized image of) self and the (derogated and subordinated) Other. The question for me has been what our alternatives are to this easy hierarchy of problem solver and problem object in relation to North Korea. In other words, if we actually want to 'solve' a problem like North Korea, we have to think about how we 'solve' a problem like the international; the two must be taken together.

How does one 'solve' a problem like 'the international'? I navigate this question by illustrating how 'North Korea' has become a rich and complex repository of our desires, myths, morality and aesthetics. Questions like, 'Whose problem is North Korea?' (i.e. is it the Koreans', the region's, the international community's?) are not merely questions involving who should get the most say in formulating and creating solutions, or who should shoulder most of the burden. They are also questions about who gets to say the most, the loudest or the most seductively about North Korea. I do not think this is an entirely rationalized or clearly delineated (or delineable) set of processes and practices, i.e. I would not say that various actors of the international community are consciously or rationally in competition with each other to secure the most privileged identity. It is more affective, more a process of enacting attachments to promises that are clustered, and more diffused in how and where these enactments occur than official narratives from sites of the international 'proper' would lead us to believe. The examples in this book attend to the diversity of these sites and the particular generic, narrative and cultural resources available from these sites to establish different versions and dimensions of the self-image.

In four chapters I examined how different cultural sites construct the 'North Korea problem' using the generic, narrative and cultural resources available from those sites to establish intimate access to and relations with North Korea(ns). While productions of mystery fiction, graphic travelogues and photography all rely on their producers' supposed possession of intimate knowledge from having 'been there', the mixed-media form that uses visual and textual representations such as the graphic travelogue and photography have additional means to generate authenticity. These visual producers are able to substantiate their proximity to the problem by *showing* 'this is what I saw in person!' through their illustrations and photographs. This is not to say visual images are more powerful than textual ones, but that the idea of immediacy is more readily accepted for visual than textual images in popular culture. Memoirs, on the other hand, establish an intimate relation to North Korea through the idea of the authentic insider, and compose a site of sentimentality, together with 'blockbuster' South Korean films that, like Hollywood films, are sites of melodrama. Interrelated narratives and affective forms – nostalgia, redemption, salvation, love (as togetherness), reconciliation – also recur and travel from one generic site to another, producing diverse effects. For instance, in the Inspector O mystery series, nostalgia for the ancient, pre-communist Korea, expressed through a North Korean policeman, works to produce the present-day North Korea as an object to be detected, policed, feared and fascinated by (Chapter 2); while the nostalgic production of rural North Korea in Ri, Man-geun's photo book points to the easy way in which North Korea is humanized by privileging our own cultural memories of the past, and thus speaks to how our desires and longings shape how North Korea is encountered (Chapter 3).

Redemption is a common narrative in cultural productions examined in all the chapters, but in North Korean defector memoirs the idea of arriving in some other place where perfect belonging and recovery from their loss and suffering is especially delimiting (Chapter 5). Not only does such a promise produce a new realm of longing and loss but it also functions to limit the demands that these figures and their narratives can make on the publics they circulate and mobilise. South Korean narratives want us to love, love and then love some more in the face of suffering, hate and a sense of helplessness, which as we see in South Korean blockbuster films crucially and violently demand North Koreans at its border, or within its embrace, to reciprocate and mirror its love, desire for togetherness, by fictionally dramatizing the world and subjectivity of the North Korea Other (Chapter 4).

North Korea enables a particular enactment of the international that makes it an especially seductive and appealing site for performing hierarchic intercultural reality. As one of the last Stalinist states (read: anachronistic, totalitarian and inauthentic to Korea), North Korea is an easy target to demonize, ridicule and relegate as a radical Other that either needs to be saved or killed off, contained or engaged, loved or hated. Whether we focus on the Oriental despot that is the Kim regime, now in its third generation, celebrate the perseverance of the human spirit despite the weight of oppression or lament the mechanized North Korean consciousness lost to the regime, these various foci give a diverse group of international bodies a wide array of roles to fill. Whether it is a solitary traveller, an empathetic onlooker, a distraught lover or a selfless saviour (among others), these seemingly diverging identities singularly occupy a privileged position in relation to a changing cast of North Korea(an)s. As outsiders, we imagine the horror and misfortune of being born a North Korean though we do not seem capable of imagining North Korea specifically, on its own terms and in the full complexity that we bestow on our own societies and realities.

This is not to echo the argument that we need to know (about) North Korea better, know the real, more authentic, historical-cultural North Korea in its full complexity as argued increasingly in numerous expert circles. I have cited a wide range of these voices (e.g. Bruce Cumings from history and Sonia Ryang and Suk-young Kim from anthropology). Increasingly, we also see expert-, expertise-driven online platforms such as 38North, Sino-NK, NKnews and non-for-profit organizations specializing in North Korea (too numerous to list) tirelessly churn out bite-size gems of insight, wisdom and observation about North Korea for popular circulation. While admirable at times, the arguments made in this book sound a slightly different cause. I focus on issues of relations, and caution against all-too-easy energetic 'doing something about North Korea' which only understands response and responsibility in terms of (self-)assertion, presence and acting upon. I think, all too often, these self-assertive actions are mistaken for acting in concert with ordinary North Koreans, but they are not. I shall return to this point shortly.

In juxtaposing Western and South Korean productions of North Korea that constitute the international, we also see how a particular strand of sentimentalism pervades the latter's photographic, cinematic and novelistic expressions. By sentimentalism, I am referring to a sense of longing for the North Korean Other, or for togetherness and a return to the 'normal' state expressed in a way that privileges presence and emotional immediacy. We see this sentimentalism in Western productions as well, but in the South Korean productions the inter-Korean interpretive framework mobilizes ideas about national unity and shared suffering that centres Korea. In Chapter 4, which examined this sentiment most directly, I argued that narratives of Korean oneness posit hope in hierarchy, order and alignment with the international in conceiving a better (a happier and a more harmonious, prosperous, peaceful) future. This hope in hierarchy functions as an attachment and alignment with the 'top' that excludes whatever is deemed as the 'bottom', which in intercultural contexts involving North Korea is an expression of colonial mentality. South Korean blockbuster films visually and spectacularly dramatize the issues of desire and anxiety that these narratives of togetherness express.

To be clear, I am not trying to establish a special position for South Korean productions; rather, I am pointing out the heterogeneous composition of the international self that gestures to the complexity of the international/North Korea hierarchy. In short, I am trying to show how South Korea and inter-Korean relations *are* part of the international, or rather they *are* international; it is this 'are-ness' that is under negotiation, construction and amplification. This formulation of South and North Koreas diverges significantly from how South Korea is prevailingly positioned in existing IR and Korean studies literature which provides it with a special status that encourages nationalist rhetoric. South Korean national(ist) fantasy is a problem because it remains squarely a male heteronormative fantasy. Rather than conceive of the 'North Korea problem' as a problem of national reconciliation and unification, or a case of geographically located conflict management and peace building, I emphasize that these cultural imaginations are engaged in issues of intercultural relations between a highly asymmetrically positioned self (South

Korea) and Other (North Korea). Besides, inter-Korean relations extends beyond peninsular processes and actors. This is a claim *despite* what is foregrounded in the South Korean productions – that is, national division and geographically specific conflict. I argue that inter-Korean relations must be understood as part of the international/North Korea hierarchy if we are to conceptualize what North Korea – as a repository of desires, myths, morality and aesthetics that circulate in an interconnected world – is doing. It is also necessary if we are to think more concertedly about displacing the North Korean Other's subordinated position in the subject/object binary.

Along similar lines, I have examined how the North Korean defectors, and more broadly the survivor-witness, occupy a particularly privileged yet highly delimited position in this international. In the international/North Korea hierarchy, North Koreans outside North Korea are privileged for what they can tell the world about the 'home' they abandoned (i.e. they are authentic 'insiders' who have escaped). I argued that what they can tell us and their subject position in the international are already mediated by existing productions of North Korea and the international. To be accepted as part of the outside world – the international that is dispersed, affective, complex and contradictory in composition – they have to occupy unambiguously a position of an innocent victim and/or witness, where the North Korean regime is reductively understood through pre-existing models of 'the perpetrator' (e.g. most clearly symbolized by Nazi Germany). At the same time, this position as a reliable informant regarding North Korea constrains how they can belong in the outside world; that is, they are always an outsider within this outside. No perfection of embrace, reduction of distance or attainment of a sense of belonging can resolve the problem of insider/outsider in relation to the North Korean defectors.

My readings of Korean productions – Kwon, Lee's *Left-handed Mr Lee* (Chapter 2), Yang, Yonghi's *Our Homeland* (Chapter 4), and Choi Zini's memoir, *The Woman who Crossed the Border Thrice* (Chapter 5) – explore how we might move beyond narratives that assume the problem of insider/ outsider, over here/over there can be solved. Rather than retain North Korean defectors as objects of our intervention, these stories help to articulate how subject/object, self/Other binaries can and must be disrupted and subjected to sustained questioning.

Emergent here is the thesis that what needs disruption is the subject/object binary more pervasively, in every sense and instance, not just in the intercultural relations involving North Korea but also in how disruption, critique and transformation are conceived more broadly. Despite the often monocultural, authoritarian and utopian enactments of translation, the concept of translation has been useful in pursuing a more sustained attention to issues of cultural mediation, how different bodies are positioned and the importance of contingency, surfaces, non-knowing in encounters. Not only does translation make explicit how mediation and intermediaries compose important dimensions of the international/North Korea problem, but they are imperative if a heterogeneity of world(s) rather than a hierarchy is to order intercultural relations. I valued translation in my analyses not as an instrument for dialogic exchanges (i.e. increased communication and improved understanding), but as an instrument and process of creation in surface-level encounters where bodies brush against each other and negotiate prevailing stereotypes. It has been seen as a creative and fictive process that helps to register the movement between cultures, the need for intermediaries, the moments of suspension of the self and the movements to 'an elsewhere, within here' that result (Trinh 2011: book title).

The final sections in Chapters 2 to 5 have been spaces to attend to cultural products that diverge in one way or another from the dominant framings, narratives and mode of engaging 'North Korea'. They have been spaces to think about and invest in alternative terms of intercultural encounters. Here, cultural productions are read for how they enable thinking about what alternatives mean if we take issues of positionality and intercultural relations seriously. Trinh Minh-ha has been helpful in these third spaces to propel cultural encounters with North Korea and our mediations of these encounters which, in their very mode of articulations, embody openness, heterogeneity and contingency attuned to and attached to specific contexts, locations and politics.

(de)Centring self

As the Rey Chow epigraph asserts, even a radical and heterogeneous development such as poststructuralist theory unfolds according to a set of unspoken rules that become clear only when it is scrutinized according to some other criteria external to itself (in Chow's case, this is cultural studies). Chow wrestles to articulate conceptually how decentring of the self and shifting of the structure of power through and in cultural productions occurs. Examined through the North Korea case, I have argued that much of how critical research goes about interrogating dominant discourses and representations remains ultimately concerned with the political agency and praxis of those 'within' a critical project: the self. Showing the binaries at work, how they unravel and produce violence, are activities pursued with the unspoken assumption that these interventions are performed in order *for us and people like us* to be reflective, interrogative and provocative about the order of things. While critical intervention in discourse and representation as pursued through poststructuralist theory is one dimension of disruption, this form of disruption too often and too easily privileges the self (albeit a critical, decentred, humbled self) as the source of action, agency and change.

This was my main criticism of photography's engagements with North Korean suffering, of love in cinematic imaginations of North Korea and of North Korean memoirs that are driven by the desire to fight the world's apathy and elicit empathy. The focus was trained simultaneously on showing the limits of interventions that re-centre the self and in illustrating new sites and modes of world making. Interrogation of North Korean voices are especially important because they further complicate and bring in 'newness' to how contingency, ambivalence and heterogeneity unfold and create.

The concept of third scenarios taken from Trinh illustrates the significance of shifting of locations and making use of Otherness. Crucially, third scenarios are a particular way of conceptualizing alternatives that privilege being always on the move to new sites of in-between-ness, expression and becoming. Chela Sandoval (2000) terms this primacy 'a methodology of the oppressed', or alternatively, 'a differential form of social movement', pointing to Trinh Minh-ha but more prominently to Gloria Anzaldua, Audre Lorde, Merle Woo and Cherrie Moraga, among others. Constituting 'U.S. third world feminism', Sandoval argues that the works of these feminists are collectively an oppositional (social) movement against Western metaphysics which works from a 'third space' and in a 'middle voice' that has been 'creat[ing] new modes of resistance, new questions and answers that supersede those that went before' (Sandoval 2000: 153). For Sandoval, 'U.S. third world feminism' has produced a 'differential *consciousness*', which effectively opposes the West through 'transforming and moving [a set of technologies that grasp meaning] on both sides, that of social reality and that of the realm of the "abyss"' (ibid.: 182, emphasis in original).

While I agree that 'U.S. third world feminism' has opened up an alternative trajectory for critical theory, I disagree that what these feminist theorists have produced is a new differential/oppositional *consciousness* or that this new theoretical trajectory comprises 'a method for generating oppositional *global* politics' (ibid.: 182, emphasis added). As rendered by Trinh, oppositional modes and practices are too fragmented to be understood as a consciousness. More importantly, a method for generating oppositional global politics involves a more *located* and 'local' understanding of subordinated spaces and cultures. Sandoval's political theory of opposition suffers from the problem of US/ self-centring, which goes uncommented, thus forgoing opportunities for reflecting/refracting this issue in how transformation of global politics is conceived.

My argument about alternatives and third scenarios has been that if what needs change is indeed the structures of power, knowledge and agency that perpetually render the North Korean Other as an object of international action, knowledge and dominance, then transforming this hierarchy requires a way of conceiving and practising disruption which, in its very conception and practice, disrupts the constitutive subject/object and 'the international'/'North Korea' binaries. I have explored the idea of shifting who gets to speak, construct, produce and act through Trinh's creative and expressive engagements with heterogeneous sources of disruption, change and alternatives. It has been a question of shifts in the terms of intercultural encounter, i.e. in how, to whom, with whom and to what end disruptions, suspensions and dissents are articulated. In other words, efforts to document, archive and produce disruptive and dissident moments and spaces must reflect – a more accurate term here might be the verb 'diffract' à la Haraway – this more foundational critical unravelling of the constitutive subject/object distinction.

Heterogeneity, simultaneity, supplementarity

Spivak's essay, 'Righting Wrongs' (2004), not only makes visible the centring of the self that plagues critical engagements but introduces a strategy to disrupt this centring. In interrupting the permanent hierarchy like that of the international/North Korea, where the latter is continually rendered an object of the international community's action, Spivak argues that the hierarchy needs to be challenged in ways that *simultaneously* attend to the agency of subordinated spaces and create alternative scenarios through it. It is a supplementary approach of 'both ends' that privileges simultaneous presences of heterogeneous sites, bodies, processes and modes. Spivak is concerned with two particular ends in her article, the metropolitan end ('the top') and the subaltern end ('the bottom'). On the metropolitan end, which she calls 'the New York end' – where she is professionally based and thus is being characteristically specific even as she makes what is undeniably a general(izing) point – Spivak echoes Chow and the tenets widely accepted in postcolonial and poststructuralist circles that promote engaging in critical interrogation and self-reflection. Here, Spivak speaks of the subterranean task of critical engagement and pedagogy of making 'unstable the presupposition that the reasonable righting of wrongs is inevitably the manifest destiny of the groups ... that remain poised to right them; and that, among the receiving groups, wrongs will inevitably proliferate with unsurprising regularity' (Spivak 2004: 530).

On the subaltern end, which in Spivak's essay is in reference to the 'rural poor', she speaks of 'activating' the subaltern agency by 'learning to weave the torn fabric in unexpected ways', and learning from below (Spivak 2004: 548). Important here is the specific way in which Spivak conceives of what defines subalternity – the long neglect, the bottom position and the permanence of this condition. Spivak specifies, 'By subaltern I mean those removed from lines of social mobility' (ibid.: 531).[1] By terming the work at this 'bottom' end an 'activation', 'learning' and 'suturing', Spivak's aim is to centre the *agency* of 'the bottom', the subaltern. Spivak understands that this agency only comes through acts of suturing the subaltern and the dominant tradition. In other words, agency comes from 'within' discourse in the sense that the long-ignored subalterns under colonialism and capitalism must become subjects of human rights, democracy and the Enlightenment tradition (i.e. become rights holders and an electorate) if they are to stop perennially becoming objects of benevolence and an alibi for domination. However, 'suturing' is a process of activating the subaltern culture, philosophies and knowledge to alter the dominant cultures that ultimately mediate and make possible the subject position of subaltern men and women. Spivak thinks we can talk about an agency of the subaltern cultural system that can be 'activated' to disrupt and alter the contours and limits of discourse.

Spivak explores the possibility of simultaneity in contexts of severe power asymmetry, i.e. what it might mean to privilege coevality of both those spaces, cultures, bodies and narratives that are rendered past, silent, blank and lost, and those that circulate within the dominant cultural system as present and active. For Spivak, accessing and activating the subaltern is conceived as an exchange between two bodies from different worlds, ends or cultures, which together reach out to a 'beyond'. Spivak explains the process as one of 'secret encounters':

> We all know when we engage profoundly with *one* person, the responses – the answers – come from both sides. Let us call this responsibility, as well as 'answer' ability or accountability. We also know, and if we don't we have been unfortunate, that in such engagements, we want to reveal and reveal, conceal nothing. Yet on both sides there is always a sense that something has not got across. This is what we call the secret, not something that one wants to conceal, but something that one wants desperately to reveal in this relationship of singularity, responsibility and accountability ... in this sense, ethical singularity can be called a secret encounter.
>
> (Spivak 1999: 384, emphasis in original)

This is not a simple retrieval of some essential past, though it is a retrieval of a kind, a type where both the subaltern men and women who 'have' access to this 'secret' act in concert with a figure like Spivak who can access it only in conjunction with subaltern men and women to create it. It is not a simple creation from nothing but a *mending* of a long disenfranchised cultural system that does not exist as a system, but only in threads, fragments, in-betweens. As with the way translation has been conceived, 'secret encounter' is a communication across a cultural divide that is a slow, attentive 'mind-changing on both sides', which in the process of 'retrieving' together, creates something 'new' (Spivak 1999: 383). This creation is not about accessing the subaltern episteme for what it is (an object that can be translated, communicated, included through her translative work within the dominant cultural system). It is creation and accessing for what comes after a disruption of the permanent subject/object divide, however momentary and fleeting the instant.

In this book I have mainly relied on the ideas of Trinh who, like Spivak, gives primacy to alternative spaces as sources of change. Trinh's expressive, poetic putting together of subordinated and subversive modes, sites, processes and practices of culture and art are efforts that are similar to Spivak's pre-occupation with the idea of learning from 'the bottom'. In short, both Trinh and Spivak are concerned with the possibility of uncoercive empowerment that is not a top-down process of educators, human rights workers or advocates acting as agents that impart something to, or do something for, the disenfranchised (Spivak 2004: 527). Both are believers in the possibility of an 'uncoercive rearrangement of desires' (ibid.: 526).

However, Trinh, unlike Spivak, relies on a wide array of visual and visionary insights and spontaneity (or are they flights of fancy?) as sources and methods of knowledge production treated as just another genre of cultural production. Trinh's choice of resources does not fall into the neat 'top end'/ 'bottom end' distinction within which Spivak works. For instance, Trinh has turned to – I haphazardly name just a few of her inspirations and interlocutors – Buddhism, Burkina Faso, Senegal, the Sumiye School of painting, Vietnamese diaspora and Japan. These sites are marginal but marginality is always relational and, moreover, their subalternity, if we use Spivak's criteria, is questionable. Yet, Trinh turns to these sites in order to learn in the manner Spivak writes about, by moving back and forth, through mutual desire to pass on a 'secret'. Trinh understands her writing and filming 'about' these practices and spaces as 'accessing' subordinated modes, sites and cultural systems.

I suggest that Trinh and Spivak ultimately have two incommensurable approaches. They identify subordinated and disenfranchised cultural systems in different ways and, as a consequence, present two diverging conceptions of what working with subordinated and subaltern spaces and cultures mean. One way to put it is to say that Trinh is less discriminatory about subordinated and subjugated sites (underappreciated aesthetic sites as well as the global underclass like refugees and tribes in Burkina Faso), and has fewer problems working in her profession (filmmaking and theory) as a producer of knowledge and culture in a conventional sense (making cultural and knowledge products). Spivak, on the other hand, privileges economic disenfranchisement and seeks out 'the lowest of the low', calling these cultural spaces and the women and men that inhabit them subalterns.

While Trinh is rather indiscriminate in her sites of creation, production and engagement, Spivak is focused primarily on two sites of engagement that require two different strategies of suturing. At the metropolitan or top end (the site of her professional work), she teaches and writes like other poststructuralist and postcolonial scholars; however, at the bottom, subaltern end, she is engaged in work that is entirely different. In the latter site, she is not involved in teaching or retrieving information for knowledge and cultural production. She is involved in *activation* and production for the other end only hinders this activation. From Spivak's perspective, engagements such as Trinh's are missing a dimension: they are not directed enough towards, and not shaped enough by, the subaltern end that on another occasion, Spivak (1999: 383) terms the 'original practical ecological philosophies of the world'. From Trinh's perspective, or perhaps it is mine, Spivak's way of dividing the world is reductive.

My response is divided. I appreciate Spivak's work for what it opens up: the possibility for exploring a greater diversity of in-between spaces and translative transactions which is attuned to issues of location, positionality and historicity. Moreover, Spivak's attention to the idea of simultaneity resonates with my account of Oh, Young-jin's graphic novel, *Pyongyang Project*: numerous episodes within it perform translative transactions to privilege co-survival and co-presence, rather than reifying North Koreans as automatons.

I also discussed simultaneity as a love that, rather than privilege reconciliation and redemption (two become one), is better understood as a project of

creating courage to stay attached that privileges heterogeneity and simultaneous survival with and in the world that causes pain. What Spivak's supplementation of 'both ends' allows me to ask relates to supplementation in
theory. In other words, what other sites, modes, processes, positions open up
when we supplement Trinh's aesthetic conception of subordinated spaces,
modes and processes with Spivak's supplementary approach of 'both ends'?
How can contingency, heterogeneity and in-between-ness be more intimately
and transformatively entangled with, and 'learn from', marginal, disenfranchised sites and the women, men and children of these sites? How can
marginality in a global context be more intimately entangled with the
productivity of contingency, heterogeneity and in-between-ness?

However, what comes to the fore in the juxtaposition are the (productive)
tensions in these two feminist postcolonial thinkers: essentially, they differ on
how power orders the world and, as a consequence, how the world can be disordered and re-ordered. In other words, Spivak's supplementary approach to
righting wrongs from 'both ends' makes visible how 'top end-focused' much
critical engagement is, especially in IR, cultural studies, film studies, area
studies and other disciplines from which I have drawn, including Trinh's
work. In a way, Spivak's supplementary approach of 'both ends' suggests a
possible limitation of my approach; that is, my exploration has been self-
contained insofar as it fails to register the absence of change from 'the bottom
end'. It gestures to some other constellation of sources, actors and processes
to usher in transformation but it does not 'activate' any specific sites and
subaltern spaces. However, to follow Spivak from this point on suggests that I
seek out 'the lowest of the low', the 'rural poor' in the North Korea/the
international case, to work with directly, personally. Not only is this a reductive way of conceptualizing the problem of hierarchy in the case of North
Korea, but it also does violence to the idea of heterogeneity in thinking about
transformation. It assumes, 'if only we streamline our political energies to an
activation of the bottom, the world will become more liveable for most of the
world's population'. Would it? There are no guarantees, Spivak might say, but
she is committed to 'licensed lunacy in the name of the unnameable other',
which always accepts self-delusion and accepts that failure as inescapable
(Spivak 2004: 564).

I think there is something to Spivak's idea of simultaneity through a supplementary strategy of 'both ends', but just as Spivak puts this phrase in
quotation marks (indicating its inadequacy, its place-holding function), there
is a need to conceptualize better what 'both ends' means.[2] What I find compelling about Spivak's 2004 essay, 'Righting Wrongs', is how her metaphors
(such as the top/bottom, centre/marginal, and the permanent class apartheid)
register a need for a more sustained interrogation of the sites, locations and
directions of disruptions, interruptions and critiques of the subject/object, self/
Other dichotomies. Spivak *expresses* the limits of current sites of theory and
how its interventions often occur in ways that fail to decentre the self radically or to attend seriously to the agency of the subordinated spaces, lives and

cultures.[3] I retain my position stated at the beginning of this book, that the dichotomy colonizer/colonized will not do in how we conceive of transformation in international/intercultural relations. However, bringing newness into the world by attending to heterogeneity, contingency, ambiguity and ambivalence must occur in ways that decentre the self that is an inescapable participant and site. Attention to subordinated spaces, cultures and sites seems indispensable *and* inadequate at the same time in intercultural engagements that seek to disrupt more intimately the permanence of relegating and subordinating 'North Korea'.

A juxtaposition of Trinh and Spivak also registers the heterogeneity of how commitments to marginal spaces and modes are negotiated and unfold. The hyphens in each poststructuralist – feminist – postcolonial theory and theorist which connect the clusters of ideas, strategies and cultures that each theoretical tradition mobilizes (which is not to say they do not overlap) are heterogeneous and heterogenizing. What the hyphens mean and affect differs in each enactment of the hyphenation in their various locations and scenes of enactment. This hyphenated theory and the attendant tensions and contradictions in what these hyphens produce are always in the process of becoming. What bringing Trinh and Spivak together underscores is the productivity of attending to the heterogeneity and becomingness of hyphenated and hyphenating practices of theory and world making.

Notes

1 She refers here specifically to the 'rural poor of the South', and even more specifically to the rural children she was teaching and encountering as part of the literacy activism work in India and China. However, elsewhere Spivak makes clear that the subaltern and 'the margins' (which she points out is the silent and silenced centre not actually the margin or marginal in spatial/material terms) include 'men and women among the illiterate peasantry, Aboriginals, and the lowest strata of the urban subproletariat' (Spivak 1999: 269).
2 I would begin by saying that Spivak's focus on economic exclusion and her conception of supplementation of 'both ends' as regarding the Global North and South needs further complication in the North Korean/international case. There is also an element of reverence for things from some distant past in Spivak's idea of 'original practical ecological philosophies of the world', which I find troubling.
3 While I do not bring in IR literature that resonates with this point I make through Spivak, this is not to say it does not exist or that this chapter has not benefited from such. Besides the works already mentioned (e.g. Sylvester 2000, 2002; Bleiker 1997), Stephan Chan (2000, 2010) has been especially inspiring.

Bibliography

Bleiker, Roland (1997) 'Forget IR Theory', *Alternatives: Global, Local, Political* 22 (1): 57–85.
Chan, Stephen (2000) 'Writing Sacral IR: An Excavation Involving Kung, Eliade, and Illiterate Buddhism', *Millennium Journal of International Studies* 29 (3): 565–89.

——(2010) 'Regarding the Pain of Susan Sontag', in Cerwyn Moore and Chris Farrands (eds) *International Relations Theory and Philosophy: Interpretive Dialogues*, Abingdon: Routledge.

Chow, Rey (1998) *Ethics After Idealism: Theory, Culture, Ethnicity, Reading*, Bloomington, IN: Indiana University Press.

Lavie, Smadar and Swedenburg, Ted (1996) 'Between and Among the Boundaries of Culture: Bridging Text and Lived Experience in the Third Timespace', *Cultural Studies* 10 (1): 154–79.

Sandoval, Chela (2000) *Methodology of the Oppressed*, Minneapolis: University of Minnesota Press.

Spivak, Gayatri C. (1999) *A Critique of Postcolonial Reason: Toward a History of the Vanishing Present*, Cambridge, MA: Harvard University Press.

——(2004) 'Righting Wrongs', *The South Atlantic Quarterly* 103 (2/3): 523–81.

Sylvester, Christine (2000) 'Development Poetics', *Alternatives* 25 (13): 335–51.

——(2002) *Feminist International Relations: An Unfinished Journey*, New York: Cambridge University Press.

Trinh, T. Minh-ha (2011) *Elsewhere, Within Here: Immigration, Refugeeism and the Boundary Event*, Abingdon: Routledge.

Index